Hard Power in Hard Times

Janne Haaland Matlary

Hard Power in Hard Times

Can Europe Act Strategically?

Janne Haaland Matlary
Department of Political Science, Blindern
University of Oslo
Oslo, Norway

ISBN 978-3-319-76513-6   ISBN 978-3-319-76514-3   (eBook)
https://doi.org/10.1007/978-3-319-76514-3

Library of Congress Control Number: 2018938125

© The Editor(s) (if applicable) and The Author(s) 2018
This work is subject to copyright. All rights are solely and exclusively licensed by the Publisher, whether the whole or part of the material is concerned, specifically the rights of translation, reprinting, reuse of illustrations, recitation, broadcasting, reproduction on microfilms or in any other physical way, and transmission or information storage and retrieval, electronic adaptation, computer software, or by similar or dissimilar methodology now known or hereafter developed.
The use of general descriptive names, registered names, trademarks, service marks, etc. in this publication does not imply, even in the absence of a specific statement, that such names are exempt from the relevant protective laws and regulations and therefore free for general use.
The publisher, the authors, and the editors are safe to assume that the advice and information in this book are believed to be true and accurate at the date of publication. Neither the publisher nor the authors or the editors give a warranty, express or implied, with respect to the material contained herein or for any errors or omissions that may have been made. The publisher remains neutral with regard to jurisdictional claims in published maps and institutional affiliations.

Cover illustration: Getty Images / Battlefield_Historian

Printed on acid-free paper

This Palgrave Macmillan imprint is published by the registered company Springer International Publishing AG part of Springer Nature.
The registered company address is: Gewerbestrasse 11, 6330 Cham, Switzerland

To our children Philip, Marie-Astrid, Francis, and Sophie-Louise

PREFACE

This book project started out as an analysis of classical strategy, meaning mainly the direction of the use of military force. It posed the question of whether European states—particularly Germany, France, and Britain—as well as the EU and NATO are able to act strategically. Use of force here does mean not only the actual deployment of troops in an operation but also force posture and political signalling—what I term *deterrence*—as well as the use of force in what is called coercive diplomacy or *coercion*. If successful, these latter two forms of use of force are far more efficient than deploying force in operations. In addition, *containment* has again become important as a general strategy, employing both political and economic tools.

I ask what deterrence in Europe today requires considering the current resurgence of geopolitics. I also ask what coercion today entails, and whether it is a viable strategy for Europe. I explore containment as a response to Russian resurgence and compare the Russian use of force with Europe's response, asking whether Europe acts strategically or merely reactively. Is there for instance a pattern of Russian strategic action met by reaction or even by appeasement, or is there a European strategy of containment at work? My interest was provoked by what I perceived to be a general lack of strategic thinking and ability on the part of European politicians. Few seem to have any notion of what strategic interaction entails and they lack experience in the unpleasantness of hard power issues since Europe has been at unprecedented peace for such a long time.

As political events unfolded in 2015 and beyond, it became clear that I also needed to discuss European strategic ability in a more *general* sense,

vii

viii PREFACE

given the multiple crises the continent has faced in recent years, including mass migration, unruly neighbours, terrorism, and populism, not to mention the unpredictability that has followed the election of Donald Trump as president of the US. Thus, I deviated from my original plan of analysing the use of military force only, expanding the scope of the book to also cover other 'hard problems' that may require hard power policy responses. The rationale for this shift in focus is not only that Europe at present faces an extraordinary array of challenges, but also that the common denominator of these challenges is the need for strategy.

It is my argument that *European politicians are particularly ill-suited for leading strategically in the face of adversaries that use various forms of hard power.* This is the opposite of the civilized, incremental, and rule-based decision-making style that has become typical of the EU and of domestic European politics, notably in Germany. The world of strategy has largely become foreign in Europe—it is one where there is interaction with adversaries and where deception, cunning, and surprises are common. There is a need for tough policy choices in this political universe. Such choices do not fare well with those whose only experience is that of liberal democracy. To mention but one example, European attempts to deport migrants are always opposed vocally by non-governmental organizations (NGOs), lawyers, and the media. It is unpleasant to become unpopular and face accusations of being hard and tough in Europe, unlike what obtains in many other parts of the world. The post-national, liberal, and human-rights based ideal type of foreign policy is the European standard today. This contrasts sharply with realism and the use of hard power, be it police closing borders or military deterrence and coercion. What counts as legitimate in the policy world differs markedly between Western European states and the states in its neighbourhood.

The work for this book started when I was a visiting fellow at the Changing Character of War Programme at Oxford University. During my sabbatical there, I benefitted greatly from discussions with, *inter alia,* professors Hew Strachan and Robert Johnston as well as with the many officer-scholars who form the backbone of this programme. Back at the University of Oslo and the Norwegian Defence Command and Staff College, I had ample opportunity to test my arguments further among colleagues there. I am also very grateful to Lt Col Kjell Sjåholm for providing a great number of articles and reports from various open sources. Having up-to-date information was particularly important because the cases analysed in this book were unfolding as I wrote. It is not easy to analyse current affairs since they are ongoing, and I have had to rely very much on news media and policy analyses of various kinds from Britain, France, and Germany. The book covers the period until the end of 2017.

The research for this book has been supported by grants from the Department of Political Science, University of Oslo and the Norwegian Institute of Defence Studies, as well as by a generous grant from the Norwegian Ministry of Defence (MOD). I am deeply grateful for the support from these sources.

All errors naturally remain my own.

Oslo, Norway   Janne Haaland Matlary
Oxford, UK
March 2018

Contents

Part I Strategic Challenges	1
1 External and Internal Shocks: Policy Needs Beyond 'Win-Win'	3
2 Strategy: Deterrence, Containment, Coercion, and Confrontation	23
3 Russian Revisionism	47
4 Mass Migration and Border Control	93
5 Confronting Terrorism and Insurgency	125
Part II Strategic Action?	149
6 Germany	151
7 Britain	175
8 France	193

xii CONTENTS

9	The EU: 'Soft Power Is Not Enough'	213
10	NATO's Deterrence and Détente Efforts	247
11	Conclusions	271
Index		285

PART I

Strategic Challenges

CHAPTER 1

External and Internal Shocks: Policy Needs Beyond 'Win-Win'

The primary purpose of this book is to examine the need for strategic action in current European security policy. The secondary purpose is to analyse the empirical state of affairs with regard to strategic ability. I examine recent cases of the use of force as well as challenges to territorial and border security to determine whether states in Europe take the lead in policy-making that concern their continent, or are mere contributors. The emphasis is not on operational art per se, but on whether governments exhibit strategic logic when they use force in one way or another. Russia, and particularly its actions in Ukraine in 2014 and onwards, constitutes a major case study of this book.

By 2014 Europe was beginning to realize—the hard way—that it faced the twin strategic challenges of global terrorism and old-fashioned geo-politics, which 'descended' on the continent around the same time. It was during that year that Putin annexed Crimea and heavy fighting in the eastern part of Ukraine ensued. The same year, Daesh, or Islamic State of Iraq and the Levant (ISIL),[1] and other terrorist actors stepped up their activity, attacking in Europe and elsewhere. The killing of almost the entire staff at *Charlie Hebdo* early in January 2015 and the massacres in Paris on Friday 13 November the same year marked a turning point. Subsequent attacks in Brussels, London, and Berlin added to the seriousness of the terrorist challenge in Europe. The values of liberal democracy were, literally speaking, under fire. Russian sabre-rattling also continued at a brisk

© The Author(s) 2018
J. H. Matlary, *Hard Power in Hard Times*,
https://doi.org/10.1007/978-3-319-76514-3_1

pace, with attempts to provoke North Atlantic Treaty Organization (NATO) reactions in the Baltics with mock attacks on American ships and planes there and transgressions of international airspace. Russia also intervened militarily in Syria in the autumn of the same year.

In many ways, Europe was 'home alone' in the face of these developments. The US had announced its so-called pivot to Asia two years before, along with major cuts in its defence spending. President Obama was reluctant to embrace a leading role in security and defence policy and asked Europeans to take much more responsibility for their own security needs.[2] He made the point that he did not want to 'follow the Washington playbook' of using military force in order to lead in world politics.[3] In not following through with a military attack on Syria after the so-called red line he had announced on the use of chemical weapons had been crossed, he did *not* weaken American extended deterrence, he argued, for his was a *different* type of foreign policy. One may add that this foreign policy looked more like Europe's—the US would no longer be the world's 'policeman'. The surprising election of Donald Trump as US president in November 2016 brought even more uncertainty to this picture. While Trump seemed to advocate isolationism and protectionism, he was also an activist and took seemingly radical positions on Russia, China, and NATO. Pointing to burden-sharing, or rather the lack of it, he demanded that the European members of NATO pay up and reach the self-imposed 2 per cent of gross domestic product (GDP) contribution very quickly. The message to Europe was clear and unmistakable: Carry the burden in terms of cost and risk in your own region.

The US's retreat from being the world's policeman was a development long in coming, but it could not have happened at a more unfortunate time: Europe was also cutting defence spending across the alliance, partly because it assumed that the US would pick up the bill, as usual, and partly because the economic crisis was so severe. Even more severe, however, was long-term youth unemployment. In addition, mass migration across the Mediterranean exploded. Greece, in particular, was inundated with migrants and refugees, unable to cope, and the European Union (EU)'s common policy did not work. It was *sauve qui peut*—every state for itself, and several European states even built border fences themselves to physically stop the flow of migrants. The Greek crisis became a Greek drama when migrants could not transit to their preferred destinations farther north. Faced with these challenges, spending on defence was certainly at the very bottom of the political list of priorities.

Under these circumstances, Europe was put in a situation where it had to react to two strategic challenges simultaneously: It became the protagonist in a strategic game with Russia while also having to deal with strategic terrorism. Instead of working in partnership with Russia, Europe had to deal with Russia as an adversary. It also had to fight terrorism, which was linked to a third crisis, brought about by the migration crisis that had to do with borders, policing, and territorial security in a very basic sense. *Russia, terrorism, and mass migration had to be dealt with by a generation of European politicians unused to thinking strategically and ill at ease with using hard power tools.*

Strategy is at the heart of statecraft, the traditional role of the statesman. The 'tools' of strategy are unitary action capacity, national interest, and the means to defend them. Strategic interaction is not a 'win-win' game, but rather one of adversarial interchange. What one actor in a strategic game does has implications for the other actor. This *interaction* is the essence of strategy itself. If a player chooses to remain passive and does nothing, this choice is also strategically relevant. Is remaining passive the same as appeasement? Or is it a rejection of the agenda that the opponent is trying to set and, as such, a true strategic move made from a position of strength?

These questions are essential for assessing whether Europe responded and continues to respond well to the challenges mentioned above. If European governments faced with the current situation were to do nothing out of the ordinary, it would not only be strategically unwise but also signal weakness and fear—it would often in fact amount to appeasement, to giving in to pressure and fear. Behaving in normal political ways with linear policy thinking is inappropriate when one's state, and indeed one's entire continent, faces fundamental strategic risks and even immediate threats.

This book considers what strategic interaction, thinking, and action require in Europe today, given the challenges at hand. It argues that European leaders have largely forgotten, or perhaps never learnt, what these entail. Politicians, who do not recall the Cold War, much less know much about the Second World War (WWII), are not likely to take much interest in security and defence issues. Although strategy is an essential part of what we call statesmanship, it is difficult, and often unpleasant, to deal with adversaries and enemies. 'Fair weather politics' is much easier and follows what we can term the 'Brussels playbook' of normal, linear, and rule-based decision-making. When European countries have gone to war in the period after 1990, it has mostly been in the form of so-called humanitarian interventions where the claim could be made that military power was a 'force for good', as Tony Blair used to say. The language of *deterrence* and *coercion*, on the other hand, has been far from common. Only with the resurgence of Russia has deterrence once again become a key word in NATO debates. It is still an awkward thing to discuss in political circles in many European states, especially in Germany.

It is frightening to Europeans that Russia can no longer be assumed to be moving in a Western direction. The assumption that Russia will become a liberal democracy is no longer tenable. Yet adversarial interaction—strategy—is not a common mode of policy among the political elites of Europe. The latest case of this kind of policy was the Cold War, which is not replicated at present, although some of the strategic elements are similar. As one NATO ambassador put it, 'we need new concepts; it is a conceptual challenge to politicians in particular'.[4]

NATO no longer works in partnership with Russia; in fact, the two entities have no interaction beyond standard diplomatic relations and the occasional NATO-Russia Council meeting. Russian leaders have labelled NATO a major threat, arguing that the sanctions imposed by the EU and the US are aimed at overthrowing the Russian government. Western leaders are, for the most part, unused to managing this kind of strategic interaction, where the name of the game is conflict, not cooperation. If, however, conflict and state rivalry are the natural features of great power politics, Western leaders need to learn, or relearn, the nature of strategic interaction.

The term *hard power* in this book describes the use of not only military but also economic means to influence the behaviour of other actors. Economic coercion in the form of sanctions or boycotts is not the main topic of this book, although sanctions often form part of the UN Security Council's (UNSC) work. In the current policy response to the case of Russian meddling in Ukraine and the annexation of Crimea there are US and EU sanctions. It has proven very difficult to uphold the EU sanctions, despite US insistence. However, what poses the most difficulty for Europe—and perhaps for every democracy—is the use of military force. European states have used military force in many operations since the Cold War, but that does not amount to having had or having a strategy for its use. The use of force to defend the state and promote its interests is something entirely different from its use in an 'optional' operation where little is at stake.

Hard power also includes police power, border controls, and anti-terrorism measures. The state's three tools of action are diplomacy, economic means, and military/police means. The conceptual opposite of hard power is *soft power*, a much more famous term, and one that Joseph Nye has written much about.[5] He points out that soft power is much more effective than hard power in most cases because it relies on persuasion and attractiveness, whereas hard power is coercive. The moment coercion is removed, the induced behaviour may stop as well. Persuasion, however, often leads to a target to accept something, or even to embrace it on an intellectual or emotional level.

This is undoubtedly true, but the policy situations that typically require hard power are conflictual and uncertain. There is little, if any, trust between parties and therefore little scope for persuasion. This typically occurs when a state and its population are threatened and the state's control of its territory is at stake. European states have, for the most part, not had to confront such situations since the end of the Cold War, and at that time there was a peaceful transition to a type of liberal-democratic order all over Europe, if in name only in Eastern Europe and the Balkans. Yet there has been no violent conflict within or between European states since the 1999 Kosovo campaign. For the most part, foreign policy has proceeded on the assumptions of the liberal model of 'win-win': We (the EU, the Council of Europe, and NATO) will teach you how to become like us, liberal democracies, and conflicts will be solved by rule of law. This is the wonderful formula of the EU—the Copenhagen criteria for membership: to join the union, a state has to have a democratic set-up, including rule of law and respect for human rights, as well as a market economy. This policy of attraction—soft power—worked as long as states wanted membership. The conditionality in the membership terms—unless you do as we say, you will not become a member—did not amount to coercion. The EU model worked very well for two decades. Even Russia was assumed to be moving in the direction of becoming a liberal market state.

However, around 2010, we notice a major change in world politics. China asserted its power and came down on critics like Norway, which awarded the Nobel peace prize that year to Liu Xiaobo, who had been imprisoned for calling for democracy in China. In 2008, Russia effectively blocked the likely membership in NATO for Georgia. Ukraine and Georgia were—unstrategically—given the option to join at NATO's summit in April that year, a move that is rather incomprehensible from a strategic point of view as NATO would incur Article 5 obligations for these states and their inclusion in NATO would certainly lead to Russian reactions. As it were, the Russian reaction was swift and hard: a military exercise turned into a small strategic attack on two so-called republics in Georgia, South

Ossetia and Abkhazia. The lesson taught was that NATO cannot expand into the vicinity of Russia without a military response; a lesson not learned perhaps, but one straight out of the realist playbook of spheres of interest. The Western reaction was nervous and evasive, and the issue of Georgian NATO membership was conveniently forgotten very quickly. There was no appetite for any military confrontation with Russia, of course; the whole business of inviting in Georgia and Ukraine was clearly a mistake in the sense that NATO—and in this case, President Bush in particular—had not taken strategy into account at all. For NATO membership entails the responsibility of collective defence, as enshrined in Article 5 in the Washington Treaty which founds NATO. Was the inclusion of Georgia so important to NATO that the alliance was prepared for major war with Russia to protect the former? The answer was clearly no, but no one seems to have thought about this absolutely vital strategic issue.

In the wake of events in Georgia, Western Europe did not invite Ukraine to join NATO, but there was a process of EU trade agreements with several former Commonwealth of Independent States (CIS). These so-called Europe agreements represent a move towards closer relations, although they do not constitute formal steps towards EU membership. Yet when Ukraine, Armenia, Moldova, and Azerbaijan were going to sign trade agreements with the EU in late 2013, the Russians stepped in and used hard economic power to stop them, including embargoes, import restrictions, and so forth. The message was crystal clear: Join us and not them. Once again, Western Europe was surprised and bewildered. The East-West conflict in Ukrainian politics came to a climax at Maidan square in early 2014, leading to the Russian occupation of Crimea.

Foreign policy requires strategic thinking when there are conflicts of interest. When the use of force is in play, there should always be a strategy because military or police force is difficult to employ for political effect as it entails risk of life and death and causes material damage. In short, while foreign policy should generally be based on strategy, the use of force most certainly ought to be, although it often is not.

As stated, the common model of European foreign policy is incentive-based, so-called win-win diplomacy. When Crimea was occupied in February 2014, then Norwegian Foreign Minister Børge Brende repeatedly said that Putin simply had not understood that the world is a 'win-win' place where dialogue and cooperation resolve problems. He was not alone among Western leaders in having difficulty understanding Putin's worldview. They have been very reluctant to accept that Putin is seemingly

EUROPE THE EXCEPTION?

serious in *not* wanting a win-win *modus operandus*. Europe is a security community with cooperative state-to-state interaction, but it now interacts with states that are not part of this community. This interaction is based on a *zero-sum* rationale—you win and I lose, or *vice versa*. In addition, the role of small states is diminished and great powers have returned as a category of states that claim special sovereign rights in what they regard as their 'sphere of interest'. This is classical *Realpolitik* or geopolitics. The relative importance of Europe and its model of integration and rule-based order are diminishing, while re-emerging great powers are beginning to claim special rights. There is a transition from Western dominance towards a multipolar system of states in which several great powers compete. This fact alone increases the risk that hard power will be used, for coercion and deterrence and in actual war-fighting.

EUROPE THE EXCEPTION?

Has the modern state system become multipolar where Europe is the exception as a soft power actor, a pole without much ability when conflicts arise? Charles Kupchan argues that the state system today, while not clearly multipolar yet, is marked by power vacuums and a lack of leadership.[6] We live in a new 'globalized world that is no longer guided by the hand of Western hegemony' and 'the next world will be populated by powers of many regime types'.[7] However, the rivalry for power and status in the state system that we are now witnessing, *in casu* the expansive foreign policies of China and Russia, comes with considerable instability, as we know from history. The state system is transitioning away from unipolarity to multipolarity, and this transition is often unstable, as some states are revisionist, challenging the *status quo*. As Kupchan notes, 'transitions in the balance of power are dangerous historical moments; most of them have been accompanied by considerable bloodshed'.[8] This is a common realist insight, and one that remains relevant today. It may be possible to achieve a stable balance of power, as with the bipolarity of the US and Russia in the Cold War. Yet both the rivalry that marks transition and multipolarity itself are unstable factors, he argues.

In terms of economic power, China and the US are more or less equal already. For a long time, neither China nor Russia seemed to put priority on military build-up and modernization, but over the last decade both states have begun spending a great deal on defence. This behaviour is also in line with realist reasoning: once a state can afford to spend on defence, it will do so, and become a revisionist state vying for power.

A counter-argument to the realist diagnosis is the liberal institutionalist one: As globalization brings about more interdependence, states will no longer compete as rivals or fight each other. Keohane and Nye introduced this argument in their famous 1979 book, *Power and Interdependence*,[9] and the subsequent literature on globalization develops this theme. In *The World is Flat*, Friedman argues that globalization will encompass all states and that it is a major driver of liberal democracy and the rule of law.[10] All states will need to work according to these principles to attract investment and create jobs, he argues. There is really no alternative to open societies, given the penetration of the internet and of capitalism. Francis Fukuyama's famous article on the 'end of history' also predicted a linear development towards liberal-democratic states and integration through peaceful means.[11]

The present state system can be divided into modern, postmodern, and failed states, and the modern states, especially China, are on the rise economically. There is no clear developmental trend in the direction of liberal institutionalism, and multilateralism suffers from a lack of trust and interest on the part of states. The UN is no longer the arena for world politics it was in the 1990s when major global conferences set the stage for a normative development of national politics. Today the UN is increasingly marginalized in world politics.

Kupchan argues that interdependence can cause conflict rather than prevent it: 'The peace-causing effects of commercial interdependence are similarly illusory. Economic interdependence among Europe's great powers did little to avert the war that broke out in 1914', he writes, and 'interdependence can actually fuel conflict by serving as a source of vulnerability'.[12] He adds that 'in the midst of strategic rivalry, commercial interdependence can do more harm than good'.[13]

Like other realists, such as Henry Kissinger, Kupchan argues that the waning powers of the West must seek ideological compromises with Russia and China, including an understanding of the need for spheres of influence. In short, if Europe does not have the power to influence Russian policy in Ukraine, it should refrain from trying to do so. This view of power assumes that hard power systematically trumps soft power, a contention that needs empirical testing.

While European states have reduced their defence budgets, China and Russia have been increasing theirs by between 10 and 15 per cent annually.[14] And although the world is already economically multipolar, as Nye points out, the US remains a military hegemon.[15] However, as time goes by, the military power balance is changing—the new economic giants are spending to modernize their defence forces and have clear security and defence ambitions.

Russia is reviving the *Realpolitik* concept of spheres of interest, exemplified by its strategic attacks on Georgia in 2008 and on Crimea in 2014. China is pursuing gunboat diplomacy in the South China Sea and shows all signs of behaving like a traditional great power in that region. In short, in some respects, the world is experiencing a return to the old great power balance system. The newly rich nations are not at all postmodern soft power adherents.

Against the backdrop of this general, and major, change in the distribution of power in the world state system, the difference between Europe as a 'security community' and the rest of the world is a stark one. After 1990, 'peace for our time' seemed a reality; it was, in the words of Francis Fukuyama, 'the end of history'. Now Europe faces the return of a multipolar world order, changes in US security and defence policy, and a reduction in its own defence budgets. In addition, it may have become so used to conducting foreign policy without a 'stick' that it has forgotten how to use one.

In his book *World Order*, Henry Kissinger argues that a new balance of power is needed, but will be extremely difficult to achieve: 'The penalty for failing will be ... an evolution into spheres of influence ... with particular domestic structures and forms of governance.'[16] Moreover, he argues, international organizations (IOs) and multilateral diplomacy do not really allow strategic action or even unitary action, and there is no substitute for American leadership in deciding on questions of order. Kissinger is quite pessimistic about the chances of a negotiated new balance of power balance or world order. Multilateralism is based on a certain number of common norms which do not exist in today's world. Therefore, the multilateral IOs are largely side-lined in decision-making at present, he argues.

The current economic crisis is weakening Europe, and globalization as a general phenomenon is making the nation-state weaker. Kupchan agrees with these two points, arguing that Western liberal democracies undermine their own ability to act strategically. The very model of integration and post-national governance makes it impossible to act as a unitary national actor in zero-sum terms.

The realist model of international relations is a multipolar one in which states remain either modern or Westphalian. Great power politics is the inevitable norm, and in periods of transition, rivalry between powers puts them at risk for war. Revisionism occurs when states become strong enough to rebalance each other. A realist would argue that we are living in such a time—Russia and China have become revisionist powers. In their book *Regions and Powers*, Buzan and Wæver point out that realist logic is not static and that the relationship between states changes.[17] They see Europe as the exception to the largely distrustful interactive pattern between states that prevails in most regions of the world. The EU has profoundly changed the norms of state behaviour, but it remains the exception and not the blueprint for the development of the current state system. With the fall of communism in 1990, it was believed that this type of state interaction would become universal as globalization surged. It seemed likely that the interdependence brought about by globalization would lead to a multilateral liberal world order.

War as Peace: The European Mindset?

As stated, the Europeans have become the main proponents of incentives-based diplomacy, sometimes referred to as soft power, as exemplified by the EU. A state may be able to 'join the club' if it behaves in the desired manner or makes the desired changes. The power of attraction, or soft power, a term coined by Joseph Nye, assumes that states are interested in visiting, studying, and investing in a given state because it is a place where the norms of liberal democracy are real—an open society with a free market.[18] The EU, as the foremost example of a group of such states, need not coerce or deter; it provides 'carrots' and does not need 'sticks'. It uses conditionality, but only in terms of incentives—a candidate for membership must act as the European Commission demands, lest it forego its chance to join. Thus, while the mode of diplomacy is one of negotiation based on conditionality, this does not constitute coercion. The 'carrots' are the main vehicles for influence, not the 'sticks'.

European states interact with each other on the basis of deep and persistent trust—the EU is the primary example of a security community.[19] The dense interdependence of member states makes it irrational for them to threaten each other, and while hard diplomacy certainly takes place here as well—notably in the euro crisis where many states have been put under pressure by Germany—European states never threaten each other with military force. The EU is therefore not only the primary example of trustful and benign interaction between states, but also the *exception* in the world: in all other parts of the globe there is currently more distrustful state interaction.[20]

The problem in Europe with regard to strategy is that of a pervasive postmodern mindset. The term postmodern can mean many things in philosophy or literature, but here it is taken to mean that the idea of nation and national history mean increasingly less and therefore the role of the nation-state also matters less. If there is no notion of *la patrie*, or of patriotism, there is little to defend and fight for. The modern state is the term applied to the so-called Westphalian state that pursues its national interest, emphasizes the nation, and is not deeply integrated with other states. The US, Russia, and China are all modern states. The EU, on the other hand, represents the postmodern state: borders matter much less and member states are so deeply integrated into one another that we speak of a 'security community'. This integration, combined with the dismantling of borders within Europe, means not only that conflicts are solved without military threats, rivalry, and attacks, but also that military force increasingly is seen as a thing of the past, often as a barbaric tool of statecraft belonging to a bygone era. The use of force is no longer relevant for European governments, most think, because Europe represents a model society in which economic and political interdependence run so deep that nation-states fade away. Force is therefore to be used primarily in instances of so-called humanitarian intervention, as a 'force for good'.

A commentator in the *New York Times* points out that current so-called identity politics, replacing the common national identity for many, is premised on a kind of relativism—there is no common human nature to agree on as the model for all persons, also for citizens. This is a marked difference from recent times where discrimination was a deviation from common human nature: 'From an identity politics that emphasized our common humanity we have gone to an identity politics that emphasizes having a common enemy' in the sense that there is no longer any known standard for common human nature.[21] This in turn means that citizenship means nothing common that is clear to all; in fact, the notion of being citizens with the same rights and obligations makes no sense if there is no common nature for all men. The postmodern condition where each group looks inwardly at itself and defines itself as a group based on some characteristic such as sex, colour, race, or sexual preference implies that there is no common national project. The nation-state makes no sense if citizens no longer recognize a common set of interests and obligations.

The integration in the EU has undoubtedly also contributed to the weakening of the concept of the nation in Europe; one could in fact say that this is a major ideology behind the EU, although integration in order to weaken nationalism as a destructive force is different from the current type of postmodern identity politics.

What does this imply for warfare? The very notion of war itself has become a problem. A lack of existential threats naturally makes populations entirely unfamiliar with war. However, the postmodern condition implies a much more profound rejection of warfare as a concept. While national defence hardly makes sense as a rationale for war, defending humanism does; but as the latter goal has nothing to do with existential defence, it seems strange and unacceptable to use military force to that end. The result is that war is relabelled peace, as in 'peace enforcement', and the conduct of war is sanitized so that its cruelty and danger, and indeed its very nature, are hidden.

Deterrence, as the major and preferred role of military force, then becomes difficult, if not impossible, because its purpose is to *instil fear*, to really send the message to the adversary that 'if you try something, we will destroy you'. This is not humanistic, but raw and brutal. Can Europeans really scare adversaries in this day and age? The only criterion for the success of deterrence is *fear*. Is the threat of death and destruction credible? This depends on two elements: capability and political will. Even if Europe has the military capability to instil fear, does it have the political will to use force in a given situation?

The other key use of force is coercion. This is much more difficult to manage. Deterrence is passive and general—we are here and we will destroy you if you attack. Coercion involves economic or military pressure to make adversary back off, like Russia in Ukraine. It involves threatening to use force unless demands are met, and the ultimatum must bring about a reversal of action. This means there is a considerable risk on the part of the coercer, for if his demands are not met, he will have to attack. Is Europe willing to accept the risk that comes with the use of coercion?

We can recall President Obama's faux pas in designating a 'red line' on Syria: if chemical weapons were used he would authorize military intervention to stop Assad. Assad did use chemical weapons, but Obama reneged on this pledge, instead asking Congress to decide for him whether or not to use force. Prime Minister Cameron made the same choice on behalf of Britain. Russia 'came to the rescue' in this matter, suggesting that Assad give up his chemical weapons and that NATO destroy them. Both Western leaders issued an ultimatum and did not follow up—they made threats to use military force on which they subsequently did not carry through. This was an utterly unstrategic action: the next time a similar ultimatum is presented, there is no reason to believe in its seriousness.

This introductory analysis of the postmodern condition in Europe underlines why it is so difficult for many Europeans to understand, much less embrace, the use of hard power. Politicians prefer to talk about peace, stabilization, peace enforcement, democratization, and development. Using force 'for good' is possible and noble, but just because the *goal* of an operation is peace does not guarantee that the *means* are peaceful. The 'newspeak' about warfare in postmodern politics risks obscuring what military force really is about. Deploying military forces in 'peace' operations, like a 'fire-brigade' which is deployed when an acute situation demands it, makes sense in the postmodern logic; indeed using force for deterrence and coercion are illogical in a worldview that sees military might as a force for good. Yet state security, which is now firmly back on the European agenda, requires the very opposite mode of using force.

If this is the situation in Europe, the adversary on the battlefield is often at the very opposite end of the moral spectrum, being terrorists and guerrillas who do not even pretend to observe the laws of war and humanitarian norms. The paradox is that while the West grows increasingly wary of using force, wars outside the postmodern world are becoming increasingly barbaric. The conduct of war, as it has evolved in the Western tradition, has had some rather constant features and is the basis of the legal norms of both *jus ad bellum* and *jus in bello* of the UN Pact of 1945. Guerrilla warfare is not one of these features. This kind of 'small' war has never been accepted by the military profession, being deemed immoral. Today's global guerrilla war adopts all the cruellest tactics and uses global communication to broadcast its actions.

This also is true for warfare waged by dictatorships in which the legal rules of war, especially *jus in bello*, are rarely observed. In a dictatorship, there is no transparency or checks and balances, and therefore no accountability when it comes to conduct on the battlefield. This benefits such regimes, if they manage to survive. The liberal democracies of the West, on the other hand, are extremely conscious of all the legal rules of war and also of the expectations of the peaceful societies that they govern. Indeed, 'lawfare' sometimes seems to be more important than warfare, remarks David Kennedy in the book *Lawfare and Warfare.*

How can Europe cope with this situation, if at all? Not only are European forces 'redefined' as 'military humanists' by their governments, which send them into battle, where they often face suicide bombers, murder, and kidnappings rather than military battles. The contrast between the 'lawfare' of the Europeans and the cruel inhumanity of the adversary's style of warfare is a stark one, and strategic logic favours the barbarians, for they are able to instil fear with their tactics. The postmodern West will not, and cannot, act barbarically, and thus is not able to instil fear in these kinds of 'small' wars. The more humane our view of warfare and the more barbaric our adversary's, the more impact the latter has in terms of deterrence, coercion, and fighting. Where there is little resilience against barbarism, there is also little resistance to it. This strategic logic does not imply that barbarism is preferable or acceptable, but is simply a description of tactical and sometimes strategic effects of the latter.

OUTLINE OF THE BOOK

In Part I (Chaps. 2, 3, 4, and 5) I analyse three of the major political challenges Europe currently faces: Russian revisionism, mass migration, and terrorism and irregular wars in and around European territory. These challenges, which we can term 'external shocks', are not the only issues that demand strategic thinking, however; with Britain having begun exit negotiations in March 2017 and mainstream political parties facing populist criticism, the stability of the EU can no longer be taken for granted.

The primary role of the state since Thomas Hobbes has been to ensure the security of its territory, borders, society, and citizens. Since the Russian annexation of Crimea in 2014, state security is firmly back on the agenda in Europe. Europe now faces a hard security policy challenge, but may be unable to deploy tools other than soft power ones. Chapter 2 analyses strategic options, Chap. 3 Russian revisionism since 2014, Chap. 4 is devoted to the migration shock of 2015 and the policy response to the latter (or lack thereof), and Chap. 5 looks at terrorism and irregular warfare on Europe's doorstep.

The external shocks described in these three chapters all require some kind of hard power response: the use of force by a revisionist Russia requires deterrence or even containment; mass migration requires stricter border controls and a crackdown on illegal immigration, both of which may bolster the strategic need to deter mass migration; terrorism, which touches the security of both the nation and the state directly and is difficult, if not impossible, to deter must be detected, confronted, and controlled.

As stated, in Chap. 2 I ask what strategic options Europe has, given the challenges it faces. Today's wars fall under the category of limited war, which is the major type of war. So-called total wars—like the world wars of the last century—started as limited wars and turned into regional and later global wars. I argue that there has not been a paradigm shift away from state wars to insurrections since 1990, taking issue with General Sir Rupert Smith's claim that 'war as we know it no longer exists'.[22] On the contrary, analysts have probably been wrong in dismissing such wars because they have neglected the fact that these wars also started as limited wars. Using force for limited political purposes and in limited ways is therefore the norm now, as before. I develop a preliminary argument about what this fact entails in today's situation where great power politics is back. What amounts to deterrence in this situation? What about coercion? What is the optimal strategy for Europe in the face of Russian resurgence and in the Ukraine case in particular?

In order to answer these questions, we need a more precise idea of what is to be deterred: I therefore move to an analysis of so-called hybrid war. The term 'hybrid war' has become common and yet may be just another fad. As the name suggests, in a hybrid war, the two traditional types of warfare, conventional and asymmetric, converge. Some use of conventional force is combined with indirect, and often non-military, methods, such as providing support to the local population, creating agitation and pressure vis-à-vis the same, and helping or even creating insurgencies, while not admitting a military presence. One example of this style of war is Putin's use of force in Crimea.

I argue that Europe faces a type of revisionism from Russia that is a mixture of conventional and asymmetric elements and therefore places new demands on actors that may want to deter and/or coerce Russia. There are elements of old-style subversion and *Finlandization* in this type of war that make it very difficult to ascertain facts and give attribution to a state actor. Faced with this kind of hybrid activity, coercion, as well as deterrence, becomes especially difficult because most of the activity takes place under the radar.

In addition to the challenges posed by Russia, Europe faces terrorist attacks from militias and guerrillas who increasingly possess conventional arms and territory, making for a mixture of conventional and asymmetric elements. The self-styled ISIL (also called Daesh which is the term used in this book) is the foremost example of this, but there are also militias in Mali, Afghanistan, Nigeria, Somalia, Yemen, and Libya that command parts of those states' territory, have sophisticated arms, and are able to launch conventional attacks. The war in Afghanistan from 2001 to 2014 was motivated by the risk analysis that terrorist groups had acquired too many tools of power: a safe haven, training grounds, conventional arms, and institutional influence. This constituted a 'red line' for the US and its allies. The same analysis applies to the operations against the guerrillas of Mali and Daesh; both sets of actors were deemed to have too many resources—territory, institutions, conventional arms—for them to be left in place. Counter-terrorism measures were not enough; these actors had to be attacked in their centres of gravity. In this chapter I argue that the types of activity these groups engage in once they possess some of the attributes of a state is better called hybrid than asymmetric.

In Part II (Chaps. 6, 7, 8, 9, 10, and 11) I turn to the actors in Europe. This book is primarily an investigation about whether there is strategic leadership in Europe. The US has led almost all the military operations in which Europe has been involved since the Cold War. It was President Obama who rose to the occasion when sanctions against Russia were decided on in 2014, and it was the US that undertook to lead the coalition against Daesh. Now, however, the US has a new policy of leading both less and 'from behind'. Moreover, it has made Asia the first priority of its security and defence policy[23] and has explicitly asked Europe to lead in its own region. The trends are very clear: Europeans must not only spend more on defence but also take the risk of leading in their own area. Therefore, it is of great importance to ask which, if any, European government can and will lead in deterrence, coercion, and operations.

Europe has two military great powers (defined in this case as having a global military posture and global interests): Britain and France. At the same time, Europe has one economic leader, whose economic and political strength is unparalleled: Germany. These three states are the key actors of this book. I ask whether they have a strategic culture in general terms. This is a key question because states without a tradition of using force rarely become leaders in using force, be it for deterrence, coercion, or operational purposes. One exception to this is Denmark, which has moved from being a so-called footnote country in NATO to displaying a clear strategic culture, to the point of perhaps being overzealous in its deployments. Denmark began strengthening its strategic culture around 1990 at the initiative of two ministers, and the Bosnian war led to major changes in the Danish military.[24]

What is meant by strategic culture is contested and varies depending not only on definitions but also on one's assumptions about philosophy of science: Can culture 'cause' behaviour or is it a contextual variable only? The original use of the term in modern political science comes from Jack Snyder's 1977 work[25] on Soviet strategic culture in which he sees strategic culture as an intervening variable between threat perception and political reaction. A similar approach is found in Graham Allison's work on the Cuban missile crisis.[26] These scholars are concerned with whether strategic culture explains some of the variance in political responses to threats that can be determined inter-subjectively beyond national cultures. In this book, I use the term in a similar way. I assume that strategic culture is a major precondition for leadership involving hard power, and that therefore Germany, with its distinct lack of such a culture after WWII, is *unlikely* to lead. But it is an open question whether other states that do have a strategic culture *will* in fact lead. Chapters 9 and 10 present an analysis of NATO and the EU as strategic actors in the three empirical cases examined in the book. I argue that states, and specifically the ones discussed above, are the main actors, and that both NATO and the EU basically are platforms or arenas of state action in hard power politics.

NOTES

1. ISIL is an acronym for Islamic State of Iraq and the Levant; Daesh is the Arabic acronym used to refer to this group. I will use Daesh in the following as this is regarded to be more correct and ISIL as such is a propaganda term as it professes statehood.
2. See Matlary, J. H. and Petersson, M., (2013) (eds.), *NATO's European Allies: Military Capability and Political Will*, Palgrave Macmillan.
3. *The Atlantic Monthly*, April 2016, Jeffrey Goldberg's interview with President Obama, 'The Obama Doctrine'.
4. Personal conversation with NATO ambassador, 5.1.2014.
5. Nye, J. (2005) *Soft Power: The Means to Success in World Politics*, Public Affairs Publishing as well as numerous later publications on the same topic.
6. Kupchan, C. (2012) *No one's world: The West, the rising rest, and the coming global turn*, Oxford University Press, Oxford.
7. Kupchan, pp. 184–185.
8. Ibid., p. 184.

9. Ibid.
10. Friedman, T. (2005) *The World is Flat. A Brief History of the 21st Century,* Farrar, Straus, and Giraud, New York.
11. Fukyama, F. (1992) *The End of History and the Last Man,* The Free Press, New York.
12. Ibid., p. 185.
13. Ibid., p. 186.
14. See *The Military Balance* 2016 (IISS, London) and SIPRI Yearbook 2013, Oxford University Press, p. 142: 'The rising trend in Russian military expenditure, which started in 1999, accelerated sharply in 2012, with a real-terms increase of 16% compared with 2011.'
15. Op.cit.
16. Kissinger, H. (2014), *World Order,* Penguin Press, N.Y., p. 371.
17. Cambridge University Press, 2009?
18. Nye, J. (2011) *The Future of Power,* Public Affairs Books, N.Y.
19. Adler, E. and Barnett, M. (1998) (eds.) *Security Communities,* Cambridge University Press.
20. Buzan, B. and Wæver, O. (2004) *Regions and Powers.* Cambridge University Press, Cambridge, UK.
21. Brooks, D. 'The retreat to tribalism', NYT, 3 January 2018, p. 9.
22. Smith, R. *The Utility of Force: The Art of War in the Modern World, Penguin Books, New York, 2006,* Introduction.
23. Kay, S. 'No More Free-Riding: The Political Economy of Military Power and the Transatlantic Relationship' in Matlary, J.H. and Petersson, M., op.cit.
24. H. Lunde Saxi, (2011). *Nordic defence Cooperation after the Cold War,* Oslo Files on Defence and Security, nr. 1. Oslo: Norwegian Institute for Defence Studies.
25. Snyder, J. (1977) 'The Soviet Strategic Culture: Implications for Limited Nuclear Operations', RAND. Corporation, September 1977.
26. Allison, G. (1969) '"Conceptual Models" and the Cuban Missile Crisis'. *The American Political Science Review,* Volume 63, Issue 3 (September, 1969), 689–718.

References

Allison, G. (1969). Conceptual Models' and the Cuban Missile Crisis. *The American Political Science Review, 63*(3), 689–718.

Brooks, D. (2018, January 3). The Retreat to Tribalism. *The New York Times,* p. 9.

Buzan, B., & Wæver, O. (2004). *Regions and Powers.* Cambridge: Cambridge University Press.

EXTERNAL AND INTERNAL SHOCKS: POLICY NEEDS BEYOND 'WIN-WIN'   21

Friedman, T. (2005). *The World Is Flat. A Brief History of the 21st Century*. New York: Farrar, Straus, and Giraud.

Fukyama, F. (1992). *The End of History and the Last Man*. New York: The Free Press.

Kay, S. (2013). No More Free-Riding: The Political Economy of Military Power and the Transatlantic Relationship. In J. H. Matlary & M. Petersson.

Kissinger, H. (2014). *World Order*. New York: Penguin Press.

Kupchan, C. (2012). *No One's World: The West, the Rising Rest, and the Coming Global Turn*. Oxford: Oxford University Press.

Matlary, J. H., & Petersson, M. (Eds.). (2013). *NATO's European Allies: Military Capability and Political Will*. Basingstoke: Palgrave Macmillan.

Nye, J. (2005). *Soft Power: The Means to Success in World Politics*. New York: Public Affairs.

Saxi, H. L. (2011). *Nordic Defence Cooperation After the Cold War* (Oslo Files on Defence and Security, nr. 1). Oslo: Norwegian Institute for Defence Studies.

Smith, R. (2006). *The Utility of Force: The Art of War in the Modern World*. New York: Penguin Books.

Snyder, J. (1977, September). The Soviet Strategic Culture: Implications for Limited Nuclear Operations, RAND. Corporation.

CHAPTER 2

Strategy: Deterrence, Containment, Coercion, and Confrontation

What is strategy? This concept is often used and even misused in general political discourse. Politicians often term everything a strategy, thereby emptying it of its use. Specifically they seem to speak about strategy when they mean policy: there is a strategy for childcare and a strategy for clean air in cities. Rarely do these uses of strategy imply *interaction* with enemies or adversaries—there is no strategic interaction, only the action of the ones making the policy. Henry Kissinger's masterly study[1] of the balance-of-power system of Europe tells a story of European pre-eminence in world politics. Yet during Cold War and ever since Europe has relied on the US for the use of force and has developed—even to the point of mastery—the ability to conduct foreign policy using only so-called soft power. The EU is the primary example of this. This policy of 'carrots only' has been a healthy diet; the EU has been extremely successful in terms of the power of attraction after 1990, peacefully integrating East-Central Europe and now the Balkans. But this has not required interaction with adversary powers.

In order to assess whether Western politicians actually act strategically, we first need to understand what strategy entails:

Strategic studies as an academic field belongs to political science, and came into being after WWII.[2] Military strategy is of course as old as war itself. The study of strategic interaction during the Cold War was completely dominated by game theoretic models of rationality. Balance-of-power theory—the essence of political realism—shared the same notion of rationality and the assumption of the centrality of the state as actor. Cold

© The Author(s) 2018
J. H. Matlary, *Hard Power in Hard Times,*
https://doi.org/10.1007/978-3-319-76514-3_2

23

War war games defined rationality within strict and clear definitions of actors and interests. According to this logic, nuclear war was irrational because there would be retaliation. The various doctrines developed by NATO during this period were thus premised on a clear existential threat picture and a clear actor structure, consisting of the two superpowers.

After the Cold War this changed. The Europeans ceased to think in strategic terms, and deterrence and balance-of-power between states was abandoned. Now the system was no longer bipolar and the threat was not all-out nuclear war. Russian resurgence as exemplified by the Georgian and Ukrainian cases signalled the return of great power politics. Yet Western security policy since the Cold War has not dealt with threats and therefore not with strategic thinking.[3] Instead Western leaders have promoted democracy or nation-building, first as a continuation of humanitarian intervention and later as the response to terrorism.[4]

Threat and risk in the post-Cold War period is often diffuse and strategic thinking is therefore not always able to concentrate on specific threats that the state should plan for. Moreover, as more non-state actors have become involved on the world stage, the state is no longer the only kind of actor. Most armed conflicts since the Cold War have taken place inside states rather than as wars between military machines owned by states. This security situation has led to increasing emphasis on *risk management* instead of strategic thinking, something which typically involves policy only, nor adversarial analysis. The risk is evaluated as either acceptable or too high, and if the latter, has to be acted upon by way of some policy. Yet one does not have to interact with the risk—that makes no sense.

STRATEGIC OPTIONS

Strategic options can usefully be classified as deterrence, coercion, containment, and confrontation. *Deterrence* combined with containment was the strategy pursued by the West towards the Soviet Union throughout the Cold War. NATO deterred with a combination of nuclear and conventional weapons, while politically it chose a long-term strategy of containment. The famous 'Long Telegram' written by George Kennan in 1946[5] when he was a diplomat in the US embassy in Moscow recommended containing the Soviet Union and waiting for results in the long run while remaining fully concentrated on deterrence in the short term.

Coercion is directed against an enemy in an attempt to make him[6] stop his undertaking. Both economic and military tools can be coercive, but the military tool is the most credible, if states are willing to use it. The strategic options for battling terrorism are much fewer than those that apply in normal strategic interaction between states. One cannot deter fanatics who are willing to die for their cause. One cannot *contain* the states where terrorists train and live, nor contain these groups directly. The best option, and perhaps the only one, is to fight terrorism in two ways: first, using intelligence as a main strategy, and second, fight directly with military means if such groups become too powerful in acquiring territory and resources. The latter strategy of *confrontation* became necessary against al-Qaida in Afghanistan after the attack on Manhattan in 2011. A similar development happened when Daesh became too powerful in terms of territory held in 2013. A coalition to fight the group was formed under US leadership and intelligence was intensified as a first line of defence in Western countries.

Strategic action also includes 'shaping' the political environment by deterring others from doing the same. A state or group of states must act strategically to prevent developments that they consider unacceptable. Thus, deterring other powers from putting pressure on one's own state is a primary form of strategic action in peacetime. This entails both the ability to define so-called red lines and to act if they are crossed. Both deterrence—a general way of communicating strength and willpower to defend red lines, and coercion, in specific cases—are primary aspects of a state's strategic ability. The use of force in deployments can be said to result from the failure of these other two forms of strategic action, either because the adversary will not be deterred or coerced, or because the acting state or group of states is unwilling and unable to act strategically to begin with. Confrontation then becomes the only option, the most risky and deadly one.

As Gray points out, 'strategy is so difficult to do well that it is remarkable that it is ever practised successfully'.[7] He adds that when operational art is all that matters, strategy is often neglected: 'when that operational grip … substitutes for strategic grasp, one is in deep trouble'.[8] This is a very salient point regarding the use of force in Europe: Operations have been the political focus, not the use of force to *avoid* them through deterrence and/or coercion. This is the point that Emile Simpson makes in his book *War from the Ground Up*.[9] There is ample use of force in Europe, but it is used like a 'fire-brigade': when things are too awful and 'something must be done', there is a 'dash' of military force thrown at the problem. This is not strategic use of force at all and therefore not *political* use of force in the sense intended by Clausewitz. There is no plan for the political effect of the use of force in such operations because there was no strategy in the first place. Strategy is 'the essential bridging function between policy ... [and war]; it is all about linking ends, ways and means'.[10] Deterrence and coercion must logically be based on a political strategy, but operations need not be. In the 'fire-brigade' *modus operandus* they are not. It is therefore not surprising that a comparative study of Europe finds 'a gradual emergence of a European strategic culture resting on a relatively narrow basis in terms of norms and social cohesion, but supporting a model of *cautious humanitarian power*' (my emphasis).[11]

Limited War as a Constant

Strategy is not a wonder cure for politics, of course. There is no point in devising a strategy in theory without putting it into practice. In fact, strategy is practice. Strachan points out that strategic theory sets out to apply rationality to what is disordered, as a tool that aids the politician.[12] He adds that we must distinguish between strategic theory and practice, and that there is no stability in strategy: it must always adapt to politics. It is always a practical tool, not a theory. The political turn of events is king; strategy that remains static is moribund. He writes: 'in the Cold War, the dynamic element of politics and strategy was lost' because theorists 'froze' the conflict between the two superpowers in time and assumed perfect rationality on the part of both actors. This became a caricature of strategy precisely for this reason, for strategy means the smart adaptation to the moves of the adversary, even to the point of choosing paradoxes' (ibid.). He points out that the Cold War shaped and still shapes our thinking about strategy, and especially about deterrence: 'the dominant instrument of cold war strategic thought, deterrence, had created the assumption that real wars were a thing of the past, not of policy'.[13]

Deterrence in this particular period was of an all-out nuclear kind, static and mechanistic rather than an instrument of policy. The importance of nuclear weapons in Cold War deterrence accounts for its 'apolitical' character, something which is ill-suited to present purposes. Today there are not two superpowers interlocked in a static manner, but various types of risks and threats where the use of force is real, in limited wars.

European leaders may have some notion of deterrence and strategy, but unfortunately it often stems from the Cold War period:

The years since the Cold War, and particularly since the 9/11 attacks of 2001, have therefore been ones of re-education for the Europeans. Armed conflict has become much more frequent. The phrase 'new wars' (whether they are really new or not) and the doctrine of humanitarian intervention are both ways of making the frequency of war comprehensible for liberal middle classes accustomed to the norms of peace. But this process has not removed the sense of fear. The trepidation in the use of war is not just a matter of war's casualties, its destructiveness and its loss of life. It is an anxiety as to its political consequences. The great powers of the 19th century, for all that they may not be the great powers of the 21st, have not lost the habits of mind which gave them that status in the first place.[14]

Thus, some states never left their strategic culture behind. Today, like before, states across the globe use force as a tool of statecraft:

> Some states remain robustly ready to use military force in the pursuit of policy goals. To name only the most obvious and immediate, Russia did so in South Ossetia in 2008, Israel in Gaza in 2008–09, and the US in Iraq and Afghanistan in 2002 and 2003.[15]

The use of force has a continuous history in all these states and they maintain a continuous strategic culture.

The wars they wage are limited, for limited political interests—this is the main mode of warfare at all times, as the disaggregation of both world wars shows. The present-day use of force is *both limited and state-to-state*—not asymmetric and civil: 'Therefore, as well as deterrence, there is another concept which has also gone out of fashion but which needs rethinking, and that is limited war.'[16]

Using Britain as an example, Strachan points out that

> Britain's insouciance about inter-state war is remarkable given that it has fought against another state five times since 1982 – to retake the Falklands from Argentina in 1982, to drive Iraq out of Kuwait in 1990–91, to protect the Kosovars from Serbia in 1999, to topple Saddam Hussein in 2003, and to bring about the fall of the Gaddafi regime in Libya in 2011. Moreover, the deployment of British troops to Sierra Leone and Afghanistan were both examples of armed conflict where the issues were both governance and state formation. *If Britain is an example, states have not abandoned using war as an instrument of policy.* (my emphasis)[17]

There is thus a difference between the mindset of the great powers—only two of which, France and Britain, are in Europe—and many of the rest of Europe in terms of strategic culture, he argues. The former have retained a strategic culture, while the rest have never had one. Yet these smaller states now use force in various operations and limited wars like never before in their history, although they lack the political tradition of thinking and acting strategically.

Strachan argues that there is no essential difference between the risk of state-to-state war in the past and today—small wars can easily escalate, and one conflict can lead to another. In fact, the commonly held view that state-to-state wars are largely a thing of the past may not be based in reality. Most wars seem to start as limited wars, but the political challenge of controlling the use of force is so great that wars tend to follow their own logic. He makes the point that 'the First World War not only began as a Balkan war, the third since 1912, but it also continued as one – even beyond 1918 ... to get to the bottom of the First World war as a global war, we first have to disaggregate it into a series of regional conflicts'.[18] If we study WWII, 'similar points can be made ... what happened between 1939 and 1941 was a series of bilateral campaigns waged by Germany to overrun each of Poland, Norway, Denmark, Holland, Belgium, and France, before it turned on Romania, Yugoslavia, Greece and Russia'.[19]

Our post-Cold War thinking has assumed that limited war will exclude major war. But what if most wars start out as limited ones? Is there really much difference between the period prior to and after the Cold War? The conception that the West uses force only in faraway lands and only for humanitarian purposes has been widely entertained since the Cold War. The so-called peace dividend and the drawing down of defence budgets were premised on the idea that military force was a largely outdated tool of statecraft. Perhaps this was mistaken; perhaps the West misunderstood the past and assumed that major wars were unthinkable because the template was the two world wars.

As Strachan and others argue, all wars as we know them have started as limited wars, inter- or intra-state that then escalated into regional and even world wars. As Dominic Tierny puts it, 'in the current strategic environment, limited interstate war is an essential option in the military tool-box'.[20]

There was really no 'paradigm shift' after 1990 from conventional inter-state wars to insurrections and asymmetric threats, but rather a quiet period in terms of great power politics and an eruption of insurrections due to Russia losing its grip in the Balkans and elsewhere. But most wars have been fought between states and eventually involved regime change, including the Bosnian and Serbian wars in the 1990s. The much-touted 'paradigm shift' away from inter-state wars of a conventional kind, like the acclaimed phrase that opens Sir Rupert Smith's book—that war as we have known it no longer exists—is an overstatement. Moreover, the asymmetric '"war among the people" has a much longer pedigree than the recent impact of the phrase as applied by another British strategic thinker, general Sir Rupert Smith',[21] writes Strachan.

A POLITICAL CLASS OBLIVIOUS TO STRATEGY

There are a number of implications that follow from the starting point that the 'new' wars are 'optional' and of lesser importance than traditional wars. One is that they do not concern national interests; another is that public opinion carries more weight than it once did. This latter consideration has become a standard feature of Western politics—re-election and therefore popularity at the polls trump security policy. Both President Obama and Prime Minister Cameron showed this in practice when they announced an exit date from Afghanistan. The course of the war played no role in deciding this, public opinion and national casualties did. There can be no better illustration of how unimportant the warfare in theatre really was. The collection of essays by British generals *British Generals in Blair's Wars*[22] is depressing reading in this respect. The major theme is politicians' lack of strategic interest in the use of force. Tony Blair, remarked General Tom Cross, 'didn't seem to ... understand the scope and complexity of what was going to be needed in the aftermath of the invasion [of Iraq]. I don't think he understood what the possible consequences could be.'[23] This means that the strategic level does not direct and that the operational and tactical levels substitute for strategy.

Strachan writes:

> Arguably strategy has been absent throughout the wars in Iraq and Afghanistan. In part that is because the political objects have been unclear, or variable, or defined in too broad terms to be deliverable in strategic terms. Because there has been no clear relationship between the ends and the limited (and often inappropriate) means, strategy is simply not possible. The result has often been shaped by platoon and company commanders, a series of ill-coordinated tactical actions, where killing and casualties define success.[24]

The implications of the lack of strategic direction to a campaign are even more dire in asymmetric warfare than in conventional and limited operations, as will be discussed below. In such operations—usually COIN (counter-insurgency)—the 'political effects are part of the immediate framework of military action'[25] and they are therefore much more difficult to plan for and to direct. The soldier on the ground may act with strategic political implications.

Yet despite this, Western governments have undertaken several such operations since 1990, some as so-called peace enforcement. Sadly the only political goals in the end seem to be to get out as soon as possible and to avoid casualties. This is another way of saying that these governments should not have become involved at all, and entails a defeatist and even unethical attitude. General Victor d'Urbal's words from 1922 are worth quoting: 'One does not prepare for war in general, but for a *specific* war, waged in order to obtain a *given* result, in a *defined* theatre of operations, against a *given* adversary, who deploys or is able to deploy in a *given* period, *given* means' (my emphasis).[26]

Simpson makes the important point that the old notion of war as the confrontation with the enemy has become replaced by a view of war as a form of 'armed politics' where war is no different from normal peacetime activity. The use of force therefore no longer requires serious strategic preparation and direction, and this explains why strategy is no longer the 'jewel in the crown' of statesmanship. The West uses its military forces like a fire-brigade: action is only taken when there is an emergency and something must be done. While we will still send in the fire-brigade to put out a fire that is actively burning, we do little to prevent fires from breaking out in the first place. This is the problem with the West's use of force, Simpson argues: on the one hand, it has become far too easy to deploy these 'forces for good' or 'fire-brigade'—we are after all never engaged in wars anymore, only in tactical operations. On the other hand the reality of the military tool is apparent—it is dangerous, destructive, not to mention deadly for our troops; but this reality cannot really be accommodated in the 'force for good'-version of things.

Governments therefore distance themselves from their own use of the military tool. This leads to cognitive dissonance and to 'stakeholder war', something which means that the war has political effects for many audiences, the effects are not only in theatre. The effects on voters might be much more important than the effects on the enemy. Simpson's highly interesting analysis concludes thus: '*liberal democracies seem to sleepwalk into the fusion of war and routine international politics,* they do not seem to grasp that ... this will challenge core aspects of the liberal tradition' (my emphasis).[27]

The main problem, Simpson maintains, is that 'currently, war is not compartmentalised as it should be. By increasingly merging it with regular political activity ... we are confronted with policy as the extension of war, that used to be the wrong way round.'[28] This is very serious; governments engage in reactive behaviour without any plan or direction. War-fighting comes first, without a strategy behind it; only later, when they see its adverse consequences, do politicians then try to justify and legitimize the use of force. Often the reasons for deploying force in the first place are not serious enough or thought through, as it is no longer the seriousness of deploying *ultima ratio*, but, as Simpson says, almost as if war has become a normal foreign policy pursuit—as long as it is on a small scale, can be justified as good and humanitarian, has a UN mandate or a coalition behind it, and troops can be withdrawn quickly.

What is so fundamentally wrong with this approach, where the focus is on the means—military force—and not on the goal—political ends—is that governments can abdicate their strategic and ethical responsibility. They wash their hands of the operation when things go badly, and in fact, they do not know why they sent in the troops in the first place. Which national interest was at stake? What warranted the use of the most serious and dangerous tools of statecraft?

For these reasons governments in Western Europe are poorly equipped for such strategic leadership—as its requirements go against the liberal-democratic model of pluralism, conflict-resolution by discussion, rejection of threats and pressure by using force, and a need for re-election that grows as the political class sees itself as a class of professionals. In addition, strategy is difficult intellectually—it requires a detailed plan, but works according to the facts as they unfold, and must be supple so that one may adjust to enemy moves and perhaps pre-empt them. There has to be immense flexibility and unity of political command, as of military command. It goes without saying that multinational organizations have even less ability to act in this manner, so when Western Europe uses the EU or NATO as their platform of action, disagreement easily becomes a permanent problem of an operation, as it did when NATO conducted its air war on Serbia in 1999. There was daily and very public disagreement between the then 19 member states about details like targeting.[29] Yet without strategy, chaos threatens in a volatile and dangerous environment: 'Strategy occupies the space between a desired outcome, presumably shaped by the national interest, and contingency.'[30]

Interacting with others who may not share your interests and intentions—and in fact, who can be assumed to differ with you on both—is the essence of diplomacy. Conflict of interest is normal, and states usually seek to advance their interests, often at the expense of other states. 'Carrots' and 'sticks' are the normal ingredients of almost all foreign policy—inducing certain behaviour and imposing sanctions if goals are not achieved through inducements.

Yet the use of military force is different from stick and carrot diplomacy because it entails both risk and unforeseen consequences. The side that threatens the use of force runs a big risk. The threat must be credible if it is to have any effect. If and when, however, the threat of force translates into real military action, there are casualties. Ending a war can be very difficult, and it most certainly has unforeseen consequences, both in theatre and at home, as Clausewitz underlined. However, the strategic logic of interaction remains the same in diplomacy as in war: states with different interests interact with one another and each seeks to influence the will of the other side. Sometimes there is a real clash of wills, and one therefore has to apply stronger pressure. Mostly this is done verbally and economically, but the military tool remains a shaper of international politics because it deters and because it may be called on in 'gun boat diplomacy' (coercion) or in actual use. Given this, general foreign policy requires strategic thinking, at least when conflicts of interests are in play. And when the use of force is relevant, there should always be a strategy, because this tool is both difficult to use in terms of getting strategic political effect, and it entails risk of life and death as well as causing material damage. *In short, general foreign policy should be based on strategy, but the use of force must be based on it.*

Strachan states that 'the nature of war ... lies at the heart of strategy',[31] and that 'war's character changes, and it does so for reasons that are social and political as often as they are technological, but war's *nature* still provides sufficient fixed points to make the study of war as a discrete historical phenomenon a legitimate activity' (324, my emphasis). This is the same point made by Clausewitz and most strategic thinkers—much may change, especially in terms of military technology and political surroundings, but the adverse and even hostile interaction in a strategic relationship among adversaries and enemies remains a constant. Clausewitz defined war as a clash of wills, a battle to force the enemy to accept our will. This same interaction characterizes political strategy as well as military strategy: 'the dynamic generated by the decisions of two sides to use armed force against each other generates recurrent features – many of them easily forgotten because they have become clichés: the fog of war, the play of friction, the role of chance, the importance of will, the function of courage and fear. Most important of all is the reciprocity in war created by the clash of wills.'[32] The statesman must know what strategic logic entails if he is to use force. However, as argued above, this is very unfamiliar in postmodern European politics.

STRATEGY AS THE DIRECTION OF WAR

Strachan makes another salient point, also unwelcome in postmodern politics, namely that it is war and the use of force that is at the heart of strategy—not diplomacy: 'the fog of war, the play of friction, the role of chance, the importance of will, the function of courage and fear'.[33] This is always war's nature which must be recognized. The tool of statecraft at the centre of both deterrence and coercion is the military tool, and strategy at its core concerns directing wars, not other kinds of activity. Precisely because so much is at stake in fighting a war, there is a need for the rationality that strategic analysis imposes. There will continue to be limited wars between states, as there have been in the past. The idea that the threat of the use of force and the use of force itself should disappear from Europe seems naïve at best, Strachan argues. There is therefore a need now to rediscover what deterrence is and to devise strategies for deterrence: 'deterrence is still in play, albeit in ways that are hardly recognised and therefore unsung'.[34] The same goes for coercion—how can this tool be effectively used?

The essence of strategy thus remains unchanged: it is the dangerous and vitally important interaction of adversaries, even enemies. Edward Luttwak, another major scholar of strategy, writes:

> The warlike dealings of national leaders and governments with one another are subject to exactly the same logic of strategy as are the interactions of their fighting forces. But it is far more difficult for national leaders to understand that logic beneath all the complications of the multiple levels of an entire war. Besides, national leaders can rarely apply whatever strategic insights they may have. To preserve their power and authority within their own societies, democratic leaders must obey the linear logic of consensual politics. That means, for example, that they cannot act paradoxically to surprise external enemies, because they must inform and prepare their public before acting [...] a *conscious understanding of the phenomena of strategy is a great rarity among political leaders.* (my emphasis)[35]

Luttwak calls our age one of post-heroic warfare: only the most important existential interest allows for deploying soldiers in wars, although, he notes, some military force is often used in 'humanitarian' operations. This means that deterrence and coercion—the vital 'shaping of the environment'—are almost impossible because serious force is used only in extreme cases, and even then only in operations, not as deterrence and coercion. This in turn means that Western leaders deprive themselves of the most effective of the military tools at hand, and also of the entire logic of strategy.

As stated before, European states are in the paradoxical situation of using military force rather frequently, but with great unwillingness for the most part. They use force in operations without having done the homework of strategy and using deterrence and/or coercion. They therefore often *react* instead of plan, and troops are deployed in reaction to events, only when things have gone so far that the infamous cry that 'something must be done' is heard. But this kind of use of force usually leads to few lasting political results, not least because of the various political caveats that Western states impose on themselves including policies of no 'boots on the ground', a preference for quick operations, and an unwillingness to take risk, therefore only using air power, and so on.

Recent operations such as Kosovo and Libya have been under such restrictions, and the International Security Assistance Force (ISAF) operation in Afghanistan included more national caveats than any previous operation. Although there were no casualties on the Western side in the air-only operations that were launched in Kosovo and Libya, there was a major loss of military effectiveness because Western governments did not make use of the complementarity of the military means. Had there, for example, been ground troops deployed in Kosovo, Milosevic would have had to counter these with armoured battalions that would have been visible from the air and easy targets to hit. However, without the need to field ground troops himself he could hide his tanks and save his troops. The war therefore lasted longer than necessary.

The lack of willingness to use the military tool according to its own logic among Western politicians today thus leads to its sub-optimal use.

It is the resurgence of Russia that has led to the return of the concept of deterrence in European politics; not the need for strategic use of force. Deterrence has returned to the vocabulary of NATO simply because Russia has shown increasing willingness to use force both as a threat and in actual operations. But deterrence also extends to other security risks, such as mass migration and possibly terrorism. A general political message of 'red lines' is also relevant in dealing with this more diffuse non-state threat since Western states cannot tolerate terrorism becoming too powerful a threat. The latter consideration was the policy of the US in *Operation Enduring Freedom* in Afghanistan in October 2001 and in the aerial attack on Daesh in Iraq in the summer of 2014. The decision to attack was not based on the fact that terrorists operated in these states, but happened because these organizations had acquired territory and state-like capacities and infrastructure. The level of risk became unacceptable.

DETERRENCE AND COERCION IN LIMITED AND HYBRID WAR

What exactly is it that Europe is set to deter and coerce? The major difference between the Cold War and the present lies in the type of threat and risk that exist today as compared to a state-to-state confrontation between the US and Europe and the USSR in Cold War scenarios. While it is clear that state-to-state existential wars are no longer likely—even if this type of conflict must also be deterred—the kinds of armed conflict that are most likely to be used today are not clearly defined.[36] A useful starting point is the concept of *limited* war, military operations carried out for limited political purposes.

Limited war thus differs from the common conception of war as total or existential war. In the latter category we would naturally put WWI, WWII, and the Cold War. Yet, as Strachan pointed out, even WWI—the so-called Great War—started as a limited war, which people though would only last for a few weeks in August 1914.[37] Moreover, the aim of the use of force today is usually not territorial gain in the old sense of extending one's borders, but rather to establish influence in a state or region. In this sense the use of force is more in line with Clausewitz than before—it is the *political* effect of the use of force which is sought, not invasion and conquest of new lands. Thus, when Russia sends forces to aid rebels in Ukraine, the aim is not to conquer and annex Ukraine but to establish a situation on the ground that makes it politically impossible for Ukraine to seek EU and NATO membership. Often a 'frozen conflict' is enough to accomplish this kind of political goal; but such conflicts can be turned into war-fighting if there is a need to underscore the political message of discord, division, and uncertainty. One exception to this approach is Crimea, which could be seen as an example of old-fashioned occupation and a change of state borders.

Limited war might be the most prevalent type of war today, but are these wars always fought in a conventional manner? Here it may be useful to think about limited war in relation to total war: while the latter is most often conducted using conventional methods, the former is more likely to involve irregular war-fighting. Total war, by necessity, is conventional when fought between states (as we assume it is), but limited war is often waged in a lopsided fashion—it is typically conventional for states and irregular for non-state actors like insurgents. Afghanistan is a good example of this: The states involved used conventional methods, wore uniforms, and followed the laws of war, while the Taliban did none of these things. Here we also see that the insurgents were fighting a total or existential war, whereas the West was fighting a limited war. This discrepancy has implications for morale and the willingness to take risk: the side fighting for existential survival is naturally more risk-willing and may therefore prevail in the long run.

HYBRID WAR

For this reason, *guerrilla* warfare between a state actor with conventional arms and non-state actors with primitive arms is once again relevant today. It was 'resurrected' in the military academies of the West when the Taliban again became a threat to Western forces.[38] 'Small wars' or irregular wars are on the agenda, not only in Afghanistan, but in the Maghreb and the Middle East. One term for small wars that exhibit a mixture of actor types and weapons types is 'hybrid war'. This has become the standard term to describe Russian warfare in the Crimea and Ukraine in 2014–15.

Wiijk argues that 'at the beginning of the 21st century, hybrid warfare has been the best concept by which to understand contemporary wars. In hybrid warfare, the distinction between large, regular wars and small, irregular wars has become blurred.'[39] It is a mixture of traditional conventional means and guerrilla warfare where non-military tools are prominent, if not the most important. Subversion, destabilization, and covert action—all the traditional 'tricks of the trade'—are used.

At a seminar with higher NATO officials at Chatham House in London in November 2014, the term 'hybrid war' was used as a descriptive classification of the type of war being waged in Crimea and Ukraine.[40] However, this term is not precise and runs the risk of being yet another label for an asymmetric type of warfare. It was used first in 2006 to describe the armed conflict between Hezbollah and Israel in which the former used asymmetric methods while the latter used conventional force. The Russian version of hybrid warfare is one in which information operations, subversion, special forces, and local uprising instigation combine with the occasional use of conventional force in the most abrasive manner, such as when forces are massed at the Ukrainian border and large exercises are carried out there without due notice given.

McDermott makes the point that we should not think that the Russians have invented a new type of modern warfare called 'hybrid'.[41] This label can mask the fact that the Russian approach consists of traditional conventional operations, including cyber operations, subversion, and disinformation campaigns. These elements are used as they suit the purpose, he argues.

The Russian Chief of General Staff (COD) Valery Gerasimov is often cited as the key thinker behind that concept. In a now-famous article, 'The Value of Science in Prediction', published in the obscure *Military-Industrial Courier* on 27 February 2013, General Gerasimov presents a blueprint for an operation like the Crimean one.

If we agree to call the most typical modern type of warfare 'hybrid', what are the strategic requirements for deterring, coercing, and fighting such wars? And how well are the liberal democracies of Europe prepared for such strategic challenges?

State-to-State Armed Conflict as a Strategic Challenge: Deterrence and Coercion

The work on coercion and deterrence as key strategies remains dominated by US scholarship from the Cold War period. The main preoccupation in a scenario that included everything from nuclear war to conventional invasion was with deterrence, and a large amount of work was written on this concept in the specific setting of the nuclear 'terror' balance between the US and the USSR.[42]

The emphasis was on a specific type of coercion, namely deterrence, and on how US foreign policy would work best. There was little general work on coercion as such. It related to the US-USSR systemic level threat situation where nuclear weapons were in play. The stakes were extremely high, higher than in an existential state-to-state war with conventional weapons. This made the strategic task different from the strategic requirements for deterrence of current Russian use of force, although the role of nuclear weapons continues to play a role also in current thinking about deterrence. Deterrence must of necessity also include high-end threats, as one cannot deter low-end threats such as 'hybrid' war (if that can be deterred) and leave it that—something which would encourage the adversary to go beyond 'low end'.

With regard to coercion—the active way of influencing someone to stop an action—there is little scholarly literature. This is because the main strategic challenge in the cold war was deterrence—using or threatening to use force was far too dangerous, given the prevalence of nuclear weapons and the nature of the strategic game where two actors confronted each other in an existential scenario. As Freedman[43] notes, coercion as a general phenomenon was studied so little in the cold war period that the scholarly literature consisted only of a few books, most notably those of Thomas Schelling,[44] and, later, of Alexander George and William Simons.[45] Schelling's *Arms and Influence* from 1966 was optimistic about the use of force as a tool of statecraft, but George and Simon's work, written after the Vietnam War, was more cautious. An inductive analysis based on case studies, the latter work came out of the important Rand Corporation intellectual milieu which was the key hub for thinking about deterrence and coercion in the Cold War period.

As mentioned, more recently, Rob de Wijk's has criticized Western powers and their ability to use force in *The Art of Military Coercion—Why the West's Military Superiority Hardly Matters*,[46] and the detailed scholarly work based on case studies by Peter Willy Jacobsen, inter alia *Western Use of Diplomacy after the Cold War: A Challenge for Theory and Practise*[47] and 'The Strategy of Coercive Diplomacy: Refining Existing Theory to Post-Cold War Realities'.[48]

Freedman has published a major volume of more than 700 pages entitled *Strategy—A History*,[49] in which he reflects on the historical understanding of and current ideas about the concept. He tends to see strategy as the art of war, 'the creative element in any exercise of power'.[50] Strategy is thus not a 'mathematical' type of calculus, but more a site of innovation and creativity where the statesman or general can undertake paradoxical moves that may or may not be successful. Luttwak has even argued that really good strategy is paradoxical in nature, outsmarting the logic of the adversary.[51]

Strategy is thus about prevailing or winning in terms of one's political aims, thereby changing the political calculus of the enemy or being his will, as Clausewitz would have termed it. *The very clash of wills that he talked about is the essence of strategy.* This point was brought home when Western state leaders still talked about Russia as a partner after the sanctions against had been adopted, as Norwegian PM Solberg did in an interview in *Dagens Næringsliv*,[52] before the NATO summit in Cardiff. When corrected, she changed her designation to 'adversary', but added that Norway wanted to re-establish partnership with Russia as soon as possible. In 2014 it was clearly very foreign and unwelcome for most Western politicians to have an adversarial relationship with Russia, and it is a situation they would like to change as soon as possible.

Strategic thinking is familiar to Western politicians in trade and economic matters where national interests are clear and often clash. The need for each country to negotiate the best regime for its business interests is evident. No one expects altruism in economic policy. It is also in this area that we find the war metaphors in modern Western politics—we have trade wars, raids, and hostile takeovers. When it comes to the much more conflictual area of security and military affairs, however, Western politicians are much less familiar with the tool of force as well as with its effects. Few have any real-life experience in this field; it is by now more than 70 years since WWII broke out and the generation that had war-time experience is mostly dead. Indeed, the period since 1990 has been peaceful on the European continent. Moreover, as Freedman states, 'Strategic coercion is not an easy option'.[53] In addition to the difficulties mentioned above, making strategy work is in itself very difficult.

What kind of strategic requirements are we talking about when we talk about deterrence and coercion? For Freedman, deterrence is a special kind of coercion that 'involves a demand of inaction and compellence a demand for action'.[54] He seems to use the term coercion for both deterrence and compellence, the latter being the active pressure and ultimatum brought to bear on an adversary, the former the passive threat inherent in being prepared to counter an attack. A useful way of defining deterrence, then, is that it aims to prevent undesirable things from happening, whereas coercion or compellence aims actively to stop someone who is already acting or using force, that is, to bend their will.

In this study I use the term deterrence to mean the defensive and general activity of stopping an adversary from doing what he otherwise may opt to do. It is not a passive activity—which is a contradiction in terms—but a *general* and *defensive* activity not aimed at anyone or any act in particular. It seeks to send the message that a 'red line' exists. The most obvious example is NATO's Article 5. Deterrence is the most preferable strategic position; it is one of strength and of little risk. Freedman says that 'indeed, we would prefer to wait forever'.[55]

Being well armed and prepared enough to scare off anyone trying to test one's resolve is the ideal position in strategy. One need not interact with the enemy and deal with the risks related to such interaction. In particular, if a state or alliance has superior military strength, this mere fact threatens to discipline and thus influences enemy behaviour. They may use other means to try to reach their goals, but not the military tool.

Deterrence is the main rationale for NATO and relies wholly on credibility. Is Article 5 credible for all member states? If the answer is yes, all is well and good. If not, the entire credibility of the alliance is in jeopardy. Will Turkey be assisted according to the terms of Article 5 if either Daesh, the Kurds, and/or Assad's forces violate its borders? The border is routinely violated already, but these incursions may be inadvertent and have so far resulted in Article 4 consultations and in the deployment of Patriot missiles. What about the Baltic states? When is Article 5 at stake, how large is the gap between a situation that should be handled at the national level and one that should involve the alliance? Does NATO really have the rapid reaction capacity to deploy to the rim of the alliance in time? What kinds of weapons are needed to deter 'hybrid' operations, such as the ones seen in Crimea and Ukraine? Special forces or tanks?—These are the questions that are pertinent to discussions of how deterrence can be made credible today. If it is not credible, the NATO alliance as such is at stake. With 28 members, of which many are poorly equipped and trained, these are the more important questions.

But deterrence is often combined with coercion of some kind, as in the Russian case discussed in this book. NATO is tasked with deterring Russia, but in the Ukraine case it is the EU and the US that coerce Russia with economic sanctions. Strategy that aims at both deterrence and coercion is complicated: 'deterrence and compellence merge when the attempt is made to deter continuance of something the opponent is already doing', Freedman remarks.[56] The difference between the two disappears once the conflict has begun. Both are forms of strategic coercion, he maintains. If NATO is the 'shield' in this effort, the EU is the 'sword'.

In the case of Russia and Europe, it is clear that deterrence and coercion happen at the same time, but European coercion is explicitly NOT military, but economic. The US and the EU impose economic sanctions on Russia, while NATO mounts a deterrent effort in especially the Baltic area. However, these sanctions, I argue, do not really qualify as coercion since the demands made are not specific enough, as we will see below in Chap. 9.

In his work on modern coercion by coalitions of Western states, Jakobsen[57] argues that 'after cold war, the demand for coercion has increased sharply. The conflicts far away are time and again placed on our agenda because of international media: the lack of threat of nuclear escalation means that we are into more and more conflicts, and R2p (responsibility to protect) also explains this.' Yet Europe's coercive diplomacy record is poor,[58] he continues, and he sets out to refine George's framework, quoting his assertion that 'knowledge of coercive diplomacy remains provisional and incomplete. It will be and should continue to be refined with the study of additional historical cases.'[59]

Jakobsen's model seeks to define the minimum conditions for success in coercion, and he takes as his point of departure coalitions of states as the actor and concentrates on cases where the adversary has already resorted to force. This makes his framework of analysis especially attractive for analysing the strategic interaction between the West and Russia. He starts by noting that coercion is more prevalent now than during the Cold War, and that it will remain a key issue in the time ahead, as it purports to reverse undesirable action.

The combination of military deterrence and economic sanctions in the Russian case arguably makes it relevant to see the sanctions as a type of coercion even if they do not expressly contain military means. Jakobsen points out that 'the stick has to instil fear in the mind of the adversary for the strategy to qualify as coercive diplomacy'.[60] In the case in question, 'adverse effects' or economic hardship are substituted for fear. In this sense, sanctions are similar to, but still different from, coercion. Coercion is more specific; it aims at stopping or undoing a specific kind of action. Both compellence and coercion stop short of the massive use of force that is war. Coercive diplomacy must give the adversary time and possibility of complying; in other words, there must be a real opportunity for diplomacy.

In sum, deterrence concerns keeping another state from doing something it may otherwise try to do, whereas coercion concerns stopping a state from doing what it has already started to do. In both cases we speak about the use of military force. Sanctions concern the economic and/or political tools of statecraft, but may occur along with the use of force.

Deterrence, in all its political and military aspects, is of the utmost importance. Writing in 2014 Haftendorn argues that politics enter much more into deterrence today than in the Cold War, and therefore 'resolve is more important than capabilities'.[61] But resolve is not enough. Solid and credible deterrence should be accompanied by a strategy of *containment*.

George Kennan's advice in the famous 'long telegram' may still hold—perhaps Russia must be contained? In the present circumstances political and economic sanctions seem to be the best method of containment, but they must be designed to have an effect, and not merely as symbolic politics. They must also be long-lasting, requiring unity of action over months and perhaps years. This is a formidable task for the EU, especially with regard to containment of terrorists. States can be contained—perhaps—but groups and individuals cannot.

What about *coercion*? Although the sanctions are intended to coerce, this objective is hard to achieve. To coerce without the threat of military force is extremely difficult, but not impossible. In Ukraine, however, it is clear that coercion without credible military threat is impossible when Russia is already using force. Diplomatic and economic means alone cannot stop an adversary that uses military force in the same theatre.

Also migration shocks must be *deterred* in order to be controllable. Deterrence in this area can be to make it undesirable to travel to Europe, a strategy many states attempt. It can also be strict border controls and even border closures, but a sustainable strategy will have to address the root causes of migration and help develop states marred by war and corruption.

Coercion is a kind of confrontation, and it is not a good option unless one is willing to threaten military force. Confronting terrorists on the battlefield is usually a poor option, but perhaps a necessary one since deterrence and containment are impossible. Attacks on terrorist groups that have too much regional power to be ignored—including those on al-Qaeda in 2001 in Afghanistan, in Mali in 2011, and in Iraq in 2013—are necessitated by the lack of other strategic options. Confrontation in the form of fighting is sometimes the consequence of a lack of other options, and sometimes the result of failed deterrence and coercion.

In the next chapters I discuss what kind of strategic options Russian revisionism, migration shocks, and terrorism call for. At the end of these chapters I suggest optimal strategies for meeting the current challenges. In Part II of the book I examine whether European great powers and international organizations act strategically in dealing with these three sets of problems.

Notes

1. Kissinger, H. (1994) *Diplomacy*, Simon & Schuster, N.Y.
2. Baylis, J. et al, (2016), *Strategy in the Contemporary World*, Oxford University Press, Oxford.

STRATEGY: DETERRENCE, CONTAINMENT, COERCION... 43

3. De Wijk, R. (2005) *The Art of Military Coercion: Why the West's Military Superiority Scarcely Matters*, Mets & Schilt, Amsterdam, 2005.
4. Lindley-French, J. (2012) 'Strategic Leadership and War', in ibid. and Boyer, *The Oxford Handbook of War*, Oxford University Press, Oxford.
5. Published in Hanhimäki, J. and Westad, O. A. (eds) (2004) *The Cold War: A History in Documents and Eyewitness Accounts*.
6. Military theory invariably speaks about the adversary or enemy as 'he', perhaps as a reflection of gentlemanly behaviour?
7. Gray, C. pp. 159–178, 'Strategic Thought for Defence Planners', p. 166.
8. Ibid., p. 167.
9. Simpson, E. (2013) *War from the Ground Up*, Oxford University Press, Oxford.
10. Gray, op.cit., p. 167.
11. Meyer, Chr. (2006) *The Quest for a European Strategic Culture. Changing Norms on Security and Defence in the EU*, p. 11. Palgrave Macmillan, UK.
12. 'Strategy in the 21st Century'.
13. Strachan, H. (2013) *The Direction of War*, Cambridge University Press, Cambridge, p. 125.
14. Ibid.
15. Ibid., p. 335.
16. Ibid.
17. Ibid., p. 333.
18. Ibid., p. 128.
19. Ibid.
20. *How we fight: crusades, quagmires, and the American way of war*, New York, p. 250.
21. Strachan, op.cit., p. 185.
22. Bailey, J, Iron, R, and Strachan, H. (eds.) (2013) *British Generals in Blair's Wars*, Ashgate, UK.
23. Ibid., p. 23.
24. Ibid., p. 267.
25. Ibid., p. 268.
26. 'L'armée qui nous faut', 2, *Revue militaire générale*, avril, 11ieme année, 4e livraison.
27. Simpson, op.cit., p. 234.
28. Ibid., p. 244.
29. Clark, W. (2001) *Waging Modern War*, Public Affairs, New York.
30. Simpson, op.cit. p. 308.
31. Strachan, op.cit., p. 325.
32. Ibid., p. 324.
33. Strachan, op.cit., p. 501.
34. Ibid., p. 516.

35. Luttwak, Edward (2001) *Strategy: The Logic of War and Peace*, The Belknap Press of Harvard University Press, p. 50.
36. The Oxford programme 'The Changing Character of War' has investigated this question for many years, and much has been written on the type of war that is typical today.
37. Strachan, H. *The Direction of War*, op.cit.
38. The literature on COIN is often referred to as 'imperial policing', written by theorists of colonial war such as David Galula, Ernest Thompson, and so on, and this literature has inspired contemporary theorists like Kilcullen, Petreaeus, and so on.
39. De Wiijk, R. (2012) 'Hybrid Conflict and the Changing Nature of Actors', p. 358, in *The Oxford Handbook of War*, Oxford University Press, Oxford.
40. '*Implementing the NATO Wales Summit: From Strategy to Action*', Chatham House, 30–31 October 2014, arranged by Stiftung Wissenschaft und Politik and Chatham House's programme 'The US project'. Attendees included top level officials from NATO, former sec-gens of NATO, and experts.
41. 'Myth and reality – a net assessment of Russia's hybrid warfare strategy since the start of 2014', *Eurasian Daily Monitor, vil. 11, issue 184*, 17 and 20 October 2014.
42. For an overview, see, for example, Part Three, 'The Future of Strategy', in Baylis, J. et al (eds.) (2013), *Strategy in the Contemporary World*, Oxford University Press, Oxford.
43. Freedman, L. (1998) Chapter 1, 'Strategic Coercion', *Strategic Coercion. Concepts and Cases*, OUP.
44. Schelling, T. (1966) *Arms and Influence*, Yale University Press, also *The Strategy of Conflict*, (1960), Harvard University Press.
45. George, A. and Simons, W.E. (eds.) (1994), *The Limits of Coercive Diplomacy*, Westview Press, Boulder, Colorado.
46. De Wijk, op.cit.
47. Macmillan, UK, 1998.
48. In Freedman, op.cit.
49. Freedman, L. (2013) *Strategy—A History*, Oxford University Press, Oxford.
50. Op.cit., p. 15.
51. Luttwak, E. (1987) *Strategy: The Logic of War and Peace?*, Belknap Pubs., Harvard University, Boston, Mass.
52. 'Solberg ser dramatiske følger av russisk maktbruk', *Dagens Næringsliv*, 31 August 2014.
53. Freedman, op.cit, p. 17.
54. Ibid., p. 19.
55. Ibid., p. 19.
56. Ibid., p. 19.

STRATEGY: DETERRENCE, CONTAINMENT, COERCION...   45

57. Peter Viggo Jakobsen, 'The strategy of coercive diplomacy: Refining existing theory to post-Cold War realities' (chap 3).
58. Ibid., p. 62.
59. Ibid., p. 63.
60. Jakobsen, P.V., 'Coercive Diplomacy', pp. 240–253, in Collins, A. *Contemporary Security Studies*, OUP, 2013, p. 241.
61. 'The Alliance and the credibility of extended deterrence', Helga Haftendorn, in A. Michta and P.S. Hilde, (eds.) (2014), *The Future of NATO: Regional Defense and Global Security*, University of Michigan Press, Ann Arbor.

REFERENCES

Bailey, J., Iron, R., & Strachan, H. (Eds.). (2013). *British Generals in Blair's Wars*. Farnham: Ashgate.

Baylis, J., et al. (2016). *Strategy in the Contemporary World*. Oxford: Oxford University Press.

Clark, W. (2001). *Waging Modern War*. New York: Public Affairs.

De Wijk, R. (2005). *The Art of Military Coercion: Why the West's Military Superiority Scarcely Matters*. Amsterdam: Mets & Schilt.

Freedman, L. (1998). *Strategic Coercion. Concepts and Cases*. Oxford: Oxford University Press.

George, A., & Simons, W. E. (Eds.). (1994). *The Limits of Coercive Diplomacy*. Boulder: Westview Press.

Haftendorn, H. (2014). The Alliance and the Credibility of Extended Deterrence. In A. Michta & P. S. Hilde (Eds.), *The Future of NATO: Regional Defense and Global Security*. Ann Arbor: University of Michigan Press.

Hanhimäki, J., & Westad, O. A. (Eds.). (2004). *The Cold War: A History in Documents and Eyewitness Accounts*. Oxford: Oxford University Press.

Jakobsen, P. V. (2013). Coercive Diplomacy. In A. Collins (Ed.), *Contemporary Security Studies*. Oxford: Oxford University Press.

Kissinger, H. (1994). *Diplomacy*. New York: Simon & Schuster.

Lindley-French, J. (2012). Strategic Leadership and War. In ibid. and Boyer (Eds.), *The Oxford Handbook of War*. Oxford: Oxford University Press.

Luttwak, E. (1987). *Strategy: The Logic of War and Peace?* Boston: Belknap Pubs., Harvard University.

Luttwak, E. (2001). *Strategy: The Logic of War and Peace*. Cambridge, MA: The Belknap Press of Harvard University Press.

Meyer, C. (2006). *The Quest for a European Strategic Culture. Changing Norms on Security and Defence in the EU*. New York: Palgrave Macmillan.

Schelling, T. (1960). *The Strategy of Conflict*. Cambridge, MA: Harvard University Press.

Schelling, T. (1966). *Arms and Influence*. Yale/New Haven: Yale University Press.

Simpson, E. (2013). *War from the Ground Up*. Oxford: Oxford University Press.

CHAPTER 3

Russian Revisionism

The topic of this book is Western strategic leadership and Western strategy, not Russian foreign and security policy. Yet, as Sun Tzu and many after him have pointed out, we need to know the adversary in order to know how to act. Were Russia's actions in Ukraine from 2014 onwards consistent with Russian foreign and security policy? Is Ukraine but one instance of a consistent Russian strategy which also involves the use of force when it serves Russian interests in other parts of Europe?

In this chapter I analyse the Russian use of force in Crimea and Ukraine and military and non-military posturing beyond these areas during 2014–17 in order to understand the strategic challenge that Russia poses to Europe. I begin by presenting a chronological account of Russian use of military diplomacy and of force from the annexation of Crimea in 2014 to the actions in Syria from 2015 through 2017. Then I proceed to an analysis of Russian political objectives and strategy, arguing that a logical and consistent pattern of political behaviour is displayed.

My chapter '*Realpolitik* Confronts Liberal democracy: Can Europe respond?' in Matlary, J.H. and Heier. T.(eds.) (2016) *Ukraine and Beyond. Russia's Strategic Security Challenge to Europe*, Palgrave Macmillan, UK, is based on excerpts from an earlier version of this chapter, as is my contribution to the proceedings of the Engelsberg seminar 2015, published as *War*, edited by Almquist, K. and Linklater, A (2016), Ax:son Johnson Foundation. There are also paragraphs on the effect of EU sanctions and general European reactions to the annexation of Crimea below in the chapters on the EU (9) and NATO (10) that are found in these publications.

© The Author(s) 2018
J. H. Matlary, *Hard Power in Hard Times*,
https://doi.org/10.1007/978-3-319-76514-3_3

Russia: A Great Power

Unlike many European states, Russia uses military force in various ways as a political tool—sometimes called 'heavy metal diplomacy',[1]—and not only as an alternative to diplomacy, as discussed in detail later in this chapter. Galeotti notes that 'it is clear that Russia's military is not just a combat force but also an instrument of foreign policy'.[2] He continues, 'although the West understandably considers itself under threat from Russia, Putin and those closest to him appear genuinely to regard themselves under attack'.[3] Russian interests are logical and consistent, according to Galeotti: 'The primary goals are to claim "great power" status while at the same time preventing the West from being able to exert any influence over Russia's domestic affairs and also those of what it considers its sphere of influence in post-Soviet Eurasia.'[4]

James Sherr's assessment is similar: 'To Russia, primacy in the former Soviet Union is an entitlement. ... Russia should define what sovereignty and independence should mean in practice. Failure to "consult" and in practice "coordinate" over such matters as relations with NATO or European integration is regarded as an unfriendly act.'[5] He adds that 'in no European country of the former USSR does Russia support the status quo'.[6]

Ukraine, along with Armenia, Georgia, and Moldova, experienced intense pressure from Russia to join the Eurasian Economic Union (EAEU) when it was offered a Europe Agreement. Sherr points out that Europe's preoccupation with Ukraine has led it to neglect Russian activity aimed at preserving dominance in other states in the region. The states of former Yugoslavia, for example, remain important to Russia, in part because all of them are likely to be invited to join the EU and NATO. Macedonia was put under direct pressure in 2017 when the Russian ambassador there stated that the country cannot do without Russia and needs to reorient itself towards Russia.[7] Russia is also reported to have attempted to hinder Montenegrin accession to NATO[8] and actively seeks to influence Serbian and Balkan politics.

In addition to trying to influence this 'near abroad', Russia perceives both NATO and the EU as aggressive actors that impose a political system based on values it rejects. Russia has no desire to become a liberal democracy with a political system based on its rules and rights. Sherr underlines this point: 'It is not as a military bloc per se, but as a military-"civilisational" force ... that NATO is deemed to pose a "danger" and potential threat to Russia.'[9] After the Orange Revolution in Ukraine in 2004 and the Kosovo intervention earlier, in 1999, 'it was clear that two normative systems had emerged in Europe: the first based on rights and rules, the second on connections, clientilism, and the subordination of law to power'.[10]

Russia, like many states were post-Versailles and post-Yalta, is a revisionist power. This term means that the state seeks a change of the *status quo*, that is, the existing order. These terms are standard in realist scholarship and make intuitive sense: states that are satisfied with the present state system, its borders and its power distribution, want to retain the *status quo*. States that are not will seek to challenge this, by seeking more relative influence in the state system and sometimes by changing borders. Commonly a peace perceived as unjust will lead to revisionism, such as in the case of German discontent after the Versailles treaty. With regard to Russia, it has always been both an empire and a great power, also in Europe. After 1990 its role was greatly reduced, yet its post-1990 revisionism came as a surprise to Europe, but could and should have been anticipated. The dismantling of the Soviet Union was never welcome in Russia, not to mention the spread of liberal democracy and NATO/EU membership. It is important to take note of Russia's rejection of the West's liberal-democratic agenda—there is no process towards becoming a liberal democracy; on the contrary, this kind of 'regime change' is rejected as Western imposition. To Western Europeans this is what is really surprising, for the spread of democracy is the major foreign policy project of the West. We think the Russians do not understand what is good for them, for how can liberal democracy be a menace? The 1990 victory for globalization and liberal order was seen by most people in the West as a normalization of their worldview and as progress in international affairs. Therefore, it is almost incomprehensible to Western audiences and politicians that others—read China and Russia—do not see it this way.

Adamsky writes that 'Moscow perceives the United States as a usurper that has been unfairly exploiting the unipolar moment since the collapse of the Soviet Union'[11], adding that it has double standards, expanding NATO and talking about humanitarian interventions like in Kosovo, something which is seen as a cover for extending its sphere of influence into that of Russia. The same thing has happened in the Middle East where, 'under the smoke screen of democratization, Washington carefully orchestrated regime changes across the region. ... From Moscow's point of view, the Arab Spring and Color Revolutions have been links in the same chain, instigated by the United States and serving its aspiration for global dominance.'[12] Moscow believes that the world has become dangerous due to American power projection. In this view, Russia, not NATO, is the defensive power.[13]

In 2008, NATO extended an invitation of membership to Ukraine and Georgia. This was not a strategic move on NATO's part: On the one hand, the alliance had not taken into account the likely Russian reaction; on the other, it had not thought about its Article 5 obligation to defend these two states in case of military conflict with Russia. Ronald Asmus' insightful book *The Little War that Shook the World*[14] exposes the sheer lack of strategy in Washington at the time. The Europeans warned against expanding NATO further to the east, arguing that the risk was high and the potential gains small. However, then President George W. Bush pushed ahead and prevailed. The Russian reaction was predictable, yet it came as a shock to NATO. Russian military exercises turned into a limited occupation of the Georgian regions of South Ossetia and Abkhazia, which were subsequently granted diplomatic recognition as independent republics by Moscow. This effectively blocked any thought of NATO accession for Georgia, in addition to telling the alliance that Russia would use force to stop NATO expansion to the east. The US reaction was to let Europe deal with the problem, and the EU was left to find a solution to the impasse. Nicolas Sarkozy, the president of the EU council at the time, was sent to Tbilisi like a modern Napoleon, albeit without an army.

Since then, Georgian membership in NATO has been on the back-burner, where it is likely to remain. This case shows that Russia will resist NATO—and perhaps EU—membership for states in its traditional and self-styled 'sphere of interest'. It also illustrates that the West—both Europe and the US—will not counter force with force in this part of Europe. Finally, the Georgian example shows a lack of strategic thinking on the part of NATO, which failed to take into account that there is an interest asymmetry between Russia and the West in this part of Europe. Ukraine and Georgia are far more important to Russia than to the West. Moreover, the extremely strange situation that NATO created then was to offer membership to states where it apparently had not considered that it also offered an Article 5 security guarantee. Was NATO prepared to go to war with Russia over Ukraine and Georgia if they had made it to become members? Luckily this issue was not brought to the fore since they are not members of NATO, but it is a very serious strategic failure indeed to extend membership to states that risk bringing NATO into a hot war. Challenging Russia with brinkmanship like this was apparently not the idea, as the US refrained from dealing with the military situation in Georgia when it happened, leaving it to France. Yet had Georgia been a member, NATO could not have rejected its Article 5 obligation. If the idea was that Russia would refrain from action in such a case, the stakes in this calculus were very high and risky, given the interest asymmetry. With hindsight we also know that NATO does not engage militarily in Ukraine after 2014 and that Georgia is left on the backburner in NATO after Russian use of force there.

This allows us to conclude that NATO was not strategic in its offer of membership to these states, and that this offer must be premised on a naïve belief that NATO membership could be extended to any given state as long as its public and government want it. This is the logic of liberal democracy, valid in liberal democracies but not beyond. It does not take into account strategic interaction and geopolitics. This is the core of the problem between NATO and Russia in general: Russia interprets expansion of NATO membership as highly strategic moves—NATO may simply follow a non-strategic logic of allowing in those that apply and qualify. Right after the Cold War this was not an issue as Russia was too weak to protest; but at present it is a highly salient one.

This case reveals a lot about Western lack of appreciation of strategic insight. In this case the American President Bush pushed for NATO extension and the Europeans, particularly France and Germany, warned against it. The Bush administration was known for its ideology of spreading democracy to the Middle East and elsewhere; something which may explain the insistence on extending NATO membership to interested countries, regardless of their geopolitical situation. The Europeans had better knowledge of how Russia perceived its security interests. Yet the fact remains that NATO as such extended a strong invitation to Georgia and Ukraine for membership, short of a membership action plan (MAP), but nonetheless rather unconditional. The text from the NATO summit in Bucharest in April 2008 was worded in a very clear way in the direction of quick membership, something uncommon in NATO.[15]

The Annexation of Crimea, 2014

The Georgian case is instructive when we turn to the case of Ukraine. Here, too, the West has a limited interest, despite its heavy rhetorical condemnation of the annexation of Crimea. Moreover, although neither NATO nor EU membership was offered Ukraine this time, Russia conducted a very strong campaign against Ukraine's turning westward in signing a so-called Europe Agreement with the EU in November 2013.

During the autumn of 2013, tension between politicians and people in Kiev mounted. The reason was the impending signing of an association agreement between the EU and Ukraine, as part of the EU's so-called European Neighbourhood Policy (ENP). The impasse became a crisis when President Yanukovych went to Moscow to sign an agreement with Russia whereby Ukraine opted to join Putin's new Eurasian Economic Union instead. The deal came with a large loan and cheap gas. Protests intensified in Kiev and people camped in Maidan Square to show their disapproval. The political crisis escalated into violence when secret police were deployed to control protesters. More than 90 people were killed, and a trio of visiting EU foreign ministers (the so-called troika) took charge of crisis negotiations between President Yanukovych and the opposition, including the Russian ambassador as a participant. Some sort of power-sharing agreement was developed, but President Yanukovych fled before the deal was signed after discovering that he no longer had command of the security forces in the presidential palace. The opposition established an interim government and the (former) president was not seen until he reappeared in Russia a couple of days later, where he gave a press conference stating that he had been deposed and was still president.

Evidence presented in a detailed study in the *International New York Times* (INYT) on 5 January 2015 shows that Yanukovych left because his security guards deserted him. They heard a rumour that they would be blamed for the killings in the Maidan square and that their commander, the president, would deny having given the command. They were also informed that weapons deliveries were on their way to Kiev from Lviv. The rational thing to do was to defect. As the leader of the security guards put it, 'when a leader stops being a leader, all the people around him fall away. That is the rule. To betray on time is not to betray, but to foresee.'[16] This is a logical political move in an autocratic system: once physical power is no longer guaranteed, there is no other source of power.

The crisis in Ukraine led to a strong and quick military reaction from Russia. In a short time, thousands of unmarked Russian soldiers appeared in Crimea, effectively occupying the peninsula. Ukrainian forces were arrested and ousted from their bases, but no shots were exchanged. The foreign forces—called 'little green men' because they were without insignia—were well-disciplined and highly professional. After several weeks, a referendum on whether Crimea should return to Russia was held against a backdrop of heavy propaganda and obstruction. Scores of people fled to mainland Ukraine. The pro-Russians dominated the referendum: the outcome was a clear 'yes' to returning to Russia, and Russia annexed Crimea in a state act a few days later.

Kristian Åtland and Una Hakvåg at the Norwegian Defence Research Establishment have undertaken a detailed analysis of the operation in Crimea.[17] They make the point that this operation was very different from the two Chechen wars and the operation against Georgia in 2008. While these three offensives were conventional, the Crimea operation was mainly a special forces (Spetsnaz) operation. The force was small by Russian standards, about 10,000 men, well organized and well-led. In a very short time, about 190 important locations—including Ukrainian military bases and the airport—were placed under Russian control. The forces at the Sevastopol naval base could move about easily while forces from Russia were flown in and transported by sea. Air domination was quickly established, and heavy materiel was then moved in from Russia. On 11 March, Grad artillery and personnel were transferred, and by 19 March, Russia had full control of Crimea.

A team of Organization for Security and Co-operation in Europe (OSCE) observers was denied access for several weeks. The Russian military build-up on the Ukrainian border at the time meant that Ukrainian forces were busy deterring an attack there. The Crimea operation was accompanied by a very aggressive information warfare operation whose central narrative was that there had been a Western-instigated military coup in Ukraine, and that it was therefore necessary to defend Russians and Ukrainians alike. This narrative was consistently presented at home, as well as abroad, and at home there was little, if any, dissent. The Crimea operation was swift, professional, and had a follow-on force of conventional arms.[18] Cyber and information operations were integrated with the military operation on the ground.

This was a new kind of military professionalism not seen before in Russia. The operation in Crimea was apparently planned and exercised long before it took place, although the triggering factor was the departure of President Yanukovych. The infiltration of Ukraine was planned from 2013, according to the *Frankfurter Allgemeine Zeitung* (FAZ).[19] So-called humanitarian mission exercises in the Russian military employed the scenario of invading Ukraine.[20]

Following the invasion of Crimea, there were extremely strong protestations from Western countries. Borders had been amended through the use of force, they claimed, making it the gravest violation of international law since WWII. Despite the strong diplomatic reaction, however, nothing more was done to punish Russia or to reverse its decision at this time. Economic sanctions were imposed only after the downing of a civilian aircraft in the summer, an event which I will discuss below.

Soon after the annexation of Crimea, local pro-Russian forces took up arms in the Donetsk region. There were strong indications that Russia had provided them with 'tanks, artillery, and infantry'.[21] A Russian aid convoy entered Ukraine without permission in August 2014, but later returned to Russia.[22] Western media reporting included pictures of armoured cars travelling across the border,[23] and paratroopers—ten members of the 331st Airborne Regiment of the 98th Division—were caught inside Ukraine.[24] Although the captured troops had documentation of active service on them when caught after a fire-fight with Ukrainian forces, Russia denied they were soldiers. The Russian news agency ITAR-TASS said that the incursion was an accident.[25] Despite persistent Russian denials, however, the facts of Russian military involvement in Eastern Ukraine were well established from the very beginning.

That troops without insignia were used to occupy Crimea shows that Russia also considered the crossing of borders to be a most serious breach of sovereignty. Were this not the case, it would not have been necessary to conceal the troops' identity. The obvious Russian interest in distancing itself from the occupation, indeed, in denying it, is a testimony to the validity of the norm of non-intervention as a standard of sovereignty.

As stated, the Western reaction was one of outrage.[26] There was unitary action, at least rhetorically, as both the EU and the US confirmed that Russia had committed a major violation of international law: 'European and American officials seemed to be speaking from an agreed set of talking points in their public remarks.'[27] Yet, as commentators pointed out, there was no strategy behind these talking points. The focus quickly became stopping Russia beyond the Crimean annexation, which was seemingly accepted as an inevitable fact, as the Russian recognition of South Ossetia and Abkhazia in 2008 had been. Prime Minister Cameron started to warn about further moves, drawing a red line only at future actions and threatening sanctions, saying 'there's a view that [the annexation] is unacceptable, but then there is another very, very strong view that any further steps into Eastern Ukraine would be even more serious and would result in much greater sanctions.'[28] The annexation that had been called the greatest violation of international law since WWII was suddenly no longer very important to Western leaders.

The Western reaction to the annexation of the Crimea was verbally very strong, but it was not followed up by sanctions beyond those of a general political nature. In international legal terms, Russia is exploiting the 'tension between a fundamental principle that prohibits the acquisition of territory through the use of force and an equally fundamental right of self-determination', as the legal scholar Burke-White writes.[29] He adds that Putin has altered the normal interpretation of this balance to the point where 'Russia's reinterpretation of these principles ... could well destabilize the tenuous balance between the interpretation of the protection of individual rights and the preservation of states' territorial integrity that undergirds the post-Second World War order.'[30]

Unlike many of his legal colleagues, Burke-White is direct about the relationship between international law and power in this area: 'In place of the era of US legal hegemony and leadership, a multi-hub structure is emerging in which a growing number of states can and do play issue-specific leadership roles in a far more flexible and fluid legal system.'[31] He points out that the tension between rights and sovereignty inherent in the UN Charter has been managed largely through Western interpretations until the present when Russia has been able to act as a legal hub along with other major and rising powers like Brazil, India, and China. When Russia vetoed a resolution in the UNSC on the genocide in Srebrenica on the 20th anniversary of that atrocity, it underlined its independence from the established interpretations of the world community. This move can be seen as an extreme demonstration of such independence, flouting the facts that the UN itself has carefully confirmed through independent analysis.

In a speech to the Duma two days after the referendum in Crimea, Putin denied having violated that country's borders, claiming, 'Russia's armed forces never entered Crimea, they were there already in line with an international agreement.'[32] According to this interpretation, the troops had been invited in to protect Russians there at a critical time. He continued to outline the general conditions for protecting Russians abroad, stating that Russia would primarily use political and legal means to protect them, while not foreclosing military ones.

In the same speech, Putin also added a threat to Ukraine: 'it should be in Ukraine's own interest to ensure that these people's rights and interests are fully protected. This is the guarantee of Ukraine's state stability and territorial integrity.'[33] In this chilling comment, the point is made that Russia determines when and if the Russian minority is mistreated. This position represents another inroad against sovereignty as it is understood in the modern state system; it is not up to the great powers to determine the sovereignty of smaller states. One cannot use protection of own nationals that live in other states as a pretext for military action, and if such nationals are offered citizenship, a conflict ensues. The problem of large minorities of own nationals in other states is a key and common one in east-central Europe, and it is generally considered impossible to revise borders or to intervene in any way to assist them. Some states grant citizenship to their own nationals, for example, Hungary which has close to two million of its nationals beyond its borders, but the use of force to protect nationals abroad is usually only talked about by great powers if at all. If there is a policy in this regard, it is one of sending special forces to extract own nationals from, for example, hostage taking, kidnapping, or similar; not to protect a group of nationals in a political struggle.

The military action on the ground in both Crimea and Ukraine was accompanied by Russian political speeches that upheld a traditional great power view of the world and the state system. The basic notion was one of Realpolitik—great powers have privileges in their near abroad—but the rhetoric also played on modern notions of human rights, in particular minority rights. The traditional nation-state being the chosen conceptual basis, minorities were deemed to belong to the Russian nation and thus to have rights akin to those of citizens, including the right to physical protection. This idea is, however, contrary to the modern understanding of human rights according to which human beings have rights because they are human beings and not because they belong to a nation or subscribe to a social contract in a given state. Minority rights are thus to be respected by all states in all territories, making it invalid for other states to claim their own nationals and grant them protection. Yet Russia cleverly used the language of modern rights, as well as that of humanitarian intervention, when it invaded Georgia in 2008 and again regarding Crimea and Donetsk.

War-Fighting in Eastern Ukraine

In Ukraine, Russian 'contributions' were less direct, making it harder to determine the facts of the incident. 'Invasion in Ukraine? It's hard to say', declared a headline in the *INYT*.[34] Politicians from the Baltic states used the term 'invasion' or 'aggression', echoed by the Ukrainian president himself, Petro Poroshenko, who rightly pointed out that the naming of the problem was a function of how the West planned to react. An 'invasion', for example, warranted a stronger reaction than an 'incursion'.

Although Senator McCain used the former term, President Obama employed the latter. International law experts pointed out that the term invasion has no special legal significance and therefore could have been used, but the key issue was its political significance and implications. The Australians called it an invasion, but that was because 'nobody [expected] them to do anything in response', as one expert put it.[35]

In terms of empirical evidence of a Russian presence, NATO released intelligence that there were at least a 4000 Russian troops and several tanks in Ukraine in the summer of 2014. In addition, up to 45,000 troops were concentrated on Ukraine's border,[36] constituting a clear threat and therefore coming under the prohibition of the use of force between states in Article 2.4 of the UN Charter. Thus, threats were made regardless of whether Russia crossed any border—by the sheer massing of forces on the other side of Ukraine's border. The Russians also held a major exercise with several non-Western states in the vicinity; the key weapons were tanks in a traditional *Panzerkrieg* invasion scenario. This unannounced exercise underscored the threat posed by the massing of troops.

As stated, the rhetorical anger on the part of Western states regarding the use of force in Crimea and Donetsk was not accompanied by any political action other than threats of sanctions. After some months, little or no attention was paid to the annexation of Crimea. MacFarlane and Menon write that

> a potent cocktail of conflicting European interests, naivety and arrogance helped to precipitate the crisis, and continues to undermine attempts to craft an effective response. Europeans have rightly been criticized in many quarters for their timorous reaction to the Russian intervention in Crimea.[37]

They maintain that the EU's approach to the East has been flawed from the beginning. The Vilnius meeting in November 2013 that was supposed to see six states sign European Association Agreements was part of the ENP, which expressly did not discuss conditions for membership in the EU. It was thus unclear to all parties—Russia, the states in question, and the EU itself—whether EU membership could be in the pipeline. In fact, there was no geopolitical analysis in the EU at all, the authors point out, whereas 'for more than 20 years, Moscow had made clear its claim to a privileged position in what it saw as its periphery'.[38] Putin created a 'counter-policy' in his customs union turned Eurasian Union, to be established by 2015. Ukraine's size made its membership in the latter essential. The EU was inattentive to risk, the authors point out,[39] likening the situation to NATO's inattention to risk at the Bucharest summit in 2008 when it invited Georgia and Ukraine to join without real preconditions.

Being naïve about risk is a sure sign of lack of strategic ability. A strategic approach will be very concerned with the adversary's moves, but in these cases neither of the two key organizations in Europe was preoccupied with any adversary. Policy was conducted in a linear manner, one-sidedly. In addition, the EU was divided: Poland and Lithuania were very keen to sign on the Europe Agreements, but most other member states did not want to risk conflict or potential economic losses from sanctions against Russia. They were decidedly frosty about the whole enterprise of association agreements, and they 'failed to generate a viable response to the Russian intervention.'[40] The lack of a NATO strategy is even more surprising given the long-term poor relationship between NATO and Russia. The missile shield negotiations where Russia was invited to join were conducted in an atmosphere of 'lack of trust'.[41]

Russia's annexation of Crimea was part of a strategy to curb Western influence and attempts to turn Ukraine in a Western direction. Russian Foreign Minister Sergey Lavrov's plan for Ukraine, which he handed to Secretary of State Kerry on 15 March 2014, the day before the referendum on Crimea, proposed the federalization of Ukraine and neutrality, as well as recognizing Russian as an official language along with Ukrainian.[42] The plan showed how Russia wanted to ensure that Ukraine would remain outside Western influence and integration, and it was soon accompanied by the large Russian military exercise along Ukraine's borders mentioned above.

Fighting continued throughout the summer of 2014 in the Russian-speaking parts of Ukraine; in the autumn, a truce was signed. It was not really respected, however, and Russia continued its involvement in the region. It was the 'war that wasn't' and the 'truce that isn't', declared *The Economist*.[43] Russia again denied involvement, but 'recognized' both the Ukrainian parliamentary election in October and the elections in the breakaway republics of Donetsk and Luhansk in November. The voters there, standing in line to vote, were given produce for free or at very low prices, something completely unheard of in normal elections where bribes of any kind are strictly forbidden. An *INYT* headline announced, 'Elections Illustrate Loss of Control in East, and Moscow's Growing Sway'.[44] Yet the main point of interest here is the simultaneous recognition of national elections and regional elections in another country. This is, of course, logically impossible as Ukraine's elections were for the entire country. Yet

Russia did not seem bothered by this, sowing further discord. Foreign Minister Lavrov suggested that the two sides should negotiate with each other.[45] At the same time there were reports of more military convoys going into Ukraine with tanks, artillery, and other heavy military equipment. The use of force was thus cleverly calibrated for political purposes, exerting pressure on the national government.

Neither Foreign Minister Lavrov nor President Putin was in any way apologetic about his political stance on Ukraine. On the contrary, a confident Putin rebuffed European appeals as he travelled to Milan to meet other leaders for the Asia-Europe summit in mid-October.[46] He stopped first in Belgrade to be celebrated, participating in a military parade reminiscent of the Cold War, and to rhetorically attack the US. Serbia, although a candidate for EU membership, having started negotiations in January 2014, opposed sanctions against Russia and seemed to support Putin far more than the EU. The 2015 Russian veto of the UNSC resolution to commemorate the genocide in Srebrenica, mentioned above, which was probably aimed at dividing the country further on EU membership, was greeted with enthusiasm in Belgrade. The refusal to call it a genocide came at a considerable political cost to Russia—if that still mattered—and indicated how far apart the UN and the Western community of states were from Russia and other states like China, which abstained. This move also indicated that it was very important for Russia to halt Serbia's bid for EU membership. It is perhaps another red line for the Russian leadership.

After leaving Belgrade, President Putin arrived hours late for a meeting with Chancellor Merkel in Milan and was also very late for a breakfast meeting the next day with President Poroshenko and Western leaders. This behaviour—quite uncommon in diplomatic settings—sent a strong political signal: Putin would determine when and with whom he would meet. At these meetings Putin reiterated that Russia was no party to the conflict in Ukraine: 'Russia, as you know, is not a party. We can only help the conflicting parties to solve their problems', he stated.[47]

At the same time, in the UN General Assembly, Foreign Minister Lavrov continued to justify Russian actions in Crimea, contending that 'Russia did not illegally seize Crimea ... but only wanted the people to decide for themselves where they wanted to belong'.[48] This was only fair after the coup d'état in Kiev, he continued, adding that it was the US and not Russia that used force unilaterally to redraw borders: 'Washington has openly declared its right to unilateral use of force anywhere to uphold its own interests. Military interference has become a norm. ... [Western] states are trying to decide for everyone what is good or evil.'[49] He added that Western states had disregarded the UNSC by intervening without a mandate, thereby flouting international law.

In July 2014, a Malaysian Airlines passenger aircraft was shot down over eastern Ukraine, in all probability by pro-Russian militias who had been supplied by Russia with anti-air weapons.[50] Although Western involvement in the conflict increased following this fatal mistake, passengers' bodies remained at the crash site for months because of the security situation. There was no real hard pressure or demands for immediate access to the site in order to retrieve the bodies. The Dutch, who lost the most citizens in the attack, did press the issue, but not as hard as one would expect, given the horrible nature of the attack. Access to the site was granted only gradually, and the Europeans seemed to be content with this state of affairs. The tepid European reaction to a situation that called for outrage could be interpreted as weakness.

In September 2014, a truce was negotiated and heavy Russian weapons were withdrawn from Eastern Ukraine.[51] Nevertheless, fighting continued on a smaller scale—for example, fighting over Donetsk Airport—as late as October. The truce was delicate and unbalanced, as Russia kept up the military pressure on Ukraine throughout the negotiations.[52] The strategically important city of Mariupol on the Black Sea remained under heavy attack until the ceasefire, and experts point out that Ukraine would have lost it had a ceasefire not been signed. The Russian demand for a decentralized Ukraine with a guarantee of non-membership in the EU and NATO had already been presented at an earlier negotiation in Minsk. The secessionists planned future moves; President Poroshenko travelled to the US to ask for military aid and planned a Western-leaning Ukraine, while the Russians demanded a federation. Russia was present at the negotiating table as an 'honest broker', it claimed, yet it was also the most powerful actor, the one wielding the military tool. This absurd situation was, of course, known to the Western participants, yet the negotiations were, as one diplomat put it, 'the only game in town'.[53]

Sherr makes the important point that the Minsk negotiations deviate from normal diplomatic practise. They amount to compromise under the barrel of a gun, he points out; the resulting agreements call into question Ukraine's sovereignty and are 'at variance with positions previously articulated by Western governments'.[54] Sherr is very critical of the mix of ceasefire agreements and political settlements: '[this combination] violates diplomatic practice. Ceasefires emerge out of urgency. Peace settlements require deliberation (which in a democracy must include representative structures of power). Constitutional changes require the same if they are to be sound, workable and legitimate. They should not be dictated by arbitrary deadlines or imposed at gunpoint.'[55]

In addition, the agreement includes actors that are not lawful: the separatists in Ukraine are not legal actors representing Ukraine, and Russia is regarded as an interested third party which is 'helping', not as a military actor on the ground. Minsk is 'an armed truce', Sherr concludes, not a negotiation based on free will. He also makes the point that 'for Moscow, the sole utility of the DNR [Donetsk National Republic] and LNR [Luhansk National Republic] is to serve as a bridgehead for securing Ukraine's transformation into a dysfunctional state: "federated", "neutral", and without European prospects.'[56]

The difference between a truce and a negotiated settlement is of key importance. A truce or ceasefire reflects relative military power on the ground, whereas a negotiation should take place without military pressure and be based on reasonable interests of the parties in conflict. The Europeans have accepted to be party to a 'negotiation' where military power plays the key role.

Meanwhile, President Putin made several statements from Moscow: 'Russia is far from being involved in any large-scale conflicts ... but naturally, we should always be ready to repel any aggression against Russia. Russia's partners ... should understand it's best not to mess with us ... I want to remind you that Russia is one of the leading nuclear powers.'[57] He went on to add that the Ukrainian army was acting like German occupiers in WWII.[58] These kinds of statements accompanied events in Ukraine throughout 2014 and 2015. They invariably cast the West, especially NATO, as the aggressor, and introduced nuclear threats to an alarming extent.

Furthermore, Russia's military doctrine continued to view NATO as a threat.[59,60] In a translated version we find that NATO and the West are classified as 'the main external military dangers' (no. 12), with particular mention of NATO expansion near Russia's borders. Military deployments in states bordering Russia are also mentioned: In the section on the use of force (no. 32) it is made clear that in order to protect national interests, as well as Russian citizens, troops can be deployed quickly outside Russian territory.

The Kremlin's warning about Russian minorities made the Baltic states fearful: 'A top Russian diplomat touched down in Riga to learn of "unfortunate consequences" stemming from alleged discrimination against the Russian minority there. The capital's mayor paid an unusually timed visit to Moscow.'[61] The Russian-friendly party in Latvia handed out leaflets comparing Latvia and Crimea, portraying them as places where Russian minorities are discriminated against.[62]

During the beginning of 2015, the fighting in Donetsk continued. NATO's Secretary General Jens Stoltenberg announced that Russian soldiers and Russian military equipment had been observed inside Ukraine as late as 21 January, but this was again denied by Russia. NATO, however, presented intelligence supporting this claim, which tallied well with Kiev's statement that several thousand Russian soldiers were present in the eastern parts of Ukraine.[63] Fighting continued with severe casualties, with the aim of gaining control of Donetsk airport, which was eventually totally destroyed. The BBC reported that on 22 January, Ukrainian forces left the airport after losing it to Russian-backed rebel forces.[64] The summit meeting that had been planned between Germany's Chancellor Merkel and France's President Hollande with Presidents Putin and Poroshenko in early January 2015 was cancelled by Germany. Chancellor Merkel announced that as the original Minsk ceasefire had not been respected, there was no reason to meet; moreover, Russia had not produced any viable peace plan, leaving nothing to negotiate about. This cancellation was another major blow to the diplomatic process, setting it back to the situation a year before. There was apparently no interest on the Russian side in making changes to the status quo. The summit in Minsk on 11 February 2015, between Putin, Poroshenko, Hollande, and Merkel led to a ceasefire agreement after 17 hours of negotiations. However, the agreement did not include the strategically important town of Debaltseve.

When the time for the ceasefire came, it was not observed. The siege of Debaltseve continued and Ukrainian forces were told to retreat. However, the retreat was not respected, and retreating soldiers were shelled and shot at by snipers. 'They were shooting with tanks, rocket-propelled grenades and sniper rifles', one Ukrainian officer reported. President Poroshenko concluded that the violence in Debaltseve amounted to 'a cynical attack on the Minsk agreement' and declared that 'today the world must stop the aggressor.'[65] According to *The Times*, however, more Russian tanks were being transported across the border even as the negotiations in Minsk were taking place.[66]

The same day, the US warned Russia that 'it would face grave consequences for the continued violation of the ceasefire.'[67] Comments from experts were harsh: 'No more appeasement', wrote *The Times'* editorial on 19 February 2015; 'Putin is happy to make a deal one day and break it the next.'[68] Former Swedish Prime Minister and Foreign Minister Carl Bildt concluded that it was time to arm Ukraine, as there was no possibility of putting pressure on Putin unless other governments were willing to use military force, at least in the case of Ukraine.[69] Yet others, including Poland, warned against doing so, even as the EU ambassador from the Ukraine pleaded for weapons.[70]

The Telegraph concluded that the West had been taken for a ride: 'it was a mistake to gamble a ceasefire on Putin's word of honour', declared one editorial.[71] The German press declared the Minsk deal, initiated by Merkel and Hollande, a total victory for Putin—it simply bought more time for the separatist forces and entrenched the view that Eastern Ukraine should have special status, circumstances which would prevent the country from turning to Western organizations. Both the ideas of a 'frozen conflict' and a federal solution with veto powers in the east could help achieve this goal, and the Minsk agreement was one more step towards realizing federalization.[72]

By mid-2015, more than a year after the troubles in Ukraine started, fighting was raging in the eastern part of the country and there was no sign of any reversal of the annexation of Crimea. Russia continued to deny both the presence of Russian troops and the flow of Russian arms across the border. The scale of the fighting was considerable, and the full spectrum of conventional weapons was used. Estimates were that about 5000 people had been killed in the fighting in 2014–15 and more than 1.2 million had been displaced.[73]

The Minsk negotiations have undergone several revisions. The economic sanctions imposed on Russia—which will be discussed in detail in Chap. 9—have taken a toll and they have been renewed several times under American pressure. According to Sherr, this has led Russia to adjust its negotiating position: 'For its part, Russia has secured two objectives, albeit more modest than those in sight after Minsk-II. First, enhancement of sanctions is now off the table ... and the obligation on Ukraine to agree elections and "special status" provisions with current DNR/LNR representatives is now unambiguous.'[74] Yet the mix of truce and political negotiations remains an uneasy one because 'no fair election can take place as long as Russia remains in occupation and controls the border'.[75] This will last as long as Russia does not achieve the federalization of the provinces it wants, along with the power to veto membership in the EU and NATO. Thus, the situation remains a kind of stand-off. The conflict sometimes flares up, and other times dies down, but it remains a political lever and Russia retains military escalation dominance. Unlike Russia and

Ukraine, the European parties involved—the so-called Normandy format consisting of Germany and France—are unable to wield any military power. As we will see below, the debate on arming Ukraine resulted in a clear rejection of the idea, both in Washington and in Europe.

Syria 2015–17

In 2015 Russia decided to enter the fray in Syria and use military force in support of Assad's government. The goals of this action were manifold: to bolster Assad and to fight Daesh, thereby filling the power vacuum left open by the US and Obama's unwillingness to get involved; and to try to retain Russian bases and a Russian stronghold in Syria. There was no breach of international law, as Russia was invited to aid Assad in compliance with Article 51 of the UN Charter which allows for such aid under self-defence. Yet Russia incurred major criticism for aiding Assad and not just fighting Daesh, although its willingness to do the latter made it a potential partner of the West. The West had long demonstrated a reluctance to getting involved, and Russia seemed bold in taking on the challenge in 2013 when it stepped in to 'solve' Obama's problem of not acting on the use of chemical weapons.

Russia's 'Syria operation has reinforced the view that not only is Russia willing and able to deploy its armed forces, but that it is prepared to use military force in situations where it perceives itself to be suffering – or to be at risk of suffering – geopolitical losses', concluded The Military Balance in 2017.[76] This operation can therefore be seen as an instance of military diplomacy, as 'a coercive tool'.[77]

Russia's engagement in Syria started in June 2016 and was declared finished about a year later. However, Russian troops continue to be present in Syria, and the naval facility in Tartus remains a key base for Russia. Russia's goals in Syria are legion, argues Adam Garfinkle: to save the Assad regime from collapse; to achieve status on a par with the US in the region; to gain leverage over the US in negotiating a truce for Syria; and perhaps also with regard to the migrants and refugee outflux which threatens to destabilize Europe (see Chap. 4). An additional political goal is probably to distract the West from the ongoing Ukraine crisis.[78]

In 2015, in a major victory, Assad's ground troops retook Palmyra from Daesh with Russian aerial support. Aerial support had similarly enabled Syrian forces to win back Aleppo, albeit with major losses of civilians and collateral damage due to the use of 'dumb' bombs. These damages led Western leaders including Obama, Hollande, and Cameron, and later Boris Johnson, to condemn Russia strongly, calling for war-crimes investigations in the middle of the fighting. While they led nowhere in terms of results, these calls show how important the political values of humane warfare are to the West. This case is interesting because it shows not only that adherence to the Geneva Conventions really does matter to Western states—as it ethically should—but also the unrealism of this criticism, as the call for war-crimes trials of Russians predictably led to harsh reactions, including the cancellation of Putin's scheduled visit to France, and a 'shouting war'. At the very moment when Western leaders needed to be able to talk with Russia, they were accusing Russia of war crimes. Moreover, these verbal attacks had no effect, especially if the intent was to influence the battle for Aleppo. If the West had been seriously engaged to stop civilian suffering there, it would have inserted itself in the fighting in order to end it, one way or the other. This was clearly never considered an option. And when Western forces were engaged in the battle for Mosul somewhat later, the very same type of civilian casualties occurred as the result of fighting insurgents in a city. The Russians justly criticized the West on this score, as a tit for tat. While there is a difference in Russian and Western ways of war, the point here is that Western criticism was not concerned with ending the siege of Aleppo, thus ending bombardment of civilians. It was only concerned with the breach of the Geneva Conventions, a strangely limited concern if the Western powers had really been moved by ethical concerns. Why not try to stop the war?

When officers of the Assad regime used chemical weapons in an attack in 2017, Russia denied that Assad's forces were behind the attack, claiming instead that conventional bombs had hit a storage base for chemical weapons. This story was not credible at all, and President Trump ordered an American response, in which 59 cruise missiles were launched against the air base that had hosted the plane carrying out the attack. This in turn led to extremely strong verbal response from Russia, including calling for an extraordinary session of the UNSC, to be chaired by Putin, because the US had violated Syrian sovereignty. These protests did not result in much, as the American attack was limited to punishment of the air base where the chemical attack originated. This event once again underlined the importance of strong norms against the use of weapons of mass destruction, something that ultimately also benefits Russia. Yet the US attack showed a new willingness on the part of the US to get involved in Syria. The Trump administration, with several generals in the lead—Mattis, Macmaster, Kelly, and Dunford—was no stranger to strategic and for that matter, tactical, insights. By punishing Assad for the attack the Americans showed that they were both principled and value-based actors, unlike Obama in an identical situation in 2013 when he failed to punish the use of chemical weapons. They also showed Russia that the US intended to be an actor in Syria and the Middle East.

Thus, by 2017 the success of Russian military diplomacy in Syria and the Middle East was not as clear as it had seemed just months earlier when commentators agreed that 'Russia is in charge in Syria.'[79] Already in 2016, the assessment was that Russia was leading, and the US following, diplomatic attempts to find a truce in Syria, and the negotiations in Astana in 2017 included the US as an invited guest, not as a major actor. While Russia is still the key player in Syria, the Trump administration's demonstration that it can and will use force there changes the political game. The Obama administration's decision to stay out of Syria, even after Obama's own 'red line' on chemical weapons was crossed in August 2013, left a power vacuum that Russia chose to fill. However, the Trump administration has signalled that it wants to return to its former role, with Defence Secretary James Mattis, an expert on the region, calling for an American strategy in the Middle East. That the first foreign stop of President Trump was in Riyadh sends a strong message that the US is back as an actor in the region. Nevertheless, Russia has thus far managed to insert itself in the key role with regard to Syria despite the fact that there is no 'end game' in sight yet.[80] By the end of 2017 the US had accepted to be an observer to the Russian-led negotiations on Syria in Astana while the UN-led negotiations in Geneva where only opposition played a key role, had failed; a fact bitterly resented yet recognized by the UN special envoy Staffan de Mistura.

Some degree of cooperation became necessary between the Western states and Russia in order to operate in the same air space over Syria, and when France was attacked by Daesh terrorists on Friday, 13 November 2015, the country took the lead in fighting the terrorists on their home turf, thus entering into much closer cooperation with Russia than the other states in the coalition. Having been hit directly by terrorism, France formed a natural alliance with Russia, which had also been attacked through the downing of a civilian air plane leaving the Egyptian resort town of Sharm-El Sheikh some weeks earlier.

By asserting itself in the Syrian war in 2015 while Western states mostly kept away, Russia continued its strategic use of military force for political purposes. Not only did this move shift attention from Ukraine to Syria, it also opened up the possibility that Russia might enter into a military coalition with the West in fighting Daesh. In terms of foreign policy goals, the Syrian intervention seemed to be very successful: Russia became the dominant player in negotiations for a solution and played a key, constructive role in destroying chemical weapons in 2013, effectively helping the West and the US, all while solidifying its bases and military presence in Syria. Moreover, Russia, France, and other Western states seemed to cooperate well in fighting Daesh in Syria. Yet by 2017, the success of Russian military diplomacy had been diminished by the severe degree of civilian losses in Aleppo and the renewed use of chemical weapons, which led to the US airstrike.

From a military standpoint, the Russians demonstrated their ability to launch missiles from afar—namely the Caspian Sea—and tested their newer weapon systems. The Military Balance provides the following assessment: 'The Syria deployment has demonstrated Russia's capability to maintain an expeditionary force for a protracted period of time. ... Russia continues to use the operation as a test bed and showcase for its military equipment.'[81]

Thus, in the Syrian case we see Russian military diplomacy at work in war-fighting to achieve real goals on the ground, but also serving other purposes: namely to place Russia on a par with the US in world politics; to make Russia the key, or at least a key, actor in the Middle East; to consolidate its base in Tartus; to fight terrorism together with the West; and to test and showcase its military power. As an added benefit, Russia's involvement in Syria distracted the West from the situation in Ukraine.[82]

From 'Hybrid War' to Nuclear Threats

Unlike many European states, Russia places great emphasis on the military tool. Military modernization continues at a brisk pace despite the suffering economy, which is puzzling to many Western observers. *The Economist* has called Russia a 'hollow superpower',[83] and economist Anders Åslund points out that 'Russia's economic prospects are looking increasingly grim'.[84] Yet Russian defence spending was 3.69 per cent of GDP in 2016, despite a 3.7 per cent decrease in GDP the previous year.[85] While this is probably not a problem in the short term, in the longer term there is a major problem for Russia here. In an authoritarian political system, the old logic of 'rallying around the flag' against an outside enemy works: If the West is portrayed as aggressive there is every reason to forgo consumption and prioritize national security. The idea that national security should come first is true even for democracies at risk. The implication of this for

Russia is paradoxical, however: the worse its economy, the greater Russia's need to view the West as a threat. Thus, a faltering economy may lead to more military posturing and sabre-rattling than in more prosperous times.

Russia continues to improve its missile technology and modernize its military. The Russians have been developing a new cruise missile that the Americans argue violates the Intermediate-Range Nuclear Forces (INF) Treaty from 1987. Signed by Presidents Gorbachev and Reagan, this treaty banned both states from deploying ground-launched ballistic and cruise missiles with a range of between 300 and 3400 miles, and resulted in the destruction of more than a thousand such missiles. However, according to the *New York Times*, the Russians began testing a new cruise missile in 2008.[86] The missile in question, the Iskander-K, has a range that exceeds the limits set by the INF Treaty.[87] At the same time, President Putin has added nuclear weapons to his political rhetoric, and on several occasions threatened their use. In the military doctrine from December 2014 the role of nuclear weapons is unchanged from the former 2010 version: they can only be used as a second-strike capability after a nuclear attack or in a conventional war where the existence of the state is at stake, although their role can be 'de-escalatory' in conventional war.[88] However, Putin's warnings to not mess with Russia are extraordinary for the head of a nuclear state. The newspaper *Pravda* used similar rhetoric in November 2014, running the headline, 'Russia prepares a nuclear surprise for NATO'.[89]

In addition to testing long-range missiles, Russia is building new nuclear submarines, which carry nuclear-tipped missiles. The American general in charge of the US Northern Command, Charles Jacoby, admitted to being concerned about this, noting that the Russians have 'just begun production of a new class of quiet nuclear submarines specifically designed to deliver cruise missiles'.[90] Tamnes provides a detailed discussion of this development in a recent study of the strategic challenges in the North Atlantic.[91] Neither US nor Russian submarines were allowed to carry nuclear warheads during the period of START I from 1991 to 2001.[92] New START, which has been in force from 2010, does not have this rule. The US is now pondering how to counter the cruise missile problem.

The NATO missile defence system, however; long in coming and open to cooperation with Russia, is viewed by the latter with strong suspicion. The opening of two missile defence bases, one in Poland and one in Bulgaria, has led to strong protests from Russia, which 'fears that the base [in Deveselu, Romania] will purportedly allow the US to eliminate president Putin and other top Russian military leaders in a surprise first nuclear strike'.[93] Putin has declared that Poland and Romania will now have to suffer the consequences of allowing these bases.[94]

Russia seems capable of using a whole range of tools, both military and civilian, in its foreign policy. Nuclear arms have been largely forgotten in NATO Europe, although its force posture still includes them, and several European states are opposed to nuclear arms, per se, including Germany. The political climate in Europe surrounding nuclear weapons contrasts starkly with the climate in Russia, where nuclear weapons are so important as to be invoked by the president as usable tools of state. Only France among the European states has a doctrine about its nuclear weapons that define them as essential to sovereignty and as usable in defence of France in a situation of existential threat.

If we move 'down' from massively destructive weapons to conventional arms, we have provided a very superficial survey of the scale and depth of Russian military modernization. Unlike NATO, Russia spends a lot on defence and does not under any circumstance seem to cut this part of the budget. The Crimea operation showed how strong information campaigns could be combined with military action. In an interesting article entitled 'Russia's ideology: There is no truth', Peter Pomerantsev describes how the Soviet legacy of manipulation and deception created a society in which truth was unknown and there was only the 'party line'. In order to survive, people pragmatically developed several 'selves' and several 'truths', he writes. This background makes it easier for the Kremlin to 'control all narratives so that all politics becomes one great scripted reality show'.[95] He mentions the downing of Malaysian Air Flight 17 as an example of the extent to which the Kremlin had retained control over people's view of the truth: 'the Russian media spread a multitude of conspiracy theories ... from claiming that radar data showed Ukrainian jets fly near the plane to suggesting that the plane had been shot down by jets aiming at president Putin's plane.'[96]

If there is no objective truth about anything, there are just various viewpoints. The narrative of a fascist coup in Kiev, aided by the EU and NATO, has been used by Russia to justify the annexation of Crimea and the 'help' given to Eastern Ukraine. Western sanctions have been presented as an attack on Russia aimed at regime change. According to Foreign Minister Lavrov, 'the West shows unequivocally that it does not want to force Russia to change its policies, but that it wants to achieve regime change'.[97] Thus, the sanctions—which I will discuss in detail below—are presented as much more than what they are aiming to be, namely as a threat to the very existence of the Russian state; therefore, they can of course be a pretext for all sorts of military action in 'self-defence'. Russia is merely defending itself and its interests after the coup in Kiev, and must also be able to do so beyond Ukraine since the West is now trying to effect regime change in Russia.

Russia's exaggeration of the alleged threat from the West is consistent and clever: NATO and the EU have extended memberships to states that belong to the Russian sphere of influence, and have even tried to do so with Georgia and Ukraine. Moreover, the EU's meddling in Ukrainian politics contributed to the fall of the elected president there. The world seen from Moscow is the very opposite of the world seen from Brussels. However, the 'truth' is not somewhere in the middle. The disagreement is total, stemming from the two sides' completely different premises for analysing international politics: Russia is a revisionist power that acts based on a zero-sum state rivalry logic and seeks to change the status quo. It stands to gain from this position because the alternative, a slow adaption to liberal-democratic norms is not palatable.

Since 2014, we have witnessed clever use of all the tools of state in Russia. Putin has kept up his rhetorical offensive, as has Lavrov. They accused the West, and especially NATO, of deception and expansionism, and called out the US for using force without UN mandates and endangering the world. This aggressive posturing is useful for Putin, who 'needs a patriotic mobilization of society against Russia's "enemies" in order not to lose his popularity because of economic problems'.[98]

RUSSIAN MILITARY POSTURE IN EUROPE

As mentioned, in 2014 and 2015 there was an increase in Russian military flights near NATO countries' borders, as well as very close to its civilian air corridors. A British report noted this increase, as well as two cases of near-collisions over Øresund, right by the large Danish airport Kastrup.[99] In one instance, in March 2014, Russian military jets with their transponders turned off came very close to an SAS flight that had just taken off bound for Rome. In January 2015, the British Royal Air Force made a similar claim about Russian incursion into European airspace: the Russian ambassador was summoned to the Foreign Office to explain why a Russian Bear Bomber along the coast near Bournemouth came so close to commercial flight paths that planes had to be redirected.[100]

The British protested that the Russians were endangering civilian air traffic although they were not doing anything illegal, but flying in international airspace with transponders off is not normal military behaviour, as it assumes that all states whose airspace is traversed have military radar surveillance and are in constant contact with civilian aircraft to warn them. Indeed, NATO Secretary General Stoltenberg warned of the dangers of flying without transponders. With their risky acts, it seems that Russian planes were testing reactions, both political and military, both in NATO countries and vis-à-vis Sweden and Finland. Although legal, this kind of flying can only be regarded as provocative.

In an analysis of all Russian sorties in 2014, James Quinlivan argues that 'Russia's military is getting more aggressive'.[101] He makes the point that

> there are military dangers to the Russian flights and the incursions. Russian fighters routinely fly armed with air-to-air missiles, as do the aircraft that intercept them. It's not difficult to imagine a pilot with an itchy trigger finger or an intimidating fly-by that gets too close – at which point many things could go wrong. ... The Russian practice of flying military aircraft in the Baltics without filing flight plans or using transponders ... shows a reckless disregard for human life. Indeed, these alarming events, such as the incidents with civilian airliners in March and December 2014, are not simply due to faulty procedures ... these kinds of near-misses will continue as long as President Putin wants them to.[102]

Yet Russia defends its behaviour. When a Russian fighter jet performed a barrel roll over a US reconnaissance plane in international airspace over the Baltic Sea, coming within 15 m, Moscow claimed this was a routine practice. Secretary Kerry, however, condemned the manoeuver: 'It is reckless. It is provocative. It is dangerous. And under the rules of engagement [the jet] could have been shot down.'[103]

François Heisbourg sums up the situation as follows:

> NATO and its EU partners have avoided any direct Russian threat: no 'little green men' have popped up in Narva, no Russian soldiers 'got lost' in the outskirts of Gdansk. But the measures taken by NATO have not deterred Russia from pursuing its most active programme of probing European air- and sea space since the end of the Cold War. During March–October 2014, 39 separate incidents were recorded. In two days in October, 26 Russian military aircraft were intercepted by NATO aircraft. Russian air-force misbehaviour included unannounced closing-in on passenger air-craft, flying in civilian airspace with transponders switched off, simulated bombing runs

and straying over sovereign territory in the Baltic and naval vessels in the Black Sea. Sweden ... which had cut its air-defence and sub-marine assets to the bone, was a favourite target.[104]

Russia's military activity beyond Ukraine is illogical if Ukraine is all that matters to Russia. If this were the case, a low profile and a simmering conflict would have served Russian foreign policy better. The West would have 'forgotten' quite quickly, as it did in the case of Georgia in 2008. Ukraine would effectively have been barred from joining the EU, and later NATO, which was the de facto result of the Georgian offensive. Yet Russia chose to keep a very high political and military profile, as well as a strong military posture, from 2014 onwards, challenging NATO on many occasions. This is a strong indicator that Russian goals go well beyond Ukraine and the near abroad.

Russian diplomacy in the period under study was self-assured and presented a coherent narrative: NATO and the US represent a threat to Russia, notably the former's expansion and the latter's unilateralism and use of force without a UN mandate. The regime change in Kiev was a coup, instigated by fascist forces in Ukraine and by the West, especially the Americans.

In October 2014 Putin gave a major speech at the Valdai Forum in Sochi in which he presented a familiar narrative about how Russia is not respected and how the US and the West violate international law and use military force aggressively.[105] The US imposes diktat, he argued, conflicts and wars are developing, military power is being used again, and the world is a dangerous place where wars can break out.

On the subject of Ukraine, he repeated that secession was simply the democratic right of the people of Crimea, as with the people of Kosovo, he said pointedly. He also talked about how 'the bear will never leave the taiga, which is our own' and praised Khrushchev, who had banged his shoe at the UN rostrum while speaking in 1953, a gesture which, Putin claimed, showed how smart Khrushchev had been to make the world fear him as a leader who commanded nuclear weapons.

The speech and comments at Valdai were very anti-American: he painted the US as unilateralist, arrogantly dominating the rest of the world without consulting anyone in an attempt to remain the world's hegemon. Russia, in contrast, simply defends itself against the aggressive behaviour of the Americans and NATO. The same arguments were trotted out in his state of the nation address in the Kremlin on 4 December of the same year. The day before, *Pravda* had written that there was still a possibility of dialogue between NATO and Russia if NATO would stop its aggression. The comment was occasioned by the cancellation of a NATO-Russia Council meeting due to the sanctions levelled by the EU and the US. The Russian narrative was that the sanctions were a hostile attack on the nation, an attempt to bring about regime change in Russia. The rhetoric about how NATO is 'encircling' Russia has been around for a long time, but it was given new life by the sanctions. Moreover, as the Duma passed laws curtailing international media ownership in Russia and making it very difficult to get foreign perspectives into the country, this narrative thus seems logical: NATO encircles Russia while the EU tries to destroy it economically in a veritable siege.[106]

Throughout this time Putin's popularity continued to soar and the Western sanctions seemed to have the opposite effect of what was intended. The average Russian praised the president for his leadership and Foreign Minister Lavrov routinely accused the West of trying to effect regime change in Russia.[107] The fall of the rouble clearly had a major impact on the buying power of Russians, but this was more due to the fall in oil prices than to the sanctions. The sanctions did have an effect, however, as they led to major capital flight by Western investors. During 2014 capital flight doubled, amounting to more than US $150 billion. There can be no doubt that the Russian economy was in a state of major crisis at the start of 2015 and that the sanctions played a part in this.[108] Yet using sanctions to put major pressure on Putin did not have the intended political effect. In a Western liberal democracy under severe economic strain, we would assume that the first cuts would come in defence spending, as all other items would have strong stakeholders in the political debate. However, as a kind of taunt to the West, the Russian state budget for 2015 came with a cut of 10 per cent in all spending with the exception of the defence sector.[109]

Foreign Minister Lavrov was vocal about Russia's position: during an official visit to Finland he warned against applying for NATO membership; he criticized the US on numerous occasions for playing a dangerous and reckless game of world domination outside of international law; and he intensified attempts to influence Eastern and Central European countries. In an article entitled 'Moscow dissects Central-Eastern Europe', Janusz Bugajski wrote about Russian attempts to influence these countries:

> Russia's revisionism targets specific neighbours for direct territorial acquisition or enforced federalization. ... Ukraine, Moldova, and Georgia are subject to violence, partition, economic warfare, and disinformation campaigns

because they have decided to follow the European path of development. ...
Belarus and Armenia are Moscow's only close European allies, primarily
because of their economic and military dependence. ... In order to preclude
broad regional opposition, Russia is also attempting to construct a belt of
neutral or supportive states across Central Europe.[110]

Bugajski pointed out that the cooperation system known as the Visegrad
Group was moribund because Poland opposed Hungary and Slovakia's positive stance towards Russia; that the latter two states also opposed further EU
sanctions against Russia and wanted existing sanctions lifted became evident
at the EU Council of Ministers meeting on 19 January 2015.[111] Along with
other countries sympathetic to Russia, such as Greece, several other EU
member states were highly critical of extending the sanctions in late June
2015. Yet pressure from the US and Germany made them acquiesce.

There are plenty of analyses of how Russia is 'behind'. Paul Krugman,
for example, cites Russia's large state debt, extensive corruption, and
effective status as a gigantic kleptocracy as evidence that Putin's bubble
has burst.[112] All this may be true, but the idea that a regime is weak or
crumbling simply because it does not develop according to the liberal-
democratic model betrays a strong bias. There are many states in the world
that are authoritarian and nevertheless continue to be stable. The same
bias is apparent in Maxim Trudolyubov's article 'Russia's lost time' in
which he laments that 'Putin excels at tripping up his enemies, but his
country is growing dangerously out of step with the rest of the world'.[113]
As I have argued, however, it is this liberal-democratic model that Russia
is challenging and this is explicitly the kind of state and society Putin does
not want. The Finnish Prime Minister Alexander Stubb was probably right
when he said that 'the integration of Russia in the West was an illusion'.[114]
He points out that Russia had a promising start after 1990 in this regard,
but that 2008 was a turning point: 'The old power politics came back. For
Moscow, foreign policy is a zero-sum game: you win, I lose.'[115] He adds
that Europe and the US should have woken up to the reality of the return
of the politics of spheres of influence in 2008, but no Western state wanted
to take this seriously. At present, Russia and China are striving to become
regional, as well as military, hegemons, but in doing so they also challenge
the predominance of the US. In his annual speech[116] in 2016, Putin
declared that although there is chaos in the world, there is order in Russia,
and the same theme was elaborated on by Foreign Minister Lavrov[117] at
the 2017 Munich Security Conference where he called for a 'post-Western'
world order. Internal stability is a sign of strength in this view.

CLAUSEWITZ REVISITED: RUSSIAN FOREIGN POLICY STRATEGY

Roy Allison's book *Russia, the West, and Military Intervention* provides a thorough analysis to date of Putin's foreign and security policy.[118] He argues that Putin's main interest lies in restoring the concert of great powers that makes up the UNSC. In line with great power politics, the very rules of the international system are at stake, in particular the rules for using force. For example, Russia was shocked when the US bypassed the UNSC in the Iraq case, Allison points out.

The world, according to Russia, is becoming more competitive and more concerned with geopolitics.[119] The key question underlying Russian foreign policy is thus 'who gets to decide what to do?'[120]

Russia wants to reintroduce spheres of influence in the near abroad, the traditional Realpolitik doctrine that great powers have special rights in the buffer states surrounding them. This amounts to geopolitics: where a state is geographically determines how much freedom it has. Sovereignty is graduated; small states have little say; great powers are the only important decision-makers and they form a 'concert' that makes decisions on behalf of small states. Allison writes that 'a consensus began to form within the Russian political elite from 1993 about the need to avert Western intrusion into this zone of proclaimed Russian interests'.[121] The CIS (Commonwealth of Independent States) states are seen as subordinate to Russia, which maintains special interests and 'drawing rights' there. Alexei Arbatov, perhaps the foremost expert on Russian strategic thinking today, explains the shift in Russian foreign policy: 'From 2011 to 2013 the drivers of Russia's foreign policy were primarily external, but since 2014 they have become primarily domestic. Challenging the West turned out to be an effective tool for domestic political consideration.'[122] The 'external enemy' then becomes a necessary driver for controlling the public at home and preventing 'colour' revolutions, but purely external events are seen as aggressive:

> Russia's assertive moves abroad began as a reaction to perceived unfair treatment by the West as well as the West's expansionism and alleged arbitrary use of force over the previous two decades. These are precisely the issues that Putin spoke about in his 2007 speech at the Munich security conference. Russia's first counter-attack with the use of military force was in Georgia in 2008, and the second occurred in Ukraine in early 2014.[123]

76   J. H. MATLARY

On the means of foreign policy-making, Arbatov reaffirms what other experts say:

> Putin's doctrine consists foremost of asserting Russia's status as a global center of political and military power ... there is a strict (often cynical) separation between rhetoric and actual policy and a profound disbelief in the sincerity of the West's declared principles ... there is a love of special effects and surprise actions ... it seems most of all that Putin hates most to look weak, which he cannot afford.[124]

Importantly, he adds that 'decisions are mostly reactive, made on a case-by-case basis, and premised on tactical considerations'.[125]

In sum, Arbatov agrees with other analysts in pointing to regime maintenance as Russia's first priority and reassertion of Russian great power status as its second. NATO, and to a lesser extent the EU, are European strongholds, and Russia would like to weaken these organizations and, if possible, see them dismantled in order for an all-European security architecture to emerge. The states that were part of the former Soviet Union are seen as areas where Russia has 'special drawing rights' in terms of political influence.

Galeotti argues that the Russian strategy is to divide, distract, dismay, and dominate, and notes that threats can be deniable if ambiguous, war games are evident but intent unclear, as is deployment, whereas intrusions are undeniable for the most part.[126] The combination of these means of military diplomacy and the goals mentioned above represent a broad repertoire in the diplomatic playbook, and we note that very few of these tools are used by European politicians.

He points out that so-called 'heavy metal diplomacy is intended to unnerve its audience, to leave foreign publics and even some politicians feeling that the risk of war is such that some kind of accommodation with Moscow ... is the best, even only option'[127] This style of diplomacy is especially important for Finland and Sweden to prevent them from joining NATO, and Galeotti cites the former Foreign Minister of Germany Frank-Walter Steinmeier, who said that the NATO exercise Anakonda 16 in East-Central Europe amounted to 'sabre-rattling and war-mongering'.[128]

Thus, not only does Russia use military force in ways that Europe does not but also its political interests are not acceptable to the West. The notion that some states are within a sphere of influence is not a norm that is compatible with the UN Pact and the modern understanding of sovereignty. The concept of spheres of influence was rejected firmly in the UN Pact of 1948[129] and is of course non-existent in international law where all states are equal in terms of sovereign rights. It is, however, contested in the real world of political life because small states have much less say over their destinies than more powerful larger ones. Yet to readmit the notion of spheres of influence as a principle of international politics is quite another matter, and something that surely will be totally rejected by Western states. The principle must remain that states themselves—which are sovereign by definition and recognized legally as such—determine whether the wish to belong in the EU, NATO, or neither. It is the challenge to this principle posed by Russian foreign policy, and not the situation in Ukraine itself, that is the key problem for the West.

The most important difference between Russia and the West is therefore how they view the rules and norms of the state system. This includes how they view both the legitimacy and the legality of the use of force. Russia maintains that only the UNSC should determine when force should be used—a position that ensures that it retains veto power over all such decisions—while rejecting humanitarian intervention as something that qualifies, and indeed overrules, sovereignty in extreme cases. If so-called failed states and dictatorships are considered less sovereign by virtue of either failing to govern or repressing the governed, thereby inviting humanitarian intervention, Russia itself would be in peril. This principled opposition to humanitarian intervention is, however, set aside when it is opportune to argue for just such intervention, as was done in Georgia in 2008 and in Crimea in 2014 when the humanitarian argument was made by Russian leaders to justify intervention in those territories.

In his book discussed above Allison examines Russian justifications of the use of force in detail and concludes that in the Georgian case they were used instrumentally. A five-day high-intensity war was justified using the language of humanitarian intervention, but Russia has 'relativized the core principles of the wider international system, sovereignty and territorial integrity, in its relations with neighbouring states', he finds.[130] The recognition of South Ossetia and Abkhazia shows this.

He highlights the importance of the Kosovo case, in which Western humanitarian intervention without a UN mandate led to a kind of international protectorate, which was eventually recognized as a new state by the West in 2008. This case is cited time and again by Russia as an example of Western arrogance and unilateral use of force. For Russia, says Allison, the recognition of Kosovo was an act that '[broke] the entire system of international relations',[131] it was both immoral and illegal, and continues to provide a pretext for Russian intervention to protect nationals wherever they are.

In his analysis of the Georgian war, Asmus points out that the West, particularly NATO, was ill-prepared to tackle the Russian response to the Kosovo case.[132] No Russian believed that this was a humanitarian intervention, he says; it was seen as a conspiracy to break Serbia. Moreover, when NATO extended the invitation for quick membership to Georgia and Ukraine in 2008, the Russians were shocked. NATO membership for these two countries was a Russian red line: 'Moscow's goal was to kill any chance of NATO ever expanding to Georgia or anywhere else along its borders and to dissuade other neighbouring countries from getting close to the West.'[133]

As discussed at the outset of this chapter, NATO's reaction to the Russian invasion of Georgia was slow and weak, suggesting that there was not much strategy behind it. Instead of an official response from NATO, the EU's High Representative of the Union for Foreign Affairs and Security Policy at the time, Javier Solana, travelled to Tbilisi. There were reactions from individual states, but NATO did not address the situation at first. Later on, it recommended partnership with Georgia, but there was no further talk of membership in the alliance. The realpolitik of the Russian reaction was clear; NATO looked the other way and did not respond. There seemed to be little strategic thinking behind NATO's membership and partnership policy, the guiding principle of which appears to have been the general idea of extending the values of democracy.[134] Only the return of Russian strength and realpolitik forced NATO to reconsider this policy.

The war in Georgia was not fought over territory, Asmus argues. Rather, it was a geopolitical struggle: 'Georgia was determined to go West and Russia was determined to stop it from doing so.'[135] He adds that 'Russia deeply opposed and resented Georgia's effort to escape its historic sphere of influence and anchor itself to the West'.[136] Similarly, the conflict in Ukraine erupted when the country took its first steps towards EU membership by signing an association agreement. The Russian reaction was already very strong, using economic means, when the issue was whether or not Ukraine, Armenia, and Moldova would sign the agreement. President Putin launched a major coercion campaign against all the three states, and the pressure not to sign was stepped up in November 2013 with the addition of harsh trade sanctions.

Considering Russia's clear and consistent policy in its dealings with both Georgia and Ukraine, it seems clear that Moscow's red lines are EU and NATO membership for the states that border on Russia. In addition, as Allison argues, Russian foreign and security policy generally aim at weakening both NATO and the EU. This goes back to the Cold War and to Russia's interest in a so-called all-European security arrangement in which it plays a partner role to the great powers of the West—an 'OSCE with guns', as Norwegian diplomats are wont to dub it. NATO poses the biggest threat to Russian power because it is backed by a military alliance with the US, but the EU is also dangerous because it solidifies liberal-democratic values in a type of integration never before seen among states. In sum, the Russian agenda extends beyond the near abroad.

In one of the early analyses of Russia's actions in Ukraine, the renowned expert on strategy Lawrence Freedman points out that 'by annexing Crimea … Russia revived some of the classic concerns of European security … the crisis represented a sharp geopolitical jolt, a reminder that hard power never quite goes away'.[137] His analysis is that Kosovo plays a key role in Russian views of what they term Western hypocrisy because 'it qualified the principle of non-interference in internal affairs, elevated the principle of self-determination and reduced the standing of the Security Council'.[138] Kosovo was, in Freedman's view, a key turning point in Russia's view of the West. Although Freedman underscores that there were never any pledges of non-enlargement made, Putin claimed that enlargement was 'a serious provocation' in an angry speech at the Munich security conference in 2007.

Freedman makes the assessment that neither side has handled the crisis well: 'It has become more of a zero-sum game rather than less', and 'Western governments failed to grasp the dynamics of change in the region and what Putin believed to be at stake'.[139]

The political relationship between the West and Russia has remained poor throughout the period under study. Under normal circumstances, it would undoubtedly have been a mistake that President Putin did not show up for the commemoration at Auschwitz on 27 January 2015, as Soviet forces played a key role in liberating the camp 70 years before; for this very reason, his absence underlined how alienated Western and Russian politicians are.[140]

In sum, when we analyse the fuller picture of events that unfolded from 2014 onwards, we see a pattern of Russian action and Western reaction. President Putin has seized the initiative and acted boldly, both in terms of political rhetoric and in terms of military testing. There has been almost no meaningful relationship on the diplomatic and political levels, and the Western reaction was reactive, at least for quite some time.

Some commentators have concluded that the main problem is that the West is too afraid to confront Putin because its politicians and publics have an absolute fear of war. This is an interesting conjecture to which I will return in Part Two. 'Europe's problem is that it is too civilised to take on a muscleman like Putin', writes Colin Freeman,[141] while Rupert Cornell contends that 'Putin is counting on the fact that the West has no desire for war'.[142] Putin's move at Minsk was another 'cynical attempt to make military gains', concluded one *Times* editorial.[143]

The House of Lords' Committee on the European Union presented its analysis on 20 February 2015, in a report entitled *The EU and Russia: before and beyond the crisis in Ukraine.*[144] The report's main conclusion about the Western reaction to the crisis is that 'there has been a strong element of "sleep-walking" into the current crisis, with member states being taken by surprise by events in Ukraine. ... The EU has been slow to reappraise its policies in response to significant changes in Russia. This lack of understanding and capacity was clearly evident during the Ukraine crisis.'[145]

After the Russian action in Ukraine the West seemed both divided and at a loss as to what to do about it. There was little real diplomatic effort over Ukraine, and no strategy developed on what to do.

No Western Strategy on Ukraine

A debate on whether to arm Ukraine erupted in US policy circles, but was rejected totally in Europe. The US has often used private military actors as proxies for arming and fighting allies of some sorts, such as when Croats were helped by a programme called "Train and equip" during the Bosnian war 1991–95. American contractors then helped decisively, making it possible for the Croats to beat the Serbs in a decisive battle called 'Flash and Storm'. But in the case of Ukraine, such involvement would have been much riskier, and the ones calling for it were mostly out of government.

The dissension among American experts seems to be over whether to engage Ukraine more, and especially over the question of arming the country with so-called defensive weapons, whatever that may mean. This issue, which had been low on the agenda throughout 2014, came to the fore in late January 2015 when it became clear that Russia was not withdrawing forces from Ukraine and that the Minsk ceasefire agreement was not being honoured. As mentioned, fighting picked up again in new offensives; Luhansk airport fell and NATO reported that thousands of Russian soldiers and armoured cars were in the country. The US Congress passed an act[146] on arming Ukraine, and major experts on security policy called for arming. Among them was Timothy Garton Ash who argued that 'only when Ukrainian military defence can plausibly hold Russian offence to a stalemate will a negotiated settlement become possible. Sometimes it takes guns to stop guns.'[147] While no one will dispute the latter fact, the key issue to be considered in this strategic move is escalation, and whether it is in the interest of Russia, which we can assume it to be since Putin talked about the 'NATO legion' in Ukraine. A real Western arming effort would provide a pretext for Russian military escalation in Ukraine and possibly beyond and could have disastrous consequences.

The West wants to avoid the use of force at almost all cost; Russia does not. A clever strategy avoids military escalation without appeasing. 'Fighting proxy wars will inevitably lead to mission creep', argues the defence editor of *The Telegraph,* Con Coughlin.[148] He recalls the many proxy wars fought by the US in Latin America and the risks involved. Yet fighting by proxy remains a way to avoid risk at home by not inserting own troops, and one could make the case that the Bosnian war was won largely due to the American 'Train and Equip' programme for the Croatian army. In the case of Russia, however, the risk of escalation is a major problem, especially since Putin seems to need more military 'victories' to sustain his popularity at home.

The Poroshenko government has been very careful not to use the term civil war and has tried its best to avoid fighting. It has been forced to fight, and is entirely inadequately equipped and trained to do so. This is clearly, militarily speaking, an asymmetric conflict. Kiev therefore terms the conflict 'an anti-terror operation'.[149] There is a fine line between engaging in war-fighting because the enemy does and insisting on non-military means only. It is the same strategic choice that the West faces, but the West can choose to fight and to win, although with a very high risk of escalation. Critics are right in pointing out that 'a political agreement, if signed, would merely confirm the military situation on the ground',[150] yet this seems to be the price the West is willing to pay because it considers the alternative too risky. In addition, there is not a major Western interest in Ukraine in the first place, regardless of Russian politics there.

As a analyst puts it, 'the Russian threat perception of NATO can be explained by Great Power rivalry and differences in state identities',[151] because Russian elites see liberal democracy and regular change of government as a direct threat to their own survival. Russian revisionism is deeply anchored in their domestic politics, and one can therefore assume that the risk of escalation both in and beyond Ukraine is great.

This position contrasts with the report by American foreign policy heavyweights including Strobe Talbott, Ivo Daalder, James Stavridis, and Charles Wald, among others. They recommended urgent lethal and non-lethal aid to Ukraine, effectively dismissing the danger of escalation: 'Some in the West are concerned that provision of military assistance, particularly of lethal arms, would cause Russia to escalate the crisis. We vehemently disagree. Russia has already continuously escalated. ... Enhanced military assistance would increase Kiev's capability to deter further Russian escalation.'[152] The authors do not discuss this issue further, but they do give a detailed analysis of the military situation on the ground, Russian support, and what the Ukrainian army lacks. This in itself is very valuable, but it is strange that such distinguished figures do not analyse the larger strategic picture.

Former Supreme Allied Commander Europe (SACEUR) General Philip Breedlove also apparently supported arming Ukraine, according to unnamed sources.[153] He increasingly came under fire from German diplomats for being too one-sided in his views, a criticism that grew in the beginning of 2015. In March of that year, Foreign Minister Steinmeier asked NATO Secretary General Stoltenberg to rein in Breedlove's statements. Breedlove is, however, double-hatted and can speak as an American general as well as NATO commander. This incident shows a certain split in how to handle the situation.

The critics of arming Ukraine are many, also in the US. Sean Kay writes that 'given the risks involved, the only realistic option is long-term, patient resolve to stay the course [the sanctions route]'.[154] He points out that the economic situation will worsen for Russia and that its political isolation will have a negative impact; both factors will grow in importance with time. If NATO succeeds in effective deterrence, the West should try to avoid the military tool as much as possible, as '[i]t is unclear how adding fuel to the fire would help'.[155] The key point, Kay argues, is the uncertainty of the risk involved, which is great.

The same position obtains in Europe. Chancellor Merkel stated that '[Germany] will not supply Ukraine with any lethal weapons'.[156] The sharpening of sanctions is the tool of choice, she says. This is, however, disputed by Wolfgang Ischinger, the chairman of the Munich Security Conference. He writes that 'we must make sure that Ukraine has a fair chance to survive, militarily and financially. ... Without external help neither will be possible'.[157] NATO should not play this role of helping Ukraine, he says, but 'Russian refusal to help implement Minsk may leave Western countries with no choice but to deliver defence equipment to Kiev – and Moscow should be fully aware of the responsibility it would then carry'.[158]

CONCLUSION

The Russia use of force in the cases of Crimea and Syria, and also including deniable involvement in Ukraine has not in any way been amended or stopped by Western reaction and action. On the contrary, the political aims of Russia apparently have been reached, despite the sanctions against the country. Russia is the key player in the post-war settlement on Syria and therefore a major player in the Middle East. Russia has effectively halted any westward turn for Ukraine because the country is destabilized with its on-and-off armed conflict in the east of the country. This situation also implies that Ukraine cannot apply for membership of the EU or NATO should it try, for these organizations require that there are no unresolved border disputes or armed conflicts in an applicant state. Like in the Georgian case, Ukraine is kept unsettled; conflict-ridden and unstable.

What about Western states? What does the West want to do about this situation? The reply is unclear. There is no Western strategy on Ukraine, as there is none on Georgia after 2008. The EU does not have any distinct policy on Ukraine after 2014; and NATO maintains a minimum of engagement along the Partnership for Peace (PfP) cooperation. The Minsk talks have not resulted in stable ceasefires or in local elections and military withdrawal, although there is now an OSCE mission of observers in place. Moreover, Ukraine remains conflict-ridden and seriously corrupt, such that in normal peaceful times the country would still be light-years from meeting EU standards.

The West has not been very interested in Ukraine. Perhaps we can ascribe this to interest asymmetry—the West has never been very interested in Ukraine in modern times. Yet with the Russian action in 2014, one may argue that interest is even less. Like in the case of Georgia, there is a fear of involvement, and certainly if this entails military aid. The West does not want to get into a potential military conflict with Russia over states outside NATO. And it clearly does not want to 'own' Ukraine, with all its problems. The Western concern in this case is the use of force as such—that Russia uses force as it did in Crimea; and also in destabilizing eastern Ukraine. I think the West understands the Russian interest in these areas of Europe and that it therefore will do much to keep this influence, but the West refuses to accept a return to the use of military force as a tool of statecraft for promoting such interests.

There is major discrepancy between the political outcry on the part of the West and actual policies to correct the problem. The reaction we have seen is primarily political, accompanied by sanctions, but as we shall see, these were insisted on by the US, not Europe. By and of itself Europe has not done anything beyond protesting. This does not amount to strategy, but as we shall see in the subsequent analysis, various European actors had different roles.

The relevant questions are: What would be a strategic response to Russia in this case? In turn this depends on what the West would like to achieve. It has demanded the reversal of the annexation of Crimea and a stop to the armed conflict in Eastern Ukraine. The means employed are sanctions, both political and economic. In addition, there is no real engagement with Ukraine. Is this because the country is hopelessly corrupt and of little interest to the West, or is it because one fears Russian reactions to such an engagement?

The subsequent chapters seek to provide answers to these questions.

NOTES

1. Galeotti, M (2016) Heavy metal diplomacy: Russia's political use of its military in Europe since 2014, European Council on Foreign relations, 19 December.
2. Galeotti, p. 1.
3. Galeotti, p. 4.
4. Galeotti, p. 4.
5. James Sherr, *The New East-West Discord. Russian Objectives, Western Interests*, Clingendael Report, December 2015, The Hague, p. 33.
6. Ibid., p. 34.
7. Ibid.
8. Ibid.
9. Ibid., p. 53.
10. Ibid., p. 54.
11. Adamsky, Dmitry *Cross-Domain Coercion: The Current Russian Art of Strategy*, IFRI Security Studies Center, Proliferation Papers 54, 2015, Paris, p. 19.
12. Adamsky, p. 20.

13. Ibid.
14. Asmus, Ronald, (2010) *The Little War that Shook the World*, Palgrave Macmillan, UK.
15. See my chapter on Norway in Matlary, J.H. and Petersson, M. (2011) *NATO: The Power of Partnerships*, Palgrave Macmillan, London.
16. *INYT*, 'Ukrainian leader was defeated even before ouster', 5 January 2015, front page and full page 4.
17. 'Russlands intervensjon på Krim – gjennomføring og konsekvenser', *Norsk Militært Tidsskrift*, vol. 184, no. 4, 2014, pp. 16–28.
18. Ibid.
19. 'Putins Schlachtplan', FAZ, 8.9.2014.
20. The Jamestown Foundation, 14.8.2014, 'Russian Military Rehearses Ukrainian Peacekeeping Operation'.
21. 'New Front opens in "Ukraine conflict", reports that "Russian forces" mount stealth invasion', NYT, 28 August 2014, front page. See also 'Ukraine says it stopped Russian incursion' through artillery strikes, *NYT*, 16 August 2014.
22. 'Ukraine braces as convoy nears' and 'Fears as Russian trucks roll on', NYT, 15 August 2014, p. 3; 'Ukraine says it destroyed Russian military vehicles that crossed the border', ibid.
23. 'A White Shining Lie', by Michael Weiss, *Foreign Policy*, 14 August 2014.
24. 'Kremlin is caught putting boots on the ground in the Ukraine', *The Daily Beast*, 26 August 2014.
25. Ibid.
26. Ibid.
27. Ibid., p. 85.
28. Ibid.
29. Burke-White, W.W. 'Crimea and the international legal order', *Survival*, vol. 56, no. 4, 2014, pp. 65–80, p. 65.
30. Ibid.
31. Ibid., p. 66.
32. Quoted in Burke-White, p. 68.
33. Quoted in Burke-White, p. 69.
34. 5 September 2014.
35. Ibid.
36. 'Hagel, Donner und Raketen', *FAZ*, 14 August 2014. The exercise in the summer of 2014 was dubbed a Panzer-Biathlon; participating states were Venezuela, China, India, Kuwait, Serbia, and Mongolia. China brought its own tanks.
37. 'The EU and Ukraine', Neil MacFarlane and Anand Menon, *Survival*, vol. 56, no. 3, pp. 95–101.
38. Ibid., pp. 96–97.

39. A contradictory view is that the 'integration dilemma' was solvable through negotiations, see Charap, S. and Troitsiy, M., 'Russia, the West and the Integration Dilemma', *Survival*, vol. 55, no. 6, 2016, pp. 49–62.
40. Ibid., p. 100.
41. Zadra, R. 'NATO, Russia, and Missile Defence', p., 55, *Survival*, vol. 56, no. 3, 2014, pp. 51–61,
42. Charap, op.cit. p. 87.
43. Ibid.
44. 'Pro-Russian voters defy Kiev at the polls', *INYT*, 3 November 2014.
45. Ibid.
46. 'Exuding confidence Putin rebuffs European appeals' *INYT*, headline 18–19.10.2014.
47. Ibid.
48. NYT, 'At UN, Russian foreign minister asserts US and allies are hypocrites', 29 September 2014, p. 5.
49. Ibid.
50. A year after the disaster on 17 July 2015, *The Daily Beast* assembled all the evidence in an article entitled 'How we know Russia shot down the MH17'. The detailed facts and analysis presented there constitute probably the most comprehensive source of what happened. See also 'Examining the Evidence of Russia's Involvement in a Malaysia Airlines Crash', Stratfor, 23 May 2006, which substantiates the claim that a Buk missile from the town of Snizhne shot down the plane, citing satellite imagery.
51. 'Ukraine and rebels agree to cease-fire', NYT, 6–7 September 2014.
52. 'Ukraine and separatists agree to cease-fire', NYT, 6–7 September 2014.
53. Interview with EU official, 23 June 2015, Budapest.
54. Sherr, p. 25.
55. Sherr, p. 26.
56. Sherr, p. 26.
57. 'Ukraine Crisis: Putin's Nuclear threats are struggle for pride and status', *The Telegraph*, 29 August 2014.
58. 'Don't mess with nuclear-armed Russia', *The Telegraph*, 29 August 2014.
59. 'Des Kremls neue Militärdoktrin' *FAZ*, 8.9.2014.
60. President of the Russian Federation, V. Putin, 'Military Doctrine of the Russian Federation', 26.12.2014.
61. 'In Latvia, fresh fears of aggression as Kremlin warns about Russian minorities', *Washington Post*, 29.9.2014.
62. Ibid.
63. See also *Aftenposten*, 17 January 2014 and other international media.
64. BBC webpage, 22 January 2015.

65. NYT, online, 19 February 2015, 'Ukraine's forces retreat from strategic town'.
66. *The Times*, 'Kiev cries foul as Putin's tanks roll over the border', 13 February, online.
67. *The Times*, online, 19 February 2015, 'US threatens Russia as battle nears end'.
68. *The Times*, online, same title and date as in text.
69. 'Hvorfor Ukraina trenger våpen', *Verdens Gang*, 20 February 2015.
70. *Die Welt*, 'Ukraine fördert tödliche Waffen con Europa', online, 19 February 2015
71. *The Telegraph*, editorial, 18 February 2015, online.
72. *Die Zeit*, online, 'Putin streicht seine Gewinne ein', 12 February 2015, see also FAZ, 'Aqud einer Position der eindrückener Überlegenheit', online, 11 February 2015 and "Pro-Russian rebels to gain ground under Ukraine deal", *The Times*, 9 February, online.
73. Ibid.
74. Sherr, op.cit., p. 28.
75. Ibid., p. 29.
76. 'Russia and Eurasia', chapter 5, *The Military Balance*, 2017, IISS, London, p. 184.
77. Ibid.
78. Adam Garfinkle, 'How to Misunderstand what didn't Happen', The American Interest, 5 April 2016.
79. War on the Rocks, 'How Moscow took control of the battlefield and negotiating table', 28 June 2016.
80. Baev, Pavel 'For Moscow, talks are about sowing discord, not solving conflicts', Eurasia Daily Monitor, vol 13, issue 35, 22 February 2016; Roger McDermott, 'Russia Raises the Stakes in Aleppo', Ibid., 9 February 2016, Crowly, PC, 'Putin's Payoff in Syria', BBC, 15.3.2916 Breaking News.
81. The Military Balance, p. 187.
82. 'Russian Actions in Syria overshadow Kremlin's Diplomatic Maneuvers on War in Eastern Ukraine', Eurasia Daily Monitor, vol 13, issue 169, 26 October 2016.
83. Leader, 19 March 2016, and main briefing 'Russia's wars' in same issue.
84. Åslund, A and Commander, S, 'Russia's Gloomy Prospects', project syndicate, 23 May 2015.
85. The Military Balance, p. 191.
86. 'A Vital Nuclear Agreement at Risk', NYT, 5 January 2015.
87. 'US and Russia in danger of returning to era of nuclear rivalry', *The Guardian*, 4 January 2015.
88. Kristin Ven Bruusgaard, 'Russian Strategic Deterrence', *Survival*, pp. 7–26, July 2016, vol 58, issue 4.

88   J. H. MATLARY

89. Ibid.
90. Ibid.
91. Tamnes, R (2017) 'The Significance of the North Atlantic and the Norwegian Contribution', pp. 8–32, in Olsen, J. A. (ed.) *NATO and the North Atlantic, revitalizing Collective Defence*, Whitehall Paper 87, RUSI March.
92. Strategic Arms Reduction Treaty (START).
93. 'INF treaty increasingly in danger as Russia balks at new missile defence base in Romania', by Pavel Felgenhauer, *Eurasia Daily Monitor*, vol 13, issue 93, 12 May 2016. See also 'Putin commits to countering new strategic "threat" to Russia', Ibid., issue 95, by Pavel Baev; and 'Putin warns Russia will respond to NATO missile shield', www.military.com, 18 May 2016.
94. Ibid., Baev article.
95. *NYT*, 11 December 2014.
96. Ibid.
97. *Die Welt*, 'Westen will in Moskau Regimestürz provozieren', 22.11.2014, online 'Der Westen zeigt unzweideutig, dass er (Russland) nicht zwingen will, seine Politik zu ändern, sondern dass er einen Regimewechsel erreichen möchte'.
98. *Die Welt*, 'Was hinter Putins geheime Krimrede steckt', 14 August 2014, online 'braucht eine patriotische Mobilisering der Gesellschaft gegen Russlands "Feinde", um bei Wirtschaftsprobleme seine Popularität nicht zu verlieren'.
99. See note 7.
100. BBC, 28 January 2015.
101. *Foreign Policy*, 30 December 2014, 'Yes, Russia's Military is Getting more Aggressive', James T. Quinlivan, pp. 1–8 online.
102. Ibid., p. 8.
103. '"Aggressive and erratic" Russian fighter jet barrel-rolls within 15 m of US plane', *The Independent*, 18 April 2016; see also 'Russia defends jet fighter barrel roll over US reconnaissance plane', *The Telegraph*, 6 May 2016.
104. Heisbourg, F., 'Preserving post-cold war Europe', *Survival*, 5 February 2015, 57, 1, pp. 31–48, p. 38.
105. The Valdai speech: 19 October, Official site of the President of Russia; Sotchi. 'The World Order: New Rules or a Game without Rules.'
106. 'Russia prepares to repel the US all fronts', The Jamestown Foundation, 26.9.2014.
107. *Aftenposten*, 19 January 2015, pp. 4–5.
108. *Dagens Næringsliv*, 'Kapitalflukten doblet', 20 January 2015, p. 31.
109. Ibid., 15 January 2015.
110. *The American Interest*, 29 December 2014, "Moscow Dissects Central-Eastern Europe".

111. *Klassekampen*, 'Klamrer seg til hard linje: EU stadig mer splittet i synet på sanksjoner og press mot Russland', pp. 14–15, 21 January 2015.
112. 'Putin's Bubble Bursts', NYT, 2 January 2015.
113. 'Russia's lost time', NYT, 2 January 2015, p. 9.
114. FAZ, online, 2 October 2014, Finnlands Ministerpräsident im Gespräch: 'Die Integration Russlands in den Westen war eine Illusion' (copyeditor's translation).
115. Ibid., p. 2.
116. *Die Welt*, 'Putin erklärt seine neue Weltordnung', 1.12.16, unity in Russia, chaos elsewhere (annual address).
117. *Die Welt*, 'Putin erklårt seine neue Weltordnung', 1.12.16, unity in Russia, chaose elsewhere (annual address).
118. Oxford University Press, 2013.
119. Ibid., p. 204.
120. Ibid., p. 118.
121. Ibid., p. 121.
122. Alexej Arbatov '*Russian Foreign and Security Policy*', Carnegie Moscow Center, 21 June 2016.
123. Ibid.
124. Ibid.
125. Ibid.
126. Galeotti, p. 5.
127. Ibid, p. 5.
128. BBC, 18 June 2016, 'German minister warns NATO against "war-mongering"'.
129. The UN Pact, which is *ius cogens*, that is, peremptory norms in international law, states that 'all members shall settle their international disputes by peaceful means in such a manner that international peace and security, and justice, are not endangered' (art 2,3), and furthermore, 'all members shall refrain in their international relations from the threat or the use of force against the territorial integrity or political independence of any state' (art. 2,4). Thus, threats are prohibited, as is meddling in the internal affairs of another state, such as 'Finlandizaton' in the Cold War and subversion in general.
130. Allison, R. (2013) *Russia, the West, and Military Intervention,* Oxford University Press, Oxford, p. 159.
131. Ibid.
132. Asmus, R. D. A Little War that Shook the World. Georgia, Russia, and the Future of the West, Palgrave Macmillan, UK, 2010.
133. Ibid., p. 5.
134. Alexandra Gheciu comes to similar conclusions, see Gheciu, A. (2005) (ed.) *NATO in the new Europe. The Politics of International Socialization after the Cold War,* Stanford University Press.

135. Ibid., p. 8.
136. Ibid.
137. Freedman, Lawrence, 'Ukraine and the Art of Crisis Management', *Survival,* 23 May 2014, vol 56, no 3, pp. 7–42.
138. Ibid., p. 15.
139. Ibid., p. 28.
140. 'Putins Fehler', Der Spiegel, 27 January 2015, online. The paper says that this is detrimental to Putin, that he isolated himself by this absence, but fails to notice the ominous signal that is sent. We can assume that Putin would have cherished such an occasion, with good reason. That he abstains from participating shows that he does not want to try to establish political dialogue.
141. *The Telegraph,* same title, online, 11 February 2015.
142. *The Independent,* online, 19 February 2015, same title.
143. *The Times,* online, 6 February 2015.
144. House of Lords, 6th Report of Session 2014–15, The Stationary Office Ltd.
145. Ibid., executive summary, p. 6, and BBC News online, 'Ukraine: UK and EU "badly" misread Russia', 20 February 2015.
146. 'The Ukraine Freedom Support Act', 2014.
147. 'Putin must be stopped. And sometimes only guns can stop guns', *The Guardian,* 1 February 2015, online.
148. Article by same name, online, *The Telegraph,* 4 February 2015.
149. 'It's time to call Ukraine a war', *The Daily Beast,* online, 4 February 2015.
150. 'Russian grinds down Ukrainian troops while Western support is elusive', *Eurasia Daily Monitor,* vol 12, issue 21, 3 February 2015, online.
151. 'Russian Threat Perceptions: Shadows of the Imperial past', *warontherocks.com,* Hanna Smith, 2 February 2015.
152. Talbott, S. et al., *Preserving Ukraine's Independence, Resisting Russian Aggression: What the US and NATO must do,* Report by the Atlantic Council, Brookings, and the Chicago Council on Global Affairs, February 2015, online.
153. 'US considers supplying arms to Ukraine forces, officials say', NYT, 1 February, online.
154. 'The escalation advocates are wrong on Ukraine', *warontherocks.com,* February 2015.
155. Ibid.
156. FAZ online, same title, 2 February 2015 'Wir liefern der Ukraine keine tödlichen Waffen'.
157. Wolfgang Ischinger, 'How to stabilize Ukraine without playing Putin's Game', *Spiegel* online, 2 February 2015.
158. Ibid.

REFERENCES

Adamsky, D. (2015). *Cross-Domain Coercion: The Current Russian Art of Strategy* (IFRI Security Studies Center, Proliferation Papers 54). Paris: IFRI Security Studies Center.

Allison, R. (2013). *Russia, the West, and Military Intervention.* Oxford: Oxford University Press.

Arbatov, A. (2016, June 21). *Russian Foreign and Security Policy.* Moscow: Carnegie Moscow Center.

Asmus, R. (2010). *The Little War That Shook the World.* London: Palgrave Macmillan.

Burke-White, W. W. (2014). Crimea and the International Legal Order. *Survival, 56*(4), 65–80.

Charap, S., & Troitsiy, M. (2016). Russia, The West and the Integration Dilemma. *Survival, 55*(6), 49–62.

Galeotti, M. (2016). *Heavy Metal Diplomacy: Russia's Political Use of Its Military in Europe Since 2014.* Brussels: European Council on Foreign Relations.

Gheciu, A. (Ed.). (2005). *NATO in the New Europe. The Politics of International Socialization After the Cold War.* Stanford: Stanford University Press.

MacFarlane, N., & Menon, A. (2015). The EU and Ukraine. *Survival, 56*(3), 95–101.

Matlary, J. H., & Heier, T. (Eds.). (2016). *Ukraine and Beyond. Russia's Strategic Security Challenge to Europe.* London: Palgrave Macmillan.

'Russia and Eurasia', chapter 5. *The Military Balance,* 2017. London: IISS.

Sherr, J. (2015). *The New East-West Discord. Russian Objectives, Western Interests* (Clingendael Report). The Hague: Instituut Clingendael.

Talbott, S. et al. (2015, February). *Preserving Ukraine's Independence, Resisting Russian Aggression: What the US and NATO Must Do.* Report by the Atlantic Council, Brookings, and the Chicago Council on Global Affairs.

Tamnes, R. (2017). The Significance of the North Atlantic and the Norwegian Contribution. In J. A. Olsen (Ed.), *NATO and the North Atlantic, Revitalizing Collective Defence* (Whitehall Paper 87, pp. 8–32), RUSI March.

CHAPTER 4

Mass Migration and Border Control

Migration has become the key political issue in Europe today for several reasons, ranging from fear of large Muslim populations in liberal Western states—so-called parallel communities—to fear of increased costs to the state as well as political instability. Yet the primary concerns are border control and internal security in an age of much terrorism. Indeed, 'the importance for a government to be perceived by its citizens to be in control of its borders cannot be underestimated', writes Koser, an expert on migration.[1] Thus it is significant but not surprising that currently, 'from Austria to the UK, Europe is gripped by border anxiety'.[2]

The dismantling of borders and their control in the EU's internal market has been the main achievement of the union, and the functioning of this extensive market depends on open internal borders. Yet the internal market was always supposed to be 'guarded' by a controlled outer border, referred to as Schengen. Migration shocks therefore have consequences not only for states and their domestic politics but also for the functioning of the internal market that Europe depends on.

In this chapter I will present and analyse the case of the external migration shock in Europe in 2015. How was this dealt with politically and which political effects did it have? Was this met with a strategy of controlled influx and control of borders, and if not, is there now a strategic response in place? My argument is that the answer to both these questions is no. Yet mass migration in an age of terrorism—where terrorists can travel into Europe under the guise of refugees—is arguably a much more

© The Author(s) 2018

J. H. Matlary, *Hard Power in Hard Times,*

https://doi.org/10.1007/978-3-319-76514-3_4

pressing security concern than Russian revisionism. Whether Russia attempts to keep a sphere of influence in non-NATO Europe in the east was really not very important to the average citizen in Europe once the shock of Crimea subsided. Major war with NATO is after all still quite unlikely, given the risk and NATO's American security guarantee. External migration shocks like the one in 2015, however, directly challenge internal stability and security of the states affected, and the EU response was a failure in terms of stopping this influx. NATO plays no direct role in this policy area, and the individual state was left to itself to respond. Citizens of stable liberal democracies experienced a totally uncontrolled influx of both migrants and refugees, their police and military seemingly could do nothing about it. The main route through the Balkans eventually saw state after state building border fences to re-route those who came, and Chancellor Merkel's welcome to all arrivals led to an initial praise from German citizens and much of the liberal world but eventually to sharp criticism at home. By the end of 2017 much of the populace wanted Merkel gone, citing her unwillingness to set an upper limit on migrants and refugees as the main reason.[3] By January 2018, there was open discussion of who might take her place as Christian-democratic Union (CDU) leader. Yet a deal with the Social Democratic Party (SPD) on 22 January 2018 led to a new coalition government. The agreement made for this included a cap of 220,000 migrants per year into Germany: Merkel finally had to defy her own principle that there can be no upper limit.

The Open Door Policy and Human Rights

As Michta puts it, 'no issue has redefined Europe's political future in the next decade more than the surge in MENA migration in 2015–15. Its effects continue to ripple across the continent, bringing into view long-term changes in European culture and politics, including the bifurcation of the EU into western and eastern halves when it comes to migration.'[4] In Germany itself the conflicts over migration continued to grow in 2017 and into 2018: 'Die Probleme, die mit der Grenz'offnung im Sommer und Herbst 2015 entstanden, haben die politische Landschaft der Bundesrepublik Deutschland ins Beben gebracht' (The problems brought on by the opening of borders in 2015 have caused an earthquake in German politics, my translation), write experts in *Die Welt*.[5] They point out that the mainstream parties do not want to deal with these problems in an honest and open manner and that they try to avoid having to deal with them.

Below we will discuss the political effects of the 2015 mass influx, which has changed the political landscape of Europe as a direct result. Mainstream political parties now have to have a strict migration policy or lose to parties of the right that are often populist. Moreover, this issue splits the EU and endangers the future of the union. First we will analyse the issue further in terms of how it was framed, or defined, as this has been extremely important to understanding its political effects. Where political elites, be it governments or the EU, have seen mass migration in human rights terms, often similar to Merkel's views; voters have seen it as a threat to both national cohesion and as a security threat.

After this discussion we present policy responses that centre on controlling borders, asking whether Europe now can control its own borders.

In addition to concerns about the security and stability of the state, debates about migration also revolve around the question of who should be allowed to become part of the national community. This is a sensitive topic because it raises questions about what a nation is, something that is rather foreign to those that have discarded the notion of 'nation' as important.

From Thomas Hobbes' *Leviathan*,[6] we learn that the state, even if unwanted as an institution in the so-called state of nature, is needed for security reasons. Security is a collective and public good that cannot be provided at the individual level, hence the need for collective security. The police, which keeps the peace internally, and the military, which guards the state and its borders, make up what Max Weber famously called a 'legitimate monopoly on violence', which is what actually defines the state.[7] Citizens pay for and contribute to this monopoly through the twin duties of taxes and conscription. They do this not because they want to, but because they have to, for the alternative, namely life in the state of nature, is, as Hobbes famously put it, 'nasty, brutish, and short'. Max Weber is the key theorist or philosopher of the modern state, and his insistence that unless a state can provide security, there is no state, is salient whenever security is at stake.

Thus, when security issues are prominent, be it state rivalry, terrorism, or a mass influx of people, as Europe experienced in 2015, the primary role of the state is that of the original Hobbesian *Leviathan*: to provide security. The state's citizens expect it and rightly demand it. If there is no security, all else is endangered and instability and 'lawlessness' quickly take hold. There simply must be domestic order and law-based conflict resolution, and it does not take much to destabilize this order, especially in a liberal state based on trust more than on policing. The mass influx of migrants and refugees into Europe in the autumn of 2015 was very threatening for this simple reason: *European governments quite clearly did not know what to do.*

Some states physically closed their borders, including Hungary, where Prime Minister Orbán spoke of an invasion. This framing of the issue was widely condemned in Western Europe where the emphasis was on the rights of migrants and refugees to apply for asylum. National, territorial, and border security seemed a foreign theme to many West European politicians who refused to even define an upper limit to how many people could come to their country and be integrated.

MIGRATION FRAMED AS A HUMAN RIGHT

'Framing' refers to defining a policy issue as 'an instance of' something. In this case, how migration was framed had extremely important implications for political action: Was this a case of economic migration, with migrants paying smugglers and ordering 'tickets', often including false identification papers, to Sweden or Germany? Or was this an instance of desperate people fleeing war and destruction? Were they migrants or refugees? The *framing* of the issue—that is, the determination of whether these persons were economic actors seeking a better state and paying a lot to get to Germany or Sweden, or whether they were refugees in danger of their lives at home—played an immense role in shaping the policy response to the problem of mass influx.

Migrants have no right to enter another country and ought to stay in their home states to build them rather than to take advantage of well-developed states; every receiving state decides itself whether it wants to take in migrants. Canada and Australia have traditionally been receiving states, and they determine who can enter, often prioritizing well-educated young people. A refugee is someone who has to leave their home country because their life is in danger and who thus has the right to seek political asylum under international law. While there is no right to enter a new state and remain there, there is a right to protection.

The human rights 'regime' that became so prominent after 1990, and which has formed a whole generation of Europeans, played a key role in framing the migration influx as a refugee issue. People who arrive in Europe must be received, taken care of, allowed to seek asylum, and possibly allowed to stay. Globalists, who tend to think that open borders are normal, were aghast at talk of closing them, and many seemed to think that there was some kind of human right to enter other countries. This attitude, or value system, led to a very strong framing of the migration influx as a question of preserving the human rights of those who arrived. Naturally every person has equal human rights, as these are universal, but it is up to one's own state to implement these rights. Foreign states have no obligation to do so; they are accountable to their own citizens and obliged to secure their human rights. Yet this idea seemed foreign to the NGOs, lawyers, and other stakeholders in this policy area who were eager to promote the rights of migrants and refugees. These actors were extremely vocal, occupying the moral high ground as migrants arrived by the hundreds of thousands. It was politically impossible for a West European government to be seen to physically close a border in this situation.

In an interesting discussion about ethics and migration,[8] Karl-Heinz Nusser cites Angela Merkel who says: 'Das Grundrecht auf Asyl für politische Verfolgte kennt keine Obergrenze, das gilt auch für die Flüchtlinge, die aus der Hölle eines Bürgerkriegs zu uns kommen'[9] (the basic right to asylum for the politically persecuted does not know any upper limit, and that is also valid for those who come to us from the hell of civil war, my translation). Since this statement in 2015, Merkel has refused to define an upper limit of how many can enter Germany, something which has become the major conflict in domestic politics since. Apparently Merkel holds an absolute principle of welcoming all who can make it to Germany and seek asylum there, and those rejected are hard to return. Yet all human rights are subject to states being able to provide their citizens with them; it is the state that is the so-called *Pflichtsubjekt*, the actor responsible for securing human rights for its citizens. Non-citizens do not have this claim on a foreign state; their human rights should be provided by their own state. Naturally many states are unable to do this and even actively deprive their citizens of their human rights, but it does not follow that foreign states acquire this obligation, as Merkel seems to assume. Moreover, the sheer inability of any state to take in a million refugees in one year—the influx in Europe in 2015 was 1.2 million—makes it clear that state capacity for integration, economic support, and so on must necessarily demand an upper limit, as has been the policy hitherto in Europe where each state has a quota policy under the UNHCR (UN High Commissioner for Refugees), where one selects refugees from camps in the their own region.

The ethics of what to do did however come to be associated with Merkel's position of open borders. Nusser points out that stable and prosperous states are the precondition for receiving refugees, and that a weakening of such states will lead to less reception as a logical necessity. Asked about this, Merkel replied that we all depend on each other in the modern, open, and interconnected world.[10] Moreover, human rights are seen not as depending on governments for their realization, but as generic and general in such a sense that states no longer matter. Hans Magnus Enzensberger calls this 'moral individualism': 'Spezifisch für den Westen ist die Rhetorik des Universalismus. Die Postulate, die damit aufgestellt worden sind, sollen ausnahmlos und ohne Unterschiede für alle gelten'[11] (universalism is a specific rhetoric of the west whereby everyone is equal, regardless and without exception, my translation). It follows from this that there is no difference between family, fellow citizens, and the whole wide world: human rights are the same for all, and the ethical fallacy inferred from this equality is that we are equally morally obligated to help everyone. This is however not the case—one has objective, legal responsibilities towards one's children and parents that are valid for them only. Likewise, there are obligations of citizenship that result in the paying of taxing to the others in the nation, not to the world, and conscription even confers the duty to die for the nation. Thus, there is no universal ethical obligation following from the postulate of universal human rights: 'Aus dem gleichen moralischen Wert, den die menschen haben, folgt nicht … dass sie auch dieselben Pflichten haben'[12] (from the same moral worth of each person does not follow the same moral obligation towards them, my translation). There are Christian obligations to help others regardless of who they are; as there also are in other religions, but elected politicians have a mandate to help their own nation or citizens before the rest of the world and parents have special and unique obligations to their children. Yet the idea that Western governments are there to 'save the world' is a common idea today, and one that seems the ethical position. The young generation has grown up in a borderless world in Europe and been able to travel the world, and they have been taught that human rights is the only ideology around. EU integration has suppressed the importance of the nation and nation-state; indeed one may argue that making the nation-state superfluous is the main aim of the EU. It is therefore not very surprising that the migration issue was primarily framed as a human rights issue, but it is surprising that a seasoned state leader like Merkel did not have a more nuanced attitude to the issue. Yet her stance came to be the 'moral' one, and this tells us much about German political culture. Was it politically impossible to close the border because pictures of police guarding borders would be associated with a so-called police state?

Thus, in 2015, migration was not framed in terms of security and the state in Western Europe, but almost entirely in terms of human rights. If we add multiculturalism to this set of ideas, we have the *ideal-typical* model that prevailed in Western Europe when the migration shock occurred: Barring a person physically from entering a state is morally unacceptable because everyone shares the same human rights and there is a duty to help everyone.

In Norway for example, the human rights framing clearly predominated. Those that pointed out that the people arriving in Europe were relatively well-off and resourceful, and therefore needed in their own states, were roundly condemned as immoral, and their arguments were seen as illegitimate.[13] This moral condemnation was very effective in excluding many from public debate. Those who tried to suggest a reconsideration of the practice of letting everyone that reached a European border apply for asylum there, and found centres outside of Europe to process such applications, were unable to get fair treatment in the debate.[14] It was extremely important to be seen as more ethical than the next debating colleague, and the debate was really about who was the most ethical, not about how to solve the problem. The self-evident facts that migration increased when open borders were 'on offer', and that Europe could not accommodate millions from the MENA region each year, were simply not taken seriously in the public debate, which was dominated by the stakeholders in the NGO and legal communities. No politician in Western Europe seemed willing to say that the human rights regime practice in asylum applications was unsustainable because European states could not take in everyone who received asylum status anyway. The physical and practical problems of major arrivals created chaos, but politicians seemed paralysed by what the lawyers said and did not address these issues.

The human rights framing was very strong in Sweden, Norway, and Germany. In both Sweden and Germany there was no willingness to discuss an upper limit to the number of migrants that the countries could absorb and integrate, whereas the governments of Norway and Denmark were more realistic and introduced border controls when the first chaotic period of mass influx abated, utilizing an exception to the Schengen rules. Sweden then followed suit, but only after a tearful press conference with Prime Minister Löfven where his immigration minister cried and the prime minister said 'we can't handle this'.[15] The sheer inability of the Swedish state to take in everyone who arrived naturally led to a need to control borders, but the government in fact regretted having to do this.

The uncontrollable influx of migrants also caused chaos in Germany, as could easily have been predicted. Sports arenas and schools were used as reception centres and had to close to normal use; train stations and public squares were unable to function normally. Yet Merkel has never said that Germany could not do any more or agreed to set an upper limit to migration, thus in effect upholding the promise that anyone that reaches the German border can enter. Apparently, she is not willing to be seen closing the German border. Border controls have improved, but this does not imply denying entry to anyone, which is seen as politically impossible.

Why is this so? All states determine who can enter via the visa mechanism. People who are suspected of planning to stay are routinely denied tourist visas if they come from poorer regions of the world. All Western states regulate who can come and exclude those that may become clients of the state, especially from Africa, the Middle East, and some Asian and Eurasian countries. If a person applies for a tourist visa at their local German or Swedish embassy, the application will be denied unless someone in these countries can serve as an economic guarantor for the visitor. This aversion to incurring welfare obligations for foreigners is so strong that even those who marry someone from one of these Western countries must have a certain income in order to be allowed to settle there.

This standard border control practice stands in stark contrast to Europe's unwillingness to close its borders in 2015. This is understandable because of the acute problems that arise from unrestricted immigration, but it also posed a major image problem for Western politicians: how do images of police closing a border in the face of thousands of people trying to get in look on TV? This move would be especially hard to justify in Germany, as it evokes images of a police state.

Yet as the crisis unfolded, public opinion changed. People naturally became sceptical of large numbers of Arab young men that seemed to arrive in organized fashion. When German women were sexually assaulted on New Year's Eve 2016 in Cologne and the police initially refused to give a full report, the public was outraged. Increasingly, even Germans and Swedes became highly critical of mass immigration, which resulted in the growth of far-right populist parties. A German investigation of media coverage showed that it had been flawed: only positive views of migration were printed.[16] The Otto Brenner Institute found that the media acted like 'public educators' instead of as critical journalists, and based this conclusion on the study of thousands of articles between February 2015 and March 2017. The report said that mainstream media supported Merkel's open door policy uncritically. They used the term 'Willkommenheitskultur' in order to put pressure on citizens and to influence public opinion: 'People who criticized the government were treated as suspect and potentially racist.'[17] The study was led by former editor in *Die Zeit*, Michael Halle, and analysed mainstream papers like *Bild, Die Welt, Süddeutsche Zeitung*, and *FAZ*. This was based on an analysis of thousands of articles in the mainstream German press, and the conclusion was very clearly that media framed the issue as one of human rights and generosity and excluded critical questions about Islam, integration, sheer numbers, and political instability. The result of this was naturally that one framing of the issue prevailed very strongly and became the politically correct one.

In addition, the Cologne attacks on New Year's Eve 2016 on women who were out celebrating were not reported until days later. When the New Year celebration in 2017 approached, the German city government of Berlin, seeking to avoid new assaults on women, suggested a 'safety zone' for women around Brandenburger Tor. This proposal was met with heavy criticism from the German police, which said that this was an adaptation to the unacceptable views of women than many migrants hold. Why should German women need to be in a safety zone in their own country?[18]

This example well illustrates the lack of clarity about own society, culture, and values in many European states in the face of the migration shock: the reality of a *security* problem for especially women, grounded in unacceptable views of them, led to a type of political appeasement in these states whereby authorities tried to accommodate the unacceptable behaviour by making victims out of their own citizens. The security problem was not handled by the punishing of offenders, but tried to be avoided by removing the offended from public squares. This is appeasement in pure form.

MIGRATION FRAMED AS A SECURITY ISSUE

The migration crisis was framed very differently in the states of East-Central Europe. These states, newly re-emerged from Communist repression, were rebuilding their own nation-states and were decidedly not postmodern in their views. The nation is definable and constant; built on long historical memory and knowledge and marked by a common Christian heritage which goes back at least a thousand years, and these states had always had invasions and incursions, wars and suppression. They did not accept mass influx from the Middle East; least of all large numbers of Muslims. The Visegrad states closed their borders and allowed people to apply for asylum from detention centres at the border. They said that risk of terrorism necessitated ID checks of everyone who tried to enter, and that those whose asylum applications were rejected—migrants— would not be allowed to enter the territory and would have to return home. These countries also said that large Muslim populations would pose problems for the values of liberal democracy and a threat to their cultures as Christian nations. Poland and Hungary said that they could accept refugees, but only Christian families. This was seen as highly unacceptable in Western Europe and the EU, but these states pointed out that they, like Western states, have the right to select quota refugees. By partially barring migrants from entering or by letting them pass through Hungary to Germany, Hungary managed to avoid having large numbers stay, but incurred major moral condemnation from its EU partners. As we shall see, however, Western Europe also resorted to closing its borders eventually, but did so by outsourcing the problem to others.

These states also rejected supranational EU refugee policy, even if this was adopted by an EU majority, and Poland and Hungary took the EU Commission to the EU court over this issue in 2017 and predictably, lost. However, they continued to oppose this particular EU policy, and along with the other Visegrad leaders, pledged to oppose EU common refugee policy in all respects: 'It is clear that the European people do not want immigration while several European leaders are still forcing the failed immigration policy', said the leaders of Poland and Hungary on 3 January 2018.[19]

For several years prior to the 2015 crisis, illegal migration was a major problem in Italy, Spain, and Greece, but other countries and the EU did not want to hear about it, much less put it on the political agenda. Repeated calls by Italy for solidarity in the EU and the creation of a common migration and refugee policy fell on deaf ears. Only with the migration shock in the autumn of 2015 did the issue force itself onto the EU agenda.

More than a million illegal immigrants and refugees came to Europe that year; in fact, more than 1.2 million crossed a European border. The EU was powerless to cope with the situation, as were most states. The German chancellor's welcoming words '*Wir schaffen das*', which translate as 'we'll manage it', or 'we can do it', naturally acted as a catalyst for more illegal migration. Migrants broke through border controls and walked on motorways as far north as Denmark. This was a *major external shock* to Europe: there was an acute need both to stop the flow of people coming into the territory and to accommodate the ones who did come in a humane manner. Europe had not faced a physical influx across its borders of this proportion for decades; there was much confusion at every level about what to do. During the Balkan wars in the 1990s there was major movement of refugees within the region, but not towards other parts of the European region.

European borders are not physical borders for the most part; they are controlled at entry points, which are not prepared for massive influxes of people. It is not possible to control all of the Schengen border, especially not at sea and between Turkey and Greece. Although the outer European Schengen border is supposed to be controlled, this has never been the case apart from the border between Russia and Norway, which is also a border between NATO and Russia. The EU abolished internal border controls in 1992 as part of the establishment of the internal market.

Europe remains a favoured destination for migrants as it offers stable political systems with little corruption, generous welfare states, and genuine human rights protections. As long as other states fare less well than Europe, Europe will remain a preferred destination for rational actors. This point is made by Paul Collier, an expert on developmental economics, who also reminds the reader that states that are solid economically and politically have been made so through citizens who have seen it as their duty to build and develop them.[20] The first duty of any person is to his own state, he points out. Yet individual economic rationality and an instrumental view based on self-interest yields the conclusion that individuals seek a better life in 'ready-made' states. International migration rose by 77 million between 1990 and 2013, and most migrants (135 million) are in the developed world. Of these some 72 million are in Europe[21] and between 5 and 10 million are illegal migrants. There is a well-developed 'migration industry' that reaps enormous profits from smuggling people and issuing false documents. 'The very poorest people', however, 'those most affected by global inequalities, simply cannot afford to move'.[22]

The main routes into Europe in 2015 were the Balkan route, the Mediterranean route, and also—curiously—routes into Norway and Finland from the High North. The influx into these Nordic states was not spontaneous, as travellers had to pass several military checkpoints *en route*. There was clearly both organized transportation and much corruption among local officials, and the influx acted as an external shock, in particular for the Norwegian government: what to do with thousands of migrants arriving during the coldest period of the year? Was this a Russian provocation? Could they be sent back? The Norwegian government clearly regarded this as a security issue and perhaps as a test of the stability of Norwegian politics, although this was of course not articulated publicly. The wave of migration in the High North stopped as suddenly as it had started. Yet Russia refused to take back people who had a multi-entry visa to Russia. Although it could have done so legally, Norway decided not to protest Russia's behaviour and accepted all these migrants, about 1500 people. The lesson learnt was that Norway and Finland could be made the object of mass influx of migrants at any time and that the closing of the border in the High North would be disastrous in political terms, especially in winter. Thus, such an influx would be a way to destabilize these states. This is an important and interesting lesson in *Realpolitik*.[23] There was a similar influx into Finland at Kandalaksha, by car, but after two months this stopped suddenly also. 'Unfortunately, this looks like a political demonstration by Russia', said Ilkka Kanerva, former defence minister and present chairman of the parliamentary defence committee. He adds 'they are very skillful at sending signals'. In the first two months of 2016, more than 800 migrants came into Finland this way. One interviewed migrant, Mussa Khan from Kabul, said that he paid US $6000 to a facilitator in Moscow who arranged a deportation order for him. Others said the same, they had paid for 'guides' who would get them to Finland and who worked closely with Russian officials, a highly organized system where only 30 persons would enter Finland every day. There were lists of names and departure dates. 'They are all in the same clique: the officials, the hotel people, the drivers. This is their business.' Apparently Putin called for this to stop the traffic on 29 February 2016.

In general, little of the travel to Europe by migrants and refugees was spontaneous, as it was organized by smugglers and paid for by their 'customers'. Media followed these groups as they crossed into new countries, walked on highways, massed in train stations, and moved from Serbia via Hungary and Austria to Germany, their preferred destination. Many also sought Sweden as their new home. Data from Interpol/Europol suggests that more than 90 per cent used smugglers and that they paid them on the average more than €3000. In a study by Koser[24] where he examined nearly 600 sources, he found that the average cost of coming from Africa to

Europe was US $6533 and for travel within Europe US $2708. Migrants are at the mercy of these smuggles who operate with total impunity.

Most migrants come without papers and therefore cannot be returned, or they disappear once their asylum application is rejected and live as *sans-papiers*. The migration industry offers false papers to those who can pay. The human rights system that Western European states observe allows everyone to seek political asylum once they reach a European country, and if rejected, they have right of appeal. In sum, the major issue is to get to Europe, to a country with a functioning welfare system and a political *praxis* of accepting refugees. Migrants, like refugees, typically do not want to stay in Greece or Italy, which offer little benefit, but to get to Germany or Sweden. The demand to get to Germany was massive among people arriving in 2015; remaining in Hungary or Greece, both EU states, was not seen as an acceptable option and most simply passed through these states. This is highly understandable based on the logic of individual preference, but not based on the logic of wanting to save one's life as would be the case for a real political refugee.

Europe, with its open borders, was completely unprepared for the influx of migrants in the autumn of 2015. European states had ignored the calls from front-line states like Italy and Greece which had been pleading common EU policy and help with burden-sharing for several years. Europe as a whole had been forewarned by the arrivals to the front-line states but chose to look the other way for as long as possible. This in itself is evidence that Europe lacked a strategic outlook.

The 1951 UN Convention on the Status of Refugees is the basis for the right to apply for political asylum. It defines a refugee as a person who, 'owing to a well-founded fear of being persecuted for reasons of race, religion, nationality, membership of a particular social group or political opinion, is outside the country of his nationality' and should be protected; it does not imply that refugees should be resettled in third countries and receive citizenship there. This convention was intended for refugees from Nazism and Communism in Europe, not for mass migration purposes. However, signatory states have also accepted that people cannot be returned to dangerous places, the principle of *non-refoulement*. Thus, people who come to Europe from war zones cannot be returned, and this means that everyone who makes it to a safe state can stay until the situation in their home country has changed. The Refugee Convention stipulates that refugees should return to their home state whenever possible, but in practice, most of those who come to Europe stay unless there is a return agreement with their home state.

The point here is that Europe's faithfulness to international law and its human rights obligations create a pull not only for refugees but also for migrants. This fact finally led to a *Realpolitik* turn, even for Germany's Merkel, who started the process of 'outsourcing' the problem of border control to Turkey in 2016. The prospect of closing borders within Europe, or at least at the entry points into Europe, has been too unpalatable to politicians in Germany, and would imply that the right to seek asylum had been suspended. Therefore, the closing of borders was 'outsourced', first in the Turkey-EU deal developed and negotiated by Germany and second in the EU's 2017 deal with Libya.

Thus, the dilemma that Europe in confronting—or failing to confront—is that the right to apply for asylum once on European territory is the major pull factor for migrants. There is currently little legal immigration into Europe as no states have a need for labour immigrants. Those that arrive as illegal or irregular migrants have either come to find work or as refugees. If granted political asylum, they can stay, at least until it is safe to return home—which is perhaps never, given the instability of many war-torn and repressive states. In any case, the application and appeals processes take a long time, and if an application is ultimately turned down, the migrant often travels on to another country or goes underground. In addition, many people are not returnable because they lack ID, and even if they have ID, their countries often refuse to take them back.

The human rights regime that is so vocally supported by lawyers and NGOs is one-sided in the sense that it privileges only asylum seekers. This is only natural since these actor groups work in the interest of these two groups. The governments of Europe face great challenges when trying to argue against taking in migrants and refugees as this is a morally contested position. It is a fact that these governments do not want migration in the current employment situation; and when it comes to refugees, they would prefer to admit only a controllable quota that allows for integration. This means letting in many fewer people than arrived in the mass wave of migration in 2015—namely a few thousand each year, mostly through the UNHCR's selection process which also allows for national selection, vetting, and control, the latter of which is very important in this age of terrorism.

POPULAR REVOLT AGAINST IMMIGRATION

Migration has indirect political effects that are already creating instability in Europe. Migration from predominantly Muslim Arab countries adds yet another layer to the issue. The question of whether Islam can accommodate and co-exist with liberal democracy is very much discussed in most Western states. There is much scepticism in this regard. Hampshire reports that polls show that many think that Islam is a problem in Europe, and that many Muslims themselves—as many as 16 per cent in France and Spain and 15 per cent in Britain—believe that violence may 'sometimes' be used against civilians in order to defend Islam, according to Pew poll data.[25] The same poll found that anti-Semitic attitudes were frequent among Muslims; for example, 'in Germany and Britain only 38 per cent and 32 per cent of Muslims had a favourable attitude towards Jews'.[26] There is, argues Hampshire, 'a potent spectre haunting the integration debate in Europe: the spectre of Islam'.[27]

Scholars have pointed out that the welfare state and political community depend on trust and social identification, and that ethnic diversity and social capital may be negatively correlated.[28] This in turn implies that multiculturalism may not be a viable model for modern democracy unless there is enough that is common in terms of values. Today the major 'culture war' in Europe seems to be over multiculturalism—should immigrants adjust to integrate into the nation-state or should the model of the nation-state be abandoned altogether? The existence of a political community, the nation, as the basis for democracy, presupposes a common identity as citizens, based in language, culture, and history. This is in sharp contrast to the multicultural model which does not recognize the need for a common culture and identity. Yasemin Soysal's 1994 book *Limits of Citizenship* argues that national citizenship is being replaced by international norms.[29] Now the tables are turned, however. Many jobs, for example, require national citizenship. Despite an increasingly globalized world, 'the nation-state remains the pre-eminent generator and guarantor of rights, and national citizenship has if anything become *more*, not less, important in the age of migration', argues Hamphire.[30]

Migration is the key uniting theme of the right-wing populist parties that have recently become quite successful.[31] Research on causes of migration scepticism has concluded that it can mostly be explained by the importance of national identity. Indeed, evidence from both Europe and North America suggests that 'identity is more important than economics as a determinant of anti-immigrant attitudes'.[32] This also explains why Islam is viewed with such apprehension, as a culture/religion/political system that is very different from the liberal-democratic set of norms based on individualism and separation of faith and politics typical of the Western Judeo-Christian tradition.

Hampshire points out that: 'to the extent that liberal states are nation-states, drawing upon deep reservoirs of feeling and emotion to underpin their authority, identity-based opposition towards immigration poses real challenges to government'.[33] I would add that even if one concedes that identities are forged over generations of historical development and experience, this means that they are real, if not material. The key point that constructivists always make is that identities are socially constructed and can therefore presumably change quickly and easily. But the opposite is the case: Identities are of course not material facts—as there is no biological or other material basis for belonging to a nation; but the national identity I am speaking about here is mostly the result of *historical evolution of a community* that shares a language and a culture, and it is therefore so real and strong that citizens of a nation-state are often willing, and sometimes required to, even die for it. This patriotism is to the homeland, the nation, rather than to the territory as such. It is the 'constructed community' that citizens love and defend more than a physical border. There is a deep irony in the constructivist claim that because identities are created, they are easy to change. On the contrary, beyond the family, little is as serious and real as one's nation. The nation is the foremost community of a citizen's life. Thus, constructivism is not helpful in explaining why national identity is so important. Reality is in a common history, culture, and language, and together these factors constitute the community that is made up of those who share this. None of these factors are material, yet they are eminently real.

National elections in 2016 and 2017 have shown how important immigration is, both in mobilizing right-wing populist parties and in causing mainstream parties to take a stricter stance on the issue than they had previously. The election of 31-year-old Sebastian Kurz as Austrian chancellor in late 2017 underscored the latter point. Kurz, representing the Austrian People's Party (ÖVP), the mainstream liberal-conservative party, was also quite populist, launching a campaign focused on himself—*Liste Sebastian Kurz*—and promising to end all illegal immigration. Indeed, immigration was at the top of the agenda during the election as Austria had been shocked in 2015 by the influx of around 1 million immigrants who came through Hungary on their way to Germany. This experience led to major outcry in Austria—law and order had been suspended all of a sudden, and the external shock of mass migration left politicians clueless as to how to handle the situation. The Austrians demanded a government that would control the country's borders.

Kurz promised strict border control, thus outflanking the right-wing populist Freedom Party of Austria (FPÖ) which bluntly declared that Islam has no place in Europe. FPÖ is an anti-immigration as well as anti-Muslim party, yet Kurz formed a government in cooperation with this party. In another move aimed at reinforcing national and European cultural values, Austria has also recently banned the use of niqabs, burkas, and the like. It is interesting to note that the FPÖ was in a coalition government in 2000, at which time it was led by the very controversial Jörg Haider. At the time major EU states boycotted Austria for six months, led by France and Germany, but followed by most EU member states and some others, like Norway. There was a public outcry against 'racists' in government, and Austria was under political boycott until a way could be found to lift the boycott. There was at the time no legal basis for such in the EU. The point here is that the present inclusion of the FPÖ in the government has not caused any protest and very few comments, something which testifies to the 'new normal'.

Populist parties gained ground in other states in Europe as well. In France, the traditional party structure was made redundant in the 2016 presidential election with the victory of the hitherto largely unknown young politician Emmanuel Macron and his newly created party, *En marche!*. The election turnout was only 43 per cent, yet Macron's victory was devastating for the traditional parties. As a popular movement without a clear party programme based on ideology, we can classify *En marche!* as populist, albeit different from the right-wing populism of the National Front, for example.

In Britain, the *Brexit* vote was also a sign that migration is important to voters there; both illegal migration across the Channel and the free movement of people in the EU's internal market played key roles in the *Brexit* campaign. The central issue was the need for sovereignty over borders, along with the rejection of supranational governance. The many attempts to label *brexiters* as populist are examples of the political misuse of the latter term. Opting to leave the EU has nothing to do with populism, although it remains true that the attitudes towards leaving were characterized by much simplicity of argumentation on both sides.

In the Netherlands, the populist Freedom Party did not succeed in winning the national elections in 2017, but came close, and Dutch Prime Minister Rutte, who received a renewed mandate, strongly emphasized the need for loyalty to the Dutch state and nation. This played out in a conflict with the Turkish diaspora in the Netherlands which wanted a Turkish minister to be allowed to campaign in the country on the occasion of the Turkish national election. When the minister tried to enter the country in order to campaign, she was stopped and deported. Rutte managed to form a government in October 2017, and strict immigration policy plays a key part in its stance.[34] This is another example of the need for mainstream parties to impose strict immigration policy and pay attention to border control.

In Germany, Chancellor Merkel was re-elected in October 2017, but the right-wing Populist Party Alternative für Deutschland (AfD) won 12.7 per cent of the vote and 94 seats in the *Bundestag*. The process of forming a government left both Social Democrats and the AfD in the opposition, but Merkel was unable to form a government in 2017 and tried to get back to the great coalition with the Social Democrats in early 2018. In her party the migration issue played a key role and was the source of conflict between the CDU and the sister party of Bavaria, the CSU. A major theme for the CSU, the Christian Democratic Party of Bavaria, was to curb migration into Germany by stipulating an upper limit of 200,000 immigrants per year, something Merkel refused to agree to. For AfD the only major issue in the election was immigration, which explains its success. Merkel's 2015 open border policy in response to the mass migration crisis has been a key point of national unrest and criticism ever since. I discuss this at length below.

The conservative leader of Hungary, Viktor Orbán, is set for re-election a third time in the spring of 2018. His ticket is very clearly national-conservative, against immigration—Muslim immigration in particular—as a threat to the Hungarian nation. Orbán emphasizes that he wants to preserve Hungary's Christian identity, which stretches back a thousand years and is written into the nation's constitution. His re-election seems to be secured.

In East-Central Europe, history is taken seriously, is known well and taught widely. These states, old nations suppressed under 40 years of communism, are determined not to let their freedom to develop their nations be undercut by Western post-national values. All four Visegrad countries (Poland, Slovakia, Hungary, and the Czech Republic) have refused EU quotas on refugees; they do not want immigration and want to decide on refugees themselves. They have explicitly said that they want Christian refugees. These attitudes are seen as discriminatory by the EU and Western European states that point to human rights that stipulate that one cannot discriminate on the basis of religion. But does this imply that a state cannot have a policy of how its nation should develop? There is no clear answer to this question; however, it is certain that every state determines whether it takes in migrants and how many refugees it is willing to take annually.

In the post-national West where multiculturalism has made a major impact, secularism is also very strong. To talk about the nation as a clear and permanent category is strange if nothing is permanent about identity and it is something one chooses freely. Therefore, the idea that the nation must be preserved is rejected, for who can define the nation? These debates are extremely different in Western states than in East-Central Europe, where nations have had to fight for their survival quite recently, something that is not the case in the West. National consciousness is particularly important in East-Central European countries because Communism—just the latest repression historically—tried to suppress and destroy their spirit of resistance, which was based on exactly national cohesion. Communism, which aims to create a society based on a community made up of the proletariat, is the ideological opposite of the nation-state. Communism therefore systematically destroyed family and national bonds, and post-Communist freedom came with search for the nation and an attempt to strengthen it.

Further, for the states of East-Central Europe, which have been physically overrun so many times in history, it is obvious that states must control their borders.

In conclusion, the mass migration influx into Europe in 2015 showed two things: First, that the closing of borders is a necessary, but not sufficient condition in order to deal with irregular mass migration. Indeed, the EU ultimately had to close its borders, although it could not bring itself to do this at home, and outsourced the problem—to be discussed below. This shows the degree of aversion to the use of hard power in Western Europe, especially when it would seem to clash with human rights. Second, this case also illustrated how different the conceptions of state and nation are in Europe, between post-national Western Europe and traditional East-Central Europe. Moreover, what started as an 'open door'-policy as the morally right position very soon came to be an issue where anti-migration parties gained massive support.

The European Policy Response: From Chaos to Outsourcing

As discussed, in the summer of 2015 the chaotic situation regarding migration into Europe became increasingly clear. Several 'flash-points' emerged—the Hungarian fence on the Serbia border and the uncontrolled influx of thousands of migrants via the Balkan land route to Hungary; the French closure of its border with Italia in Ventimiglia where hundreds of migrants stayed attempting to enter France, as well as the situation regarding the Channel tunnel between Calais and Dover. Thousands of migrants camped near the tunnel entrance, trying to get onboard trucks and even to get into the tunnel to traverse it on foot. In the NYT of 30 July the major headline on the front page was devoted to this issue.[35] 'Here we see clear evidence of "buck-passing" – the French think that the English should secure their border at Dover rather than criticizing the French for not doing enough in Calais: "Where is the border?" For me, it isn't in Calais, it is in Dover', says a local French politician in Calais and former minister of labour under Sarkozy, Xavier Bertrand.[36]

During the spring of 2015, hundreds of people drowned in the Mediterranean Sea on their way to Europe from chaotic and dangerous Libya leading to an outcry, at least in the international news and among rights groups: 'EU leaders don't care about drowning immigrants'.[37] Amnesty International attacked European governments for neglecting the crisis, which, they claimed, led to more deaths,[38] and when empty boats were found at sea, criticism was strong on account of the discontinuation of the Italian-run rescue service Mare Nostrum. In two days, more than 6500 migrants were taken to Lampedusa, and Human Rights Watch stated that the 'intolerable number of victims is only going to grow if the EU does not guarantee rescue operations in the Mediterranean'.[39]

The EU's foreign policy head, Federica Mogherini, admitted that the EU could do more, pointedly saying that the Dublin rule which says that asylum can only be applied for at point of entry into Europe could be practiced in a more consistent way and calling for more solidarity among EU states.[40] Now that the policy issue had become what the Commission described as a crisis, it could no longer be ignored.[41] The EU called an extraordinary summit to discuss measures 'to prevent more people from dying at sea'.[42] The agenda was thus emergency measures in a crisis, not migration policy in general.

There was agreement on a few points, all related to the halting of migration flows; leaders agreed that it was necessary to strengthen the EU's presence at sea to stop boats bound for Europe and return them; to fight traffickers according to international law; and to prevent illegal immigration. Member states wanted the EU to be able to stop illegal migration at the outer border, as agreed in the Schengen treaty, but they did not want a common EU burden-sharing policy determining the distribution of refugees. The EU used majority procedure to decide on the redistribution of 160,000 refugees in 2015, but as of 2017 only 5 per cent of those have been taken in by various member states. The Visegrad countries were adamant that they would never accept a supranational refugee policy of quotas, and have steadfastly refused to accept the EU decision. Nevertheless, all member states agreed that the outer Schengen border needed to be controlled and pledged funds and resources to make this a reality. Yet there was no agreement on burden-sharing in the form of quotas despite the use of majority voting. The president of the European Commission, Jean-Claude Juncker, argued in favour of a common migration policy in the EU, whereby states would agree to quotas, to no avail. It was very clear that member states first and foremost wanted controlled outer borders, not a common EU policy of burden-sharing.

This goal was accomplished by implementing visa arrangements that would stop potential migrants from boarding planes to European states, but in terms of physical control of borders the task seemed impossible. As migrants continued to come, some individual EU states closed their national borders. In the summer and autumn of 2015, Hungary built a border fence that was effective, albeit controversial, and Austria and Croatia only allowed migrants and refugees to pass through on their way to Germany. No state wanted to accept large numbers of arrivals; national actors tried to make themselves the least attractive destination in what is commonly called the 'race to the bottom'. As Sophie Matlary found in her study of EU policy on migration, the logic of a 'decision trap' is evident: although states see the need for a common EU policy they will follow their own self-interest by not accepting a policy that deprives them of national sovereignty.[43]

The EU failed to achieve anything in the way of supranational migration policy—so-called burden-sharing—but was tasked with patrolling and controlling borders.

The EU Outsources Border Closure to Turkey and Libya

Despite broad agreement that stricter border controls were necessary following the mass influx in 2015, Europeans governments largely avoid implementing such controls and closing borders—the two measures that combined would end migration and the smuggling business by ensuring that people would not be able to enter Europe. Instead, they outsourced the border control and asylum processes to regimes with awful records on human rights, namely President Erdoğan's regime in Turkey and the lawless regime—or lack of such—in Libya.

In 2016 Chancellor Merkel, acting for the EU, negotiated a bilateral agreement with Turkey in an attempt to stop the influx of people into Europe through the so-called Balkan route.[44] All migrants and refugees were to be sent back to Turkey, which was declared a 'safe country of return', when they arrived in Greece. Those that wanted to apply for political asylum would have to do so in Turkey, and the many who had already made it to Greece, would have their applications processed there. The agreement was signed on 18 March 2016 and took effect two days later. The deal, brokered by the 28 EU member states, was 'forged with their backs seemingly against the wall, and in an atmosphere of palpable panic'.[45]

During the previous month, more than 57,000 migrants had arrived in Greece, and states farther north including Macedonia, Austria, and Hungary had already closed their borders. There were domestic protests in Germany, and populist parties were on the rise everywhere. Popular revolt against the mass arrivals was mounting by the day, and governments simply had to do something drastic to halt the steady stream of both Syrian refugees and African and Afghani migrants. There was only one alternative to closing the Schengen border itself: closing the borders in other states beyond Europe.

The 'EU-Turkey Refugee agreement' was reached with a heavy presence of German negotiators. In 2015, 84 per cent of illegal border crossings took place between Turkey and Greece. There was a dramatic fall once this agreement was made, between March and April 2016 the numbers were down by 90 per cent. Yet the returns to Turkey are very few indeed, as Greek lawyers are slow to process applications and do not agree that Turkey is a safe country of return. The result is that many thousand are in limbo in the Greek islands at present.

The EU-Turkey deal consists of an arrangement whereby people arriving in Greece after 20 March 2016 would be turned away and returned to Turkey, from where they could seek political asylum in Europe. If granted, the EU would take them in as refugees, up to a limit of 72,000 persons. It is unclear how this number was arrived at, but it was very clear that most European states, including EU states, refused to commit to taking in many new refugees, especially given the many irregular arrivals up to that point. The EU plan for quotas that had already been adopted—the 160,000 people who were to be redistributed from Germany and Hungary in particular, which had received the most—was met with massive resistance. The pledge of taking in ever new applicants from Turkey therefore seemed wholly unrealistic. EU states acted in their self-interest in a consistent manner in the face of this challenge; they wanted as few refugees and migrants as possible. When France and Britain were in conflict over the Calais 'jungle' and controlling the Channel crossing, they found an EU solution preferable and called for one, as Sophie Matlary shows in her thesis.[46] When Italy and Greece carried the brunt of the burden of new arrivals, they also wanted an EU solution, something other states like Germany did not want, and so on. Based on this logic, Germany now wanted much more burden-sharing since it was hosting the lion's share of the arrivals, but the other states certainly did not want to help with this. They all wanted the Schengen borders to be strictly controlled, and possibly even closed, to stop migrants, but they did not want to share the burden of taking in refugees beyond the modest numbers they themselves opted for.

The Turkey deal worked very well in terms of stopping the influx into Greece. The cost to the EU was, however, considerable: €6 billion to pay for camps and maintenance in Turkey and, we can assume, to pay Turkish authorities. Furthermore, Europe promised to reopen membership negotiations with Turkey and visa-free travel for all Turkish citizens—100 million—into the EU. Apart from the payments, however, these promises have so far not become reality: Turkey is still formally a candidate for EU membership, but even Chancellor Merkel has now stated that it is time to remove this offer from the table, given the massive repression of democratic values and principles in Turkey after the attempted military coup in the summer of 2017. Visa liberalization is also out of the question currently, and if implemented could led to a massive influx of persecuted Kurds, something which would paradoxically present Europe with large numbers of traditional political refugees. Now, at the end of 2017, the relationship between Germany and Turkey, in particular, is as poor as it can be. This implies that the dependent party—the EU in this case—is extremely vulnerable to a new massive influx of migrants and refugees. Whether Turkish trade interests with Europe will prevent this remains to be seen. *The point here is that outsourcing its border control to a state like Turkey has made Europe extremely vulnerable.*

An additional point is that by making this deal, the EU seemed to distance itself from some of its human rights obligations. As NGOs and think tanks have underlined, 'the deal has also unveiled a paradox for a European Union that has spent decades preaching its own high asylum standards to neighboring countries'.[47] NGOs and refugee lawyers argued, among other things, that Turkey was not a safe country of return, that it interred refugees, and that there were 'bulk returns' rather than returns based on individual assessments of applications in Greece.

Those who were already in Greece, and the few who have arrived since, have been unable to move on to other European states; they have been detained in Lesbos, and the slow legal process of applying for asylum has not led to any quick returns to Turkey and then back to Europe as a quota refugee. Most have been stuck in appalling conditions in Greece—so appalling that EU officials fear to serve there as legal counsel.[48] It is too dangerous for EU officials to work in the refugee camps in Greece.

Meanwhile, President Erdoğan has survived an attempt on his life during an unsuccessful military *coup d'etat* in the summer of 2016; since then conditions in Turkey have gone from bad to worse. Human rights are being violated in almost all respects: people are being arrested in the thousands on trumped-up charges, mock trials are being held, foreigners are being held as hostages, and all power is concentrated in the dictator's hands. Turkey's relationship with Germany is as bad as it can be, short of severing diplomatic ties. German politicians are not allowed to visit their own soldiers at Incirlik military base, which amounts to a major provocation on Turkey's part, and German human rights activists and journalists have been arrested in Turkey. The two countries are close to freezing bilateral relations, yet they are the main partners in the European refugee and migration policy that aims at stopping the mass influx of people into Europe. The vulnerability of Germany and the EU is considerable and increasing by the day as Erdoğan issues threats to inundate Europe with millions of migrants and refugees and challenges democratic values. Turkey, a NATO member, allies itself with Russia and buys Russian anti-aircraft systems and fights Kurds rather than ISIL. As of late 2017,

Chancellor Merkel had ruled out Turkish EU membership and was on the brink of discontinuing diplomatic relations. The relationship between these migration management partners could not be worse.

Thus, a way to avoid making policy choices that imply changes to the asylum rights regime and also closing of borders is to pay others to do both. This is what both the Turkey deal and a new deal with Libya are about. In 2017, the EU adopted a so-called action plan for stopping migration from Africa through the lawless and war-torn state of Libya. This ten-point plan gives money to militias that stop migrants from arriving into Libya from the south, to the Libyan Coast Guard for intercepting and returning boats, and to various actors in the smuggling business. The deal is between Italy and Libya, France and Libya, and the EU and Libya. The EU describes the programme as 'support of the Libyan Border and Coast Guard in order to enhance their capacity to effectively manage the country's borders [with] a particular focus on the Southern regions of the country'.[49] This rather neutral wording covers the active support by the EU of a corrupt coast guard suspected of being smugglers themselves and to militias in the south that can control borders there, both far from the normal state representatives with which the EU normally cooperates. These actors definitely do not possess the 'legitimate monopoly on violence' that Weberian statehood entails.

There is currently no functioning government in Libya, only competing factions and a nominal government called the Government of National Accord, recognized by the UN,[50] but powerless. But the desperation over large numbers of people coming across the Mediterranean, especially after the closure of the Balkan route via Greece as a result of the EU-Turkey deal, has led to an even more precarious policy deal with Libyan actors. The agreement, finalized in the summer of 2017, basically involves paying various border agents in the south of Libya, as well as the Libyan coast guard, to stop migrants. In addition, the deal provides support for the International Organization of Migration (IOM) to return people home. The extremely dismal and dangerous conditions in Libyan detention centres make people willing to be returned to their country of origin. Most arrivals in Libya come from sub-Saharan Africa, mainly from Nigeria, and few qualify for refugee status.[51] There was a desperate call from Italy both to stop the traffic across the Mediterranean and for EU burden-sharing in the summer of 2017, to no avail: neither France nor Germany wanted to discuss taking in more people. The Italian president of the European

Parliament, Antonio Tajani, called for a deal with Libya similar to the EU-Turkey deal, based on a grant of €6 billion.[52]

One analyst writes:

> Libya is embroiled in civil war. Currently there are three rival 'governments' battling for control of Libya's security services. To this effect, expecting Libya to be in a position to implement the EU deal is gross disregard for Libya's capacity as a country. Whilst UNHCR and IOM officials are envisaged to be the main processors of migrant issues, the fact is they cannot do this solely as migrants numbers are too large for them. This deal also fails to acknowledge the deplorable migrant conditions in Libya. Essentially, migrants who shall be returned to Libya are likely to end up in detention centers. Of intrinsic concern is Libya's negative track record on human rights; the country has failed to ratify international conventions on human rights. UNICEF's 'A Deadly Journey Report' released recently captures gross violations of human rights in Libya as one of the central push factors for migration to Europe. Migrants who make it to Italy have often recounted being abused, starved and even raped in detention camps.[53]

The states most affected by migration from Africa held a meeting in Paris in early September 2017 led by President Macron. From the European side, Italy, Spain, France, and Germany were present, and from the African side, Libya, Chad, and Niger. They agreed on a plan to reduce migration, and it seems that a possible format for future such deals will entail tying EU aid money to border controls and return acceptance.[54]

Italy made its own very muscular policy, designed by Interior Minister Marco Minniti. He travelled to Libya and met with various tribes and militias in the south, agreeing to pay them to keep migrants out: 'The southern border of Libya is crucial for ... Europe as a whole. So we have built a relationship with the tribes of southern Sahara. They are ... the guardians of the southern border.'[55] In the same interview, he said that he brought tribe leaders to Rome and negotiated with them for 72 hours, and then he went to Libya and talked with the mayors of 14 towns, offering them economic assistance if they stopped migrants. This policy had led to an 87 per cent reduction in arrivals in Italy, a major change to say the least. More than 60 per cent of boats leaving Libya were turned back by the coast guard before they reached international waters.[56] Yet the deal is very fragile—at one point in-fighting among militias led to a breakdown in the agreement.[57] Minniti is mindful of the domestic political situation: more than 12,500 people arrived in one day, which meant a boost for populist parties and a major threat to stability in Italy. Therefore, something very drastic had to be done.

Like the EU-Turkey deal, the deal with Libyan actors has received major criticism from human rights organizations, as well as from the UN High Commissioner for Human Rights, Zeid Ra'ad al-Hussein, who said that although there is proof that migrants are severely abused in detention centres in Libya—including being raped, extorted for more money, and even killed—'memories are short when facts are inconvenient'.[58]

The facts on ground continue to make trouble, not surprisingly. The coast guard head A Milad is accused of being a key trafficker, writes *the Times*. Despite the lack of accountability of key partners like this person, and physical government control of Libya, the EU will spend €200 million to stop migration, by 'breaking the business model' of the traffickers. EU Council President Tusk even stated that 'now is the time to close down the route from Libya to Italy'.[59]

In sum, both the EU and individual European states have moved forwards with drastic policy in order to close borders beyond Europe. Rather than trying to close the Schengen border, the EU has chosen to outsource both border controls and asylum applications to Libya and Turkey, and seeks to form similar agreements with other states in Africa. This policy has so far been very effective in stopping migrants and refugees before they enter Europe, but it has come at a considerable cost in terms of human rights and makes Europe very vulnerable and dependent on rogue regimes and actors. As neither present-day Turkey nor Libya constitutes a partner that can be trusted, the deals are extremely fragile. Moreover, the human rights situation in these countries is best described as deplorable. Thus the EU has not only exposed itself to new migration shocks if these partners are displeased and renege on their part of the agreement, but also compromised on its human rights standards. Finding itself in the desperate situation of needing to stop migration into Europe, but being unwilling to do so itself, the EU has taken these risks. It would have been much safer for the EU to control and close its own borders rather than rely on outsourcing, but apparently this was so unpalatable that it was not done. Only political 'outcasts' like Hungary dared to close their borders. Perhaps ironically, this is what Germany and the EU, and later Italy and the EU, have done by outsourcing the migrant problem to others in exchange for payment. One may ask which is the more ethical choice.

The Strategic Imperative: Stop Migration and Help Build Sustainable States in the MENA

European governments must dissuade and if possible, stop illegal mass migration into Europe. They must hinder the physical arrival of migrants who will then apply for asylum and, for the most part, stay in Europe, regardless of the outcome of their applications. Return rates are very low and returns are very costly, both in terms of establishing a person's identity and in terms of the actual return itself, which often involves a police escort from Europe. Further, as European governments will in no circumstance be able to accommodate everyone who qualifies for refugee status, it makes sense to outsource the application process to centres in the regions from which the refugees originate. There is also the added and very important argument that those who travel illegally, assisted by smugglers, risk death and injury on the way, especially when crossing the sea. Finally, there is the major argument that smuggling must be stopped so that the business will be quelled. If 'clients' are no longer able to reach Europe, this dreadful business will disappear.

Taken together, the factors suggest that the most important *strategy* in stopping illegal migration is to change the practice of allowing people to apply for political asylum once in Europe or at a European border. Indeed, this policy mostly explains the attraction of coming. As for the refugees, while some of them will come to Europe, not all of them will be granted refugee status. It is therefore unjust that only those refugees who can afford to pay smugglers to get them to Europe should be the ones let in. It would be fairer to select people in camps in their regions, and this would also let European governments have a say in which refugees they want to allow to settle—families, the handicapped, the poor, and so forth. Strong young men like those who made up the bulk of the influx into Europe in 2015 would not take precedence, and older, sicker, and perhaps weaker individuals would be given a chance.

Thus, all aspects of the *problematique* point to one strategy: the closing of the outer European border combined with the announcement that political asylum must be applied for from locations outside of Europe. Such a policy would quickly discourage migration, and Europe could use its resources on refugee centres and camps in regions of conflict and let the UNHCR continue its expert work as lead agency in this field. European states would certainly be expected to accept refugee quotas as before and also to help develop failed and impoverished states to make it attractive for citizens of those states to stay there and help rebuild. As for refugees, all wars end and war refugees can therefore return someday. European diplomatic efforts and money are being directed towards ending wars and rebuilding states, and this work must continue. After all, money spent on the root causes of these problems is money well spent—and money spent on refugees in the local regions helps many more than spending on those who arrive in Europe, as the difference in the cost of living is vast.

Thus, the main element of a strategy to counter migration shocks and to stop and dissuade migrants and smugglers is a strict border control policy, notably of the outer Schengen border. This must be accompanied by a policy that limits applying for political asylum to specific extraterritorial locations. In addition, European governments must do much in the regions migrants and refugees come from, not only to stop wars but also to rebuild states. There is no longer a clear distinction between war refugees and migrants, and the solution to the problem of mass exodus is development and stability.

Did European states act strategically in dealing with the 2015 migration crisis? I will discuss this in detail in Part II. Here I present what happened politically, the crisis in *general* terms.

NOTES

1. Khalid Koser, *International Migration. A very short introduction*, Oxford University Press, 2016: 53.
2. Article by same title, same date.
3. 'Merkel's popularity is faltering in Germany, polls show', *Huffington Post*, 24 September 2017.
4. Michta, A. 'The Twilight of an Era in Europe', *The American Interest*, 16 October 2017.
5. 'Ausgeblendete Realitäten', Aust, S. and Büchel, H., *Die Welt*, 22 January 2018.
6. Thomas Hobbes *Leviathan*, 1651, edition of 2004 by Barnes and Noble, New York.
7. The most famous quote from the Introduction to the book.
8. Karl-Heinz Nusser, 'Menschenrechte, Flüchtlinge und Migration. Zwischen Gesinnung – und Verantwortungsethik', *Die neue Ordnung*, 71:6, December 2018, pp. 429–437.
9. Ibid., p. 429, citation from *Rheinische Post*, 12.9.2015.
10. Ibid.
11. Ibid., p. 430.

12. Ibid., p. 433.
13. A colleague, Dr. Asle Toje, experienced that the fact that he did not share the 'human rights' exclusive framing of the migration issue on Norwegian public radio made him an object of scorn as being immoral. He therefore refused to appear in debates as long as the radio hosts did not apologize for their bias.
14. The director of the Norwegian Authority on Migration (UDI), Frode Forfang, has suggested that asylum applications be made in UN-run centres beyond Europe, in the regions which have many refugees.
15. http://www.independent.co.uk/news/people/refugee-crisis-sweden-deputy-prime-minister-cries-as-she-announces-u-turn-on-asylum-policy-a6749531.html.
16. Report from the Otto Brenner Institute, discussed in *Die Zeit*, 10 August 2017.
17. *Die Zeit*, 10 August 2017.
18. *Die Welt*, 'Polizeigewerkchaft spricht vom "Ende dere Freizügikeit"', 2 January 2018.
19. 'We'll defy asylum seeker quotas', pledge Hungary and Poland, *The Times*, 3 January 2018.
20. Collier, P. (2014) *Exodus. Immigration and Multiculturalism in the 21st century*, Penguin Books.
21. Koser, Khalid, *International Migration, a very short introduction*, Oxford University Press, 2016.
22. Ibid., p. 35.
23. 'EU suspects Russian agenda in migrants' shifting Arctic route', INYT, 2.4.2016.
24. Op.cit., p. 60.
25. Quoted in Hampshire, James; *The Politics of Immigration*, Polity Press, 2013, p. 151.
26. Ibid., also a Pew poll from 2011 which showed similar results.
27. Ibid., p. 150.
28. Putnam, Robert (2007) '*E pluribus unum?* Diversity and Community in the 21st century', Scandinavian Political Studies, 30, 2, pp. 137–174.
29. Soysal, Y. (1994) *Limits of Citizenship. Migrants and Postnational Membership in Europe*, University of Chicago Press, Chicago.
30. Ibid., p. 116.
31. Populism is a derogatory term, hence a normative one, whereas democratic is a positive term, while also being a descriptive one. In this book, I define populism as a simplistic political response to complex questions, based on emotional reactions, prejudice, and sometimes fear. Populism exists on both the right and the left of the political spectrum. There is no agreement on which parties deserve the populist label and which should be classified

as 'mainstream'. Here I will consider anti-Muslim, anti-Jewish, and pro-Nazi parties in the former category.

32. Hampshire, James (2013), *The Politics of Immigration. Contradictions of the Liberal State*, op.cit., p. 23.
33. Ibid., p. 24.
34. *NYT* weekend issue 27–28 October 2017.
35. *NYT*, 31.7.15, 'Migrants turn Channel into crisis flash point', front page and p. 3.
36. Ibid.
37. www.euractiv.com, same title, 16 April 2015.
38. www.amnesty.org/ 'got a sinking feeling they don't care', 2015/04.
39. Euractiv, ibid.
40. Ibid.
41. 'Juncker suffers double blow on immigration summit', 24 April 2015, www.euractiv.com.
42. 'Wrap-up: Special EU summit on the Mediterranean crisis', www.euractiv.com, 23 April 2015.
43. Matlary, Sophie: *A Joint-Decision Trap? The EU and Migration* MA thesis King's College, London, 2015.
44. 'EU and Turkey reach refugee deal', Barigazzi, K, *Politico*, 18 March 2016, 'Merkel has been courting Turkey since last Fall', p. 2.
45. Comment by E. Collett, 'The Paradox of the EU-Turkey refugee deal', *Migration Policy*, March 2016.
46. Matlary, S., op.cit.
47. Ibid., p. 2.
48. 'Asylchaos in Griechenland. EU-Staaten verweigern Entsendung ihrer Beamten', *der Spiegel*, 29.10.2016.
49. 'EU-Libya relations', EU Fact Sheet, 5 September 2017.
50. UN Security Council Resolutions 2259 and 2278.
51. Arrivals in Italy in 2017, by June, count 15,000 Nigerians, 9000 from Bangladesh, 7700 from Guinea, the same from the Ivory Coast, then around 5000 each from Gambia, Senegal, Mali, Eritrea, Morocco, and Sudan (Source IOM).
52. 'EU should reach "Turkey-like" migrant deal with Libya', Politico, 28 August 2017.
53. E-int relations, D Nakache, The EU-Libya migrant deal, 25 June 2017.
54. See for example, 'Architect of EU-Turkey refugee pact pushes for West Africa deal', Delcker, Janosch, *Politico*, 28 July 2017.
55. 'Italian minister defends methods that led to 87% drop in migrants from Libya', *The Guardian*, 7 September 2017.
56. 'Italy's deal to stem flow of people from Libya in danger of collapse', Wintour, Patrick, The *Guardian*, 3 October 2017.

57. Ibid., Clans paid by Italy were challenged by contenders in the key port for migrants, Sabratha, and many were killed or displaced.
58. 'UN rights chief says EU deal on Libya migrants falls short', Reuters, 8 September 2017.
59. 3 March 2017, 'Libyan coastguard chief accused of being a key trafficker'.

REFERENCES

Collett, E. (2016, March). The Paradox of the EU-Turkey Refugee Deal. *Migration Policy*.

Collier, P. (2014). *Exodus. Immigration and Multiculturalism in the 21st Century*. New York: Penguin Books.

Hampshire, J. (2013). *The Politics of Immigration. Contradictions of the Liberal State*. New York: Polity Press.

Hobbes, T. (1651). *Leviathan*, edition of 2004 by Barnes and Noble. New York.

Koser, K. (2016). *International Migration. A Very Short Introduction*. Oxford: Oxford University Press.

Matlary, S. (2015). *A Joint-Decision Trap? The EU and Migration* (MA Thesis). London: King's College.

Nusser, K.-H. (2018). "Menschenrechte, Flüchtlinge und Migration. Zwischen Gesinnung – und Verantwortungsethik", *Die neue Ordnung*, Germany.

CHAPTER 5

Confronting Terrorism and Insurgency

In this chapter I discuss how European states fare in confrontations, that is, military use of force in operations to fight terrorism in the home area, mainly in the Middle East and North Africa (MENA). I am not interested in whether anti-terror constituted the reasons for confronting the enemy, although one may notice a pattern starting with Afghanistan in 2001 via Mali to Iraq in 2014: all three are cases where terrorist groups have grown too powerful to be left alone in their quest for territory and state-like features. This is a disconcerting development indeed. The distinction between terrorists and insurgents is important, albeit unclear. Bjørgo defines the difference thus: 'What distinguishes terrorist violence from other forms of violence used in waging political and armed conflict is its criminal and normless character, with deliberate attacks on civilians, indiscriminate bombings, the taking of hostages – tactics that would qualify as war crimes in conventional armed conflicts.'[1] Both al-Qaida and Daesh are terrorist groups, but they also fight irregularly as well as sometimes using conventional weapons. Other national movements, like the Taliban, are also both insurgents and terrorists.

In this chapter I do not study how the actors in this book do their anti-terrorism work at home. All the three states in this book have suffered major terrorist attacks in the period under study: Britain has been attacked by solo terrorists using cars several times; the same has happened in Berlin and Nice with many more killed. France has also been attacked twice in major ways: the staff of Charlie Hebdo was massacred in January 2015,

© The Author(s) 2018   125
J. H. Matlary, *Hard Power in Hard Times*,
https://doi.org/10.1007/978-3-319-76514-3_5

and on Friday, 13 November the same year the concert at Bataclan was attacked, leaving 129 dead and many wounded. France then declared a state of emergency which lasted for two years, until legislation empowering the security service and the police was passed. But even if the other two states in this study did not do the same, they also have intensified police and intelligence work and cooperation. The nature of this work is hidden, but it is seemingly effective in having stopped many planned attacks. There is also ample cooperation on a 'need to know basis' between Western states. Thus, the focus here is rather *which* states *led* and *fought* in the MENA region, especially against Daesh, but also other terrorist groups. Having to choose confrontation as the strategy, did these actors act and lead? Or did the US take on the leading role?

The challenges Europe faces today come from the North (Russia) and from the South (Middle East and the Maghreb/Sahel). As discussed, there is one similarity in these two very different types of risks: hybrid methods. Both actors in classical Guerrilla fashion and Russian 'little green men' combine unconventional warfare and asymmetric indirect approaches. Yet the similarity stops there. The Russian actors are state actors and have a 'home address', whereas insurgents and terrorist groups do not—at least for the most part. In Afghanistan there was a 'home address', and al-Qaida was in fact attacked in that country in 2001. The UNSC deemed that Article 51 of the UN Pact applied and that the attack was in self-defence.

The current threat from Daesh is also from a terrorist group with 'an address'—it has taken territory in Iraq and Syria, has acquired weapons of a conventional kind from the old Iraqi army, and calls itself a state in its English rendering, Islamic State—clearly aspiring to be one. Neither al-Qaida nor Daesh can be deterred despite having territorial 'havens', however. This is because their ideology is apocalyptic, involving suicide missions and a total rejection of the West, the object of attack. They are for the same reasons not amenable to coercion and negotiation. Terrorist actors, even if they acquire safe havens and even large territorial areas, are thus as a rule not deterrable, coercible, or indeed containable. National terrorist groups could in some cases be negotiated with after long periods of fighting. Thus, both the IRA in Ulster and ETA in Spain have been disarmed and converted into political actors. But the type of terrorism originating in the MENA today does not invite any such negotiation. The only strategic choices left are to defend European societies as much as possible through increased intelligence and police work as well as to opt for confrontation in the rare case that the territorial gains of such groups are so substantial that they pose a threat that is considered too high by Western actors. This is the reasoning behind the attack on Afghanistan in 2001— the US and allies could not allow this terrorist organization to have training grounds in such a 'safe haven'.

A similar situation occurred in 2014 when Daesh decapitated prisoners, also from the West, massacred and otherwise persecuted Iraqis, and in general, showed a degree of barbarity that must be close to being unparalleled in human history. The fact that this organization had acquired territory and territorial resources, institutional structures, and conventional weapons made it necessary to confront it in similar fashion to the decision to attack al-Qaida in Afghanistan in 2001. The same reasoning was behind the French-led attack on Tuareg turned terrorists in the north of Mali in 2011 and other similar and recent operations in Africa.

As discussed in Chap. 1, Europe quite often uses force in operations in the period after the Cold War. Afghanistan was a turning point in this regard, and as will be shown in Part II, there are major differences in fighting ability and political will among the countries analysed in this book.

Insurgency as a Strategic Challenge: Why the Weak May Win

Arreguín-Toft has written an important analysis of how states can prevail in asymmetric conflict, *How the Weak Win Wars: A Theory of Asymmetric Conflict*.[2] In this book he investigates the phenomenon of modern asymmetric warfare, noting that weak actors tend to win these wars to an increasing extent starting from about 1950. In a survey of more than 200 wars, he finds that the strongest actor wins by clear majority in the period 1800–49, and that this continues with decreasing trends until 1950. For the 43 wars after 1950, however, the weaker party won in 51.2 per cent of the cases.[3] He sets out to find explanations of this counter-intuitive development: What can account for the weaker party winning wars?

In the Afghanistan case, the overarching question was what the outcome would finally be. The initial attack by the US and its coalition in 2001, known as Operation Enduring Freedom (OEF), was itself an example of hybrid war—a brilliant combination of special forces operations and advanced technological shock-and-awe, in which members of the Afghan Northern Alliance on horseback were backed up by drones and the most sophisticated precision-guided missiles. The Taliban was effectively driven back and a period of consolidation for the Western forces ensued. However, as in many similar cases in history, the enemy came back: in 2006 the Taliban returned and started to operate very effectively from bases in Pakistan. Throughout the war this pattern of back and forth has continued, and the Taliban has been quite successful in guerrilla-style warfare. By 2014 it had regained control of Kunduz in Northern Afghanistan, which had been held by NATO forces for as long as they had been present in the area. Yet this was not a lasting victory; by 2017 Kunduz was back in government hands.

Arreguín-Toft presents an overview of the literature on winning small wars. All outcomes of war are political in the end; winning militarily but losing politically makes no sense to Clausewitz or to anyone else. All strategy related to hard power is political from beginning to end; there is no 'political' versus 'military' solution. In *guerrilla* warfare, especially, it is important to retain this holistic picture because the political dynamics and effects are the main lines of the operation.

In today's global world the Western state party may win militarily in theatre and lose politically on the 'home front', so to speak. The political effect of barbarism and of killing civilians in combat is extremely significant in Western democracy. Furthermore, however much the Taliban or other adversaries use torture and other barbaric methods, the West cannot respond in kind. The refusal to engage in such conduct is an absolute norm in liberal democracies. It is for this reason that Israel can be said to have lost all three of its recent wars—in Southern Lebanon in 2006 and in Gaza in 2008–09 and 2014—despite the fact that, it could be argued, they won militarily in all the three cases in terms of destroying insurgent capacity for launching missiles against Israel. The political cost, however, was however too large. All strategic thinking involves attention to the dynamic nature of politics, and today, when many of the wars we fight are 'wars among the people', to use the famous phrase of General Sir Rupert Smith, there is no distinction between war and peace as in former times.

Arreguín-Toft points out that in asymmetric wars, the domestic public and the political situation in the country of the militarily strong state actor play a key role in the 'real' political outcomes of such wars. Whereas domestic support can be assumed and counted on for existential wars, this is not the case in non-existential wars. In fact, the weakest link in the asymmetric conflict may be the lack of domestic support for the war in the strong state. Thus, interest asymmetry—where the weak party is the less interested party—is an important variable. As all use of force by European

CONFRONTING TERRORISM AND INSURGENCY   129

states since 1990 has been 'optional' (i.e., not about existential survival), Europe is the weaker party for this reason. Political resolve is a key issue in deterrence, coercion, and confrontation. The issue of interest asymmetry is very central to the Western response to Putin's assertiveness in Ukraine, as we will see in Part II.

The political science literature on this topic is scant.[4] The same can be said for the military theory on how to win asymmetric conflicts. There are many books about *guerrilla* warfare and 'imperial policing', as well as manuals about how to fight counter-insurgency operations (COIN), but there have been few attempts to integrate the military analysis into the larger political picture. There are however a few contributions to this virgin territory of strategic thinking. Two authors in particular, A. Mack[5] and G. Merom,[6] have explored the role of domestic political support in the militarily strong state actor. Mack argues that because militarily strong actors in asymmetric wars often have a low political interest in winning, they tend to lose. The weaker party in the war is typically fighting an existential war while the stronger party is fighting an optional war. The strong actor is therefore politically vulnerable as compared to the weak party. This is clearly the case in the fight between the various NATO states in Afghanistan. For example, because Germans had low political interest in the war's outcome, one could expect them to be the more vulnerable to Taliban attacks. This is also the case with the conflicts between the West and Daesh and between the West and Russia over Ukraine. However, were Daesh to become more active in Europe and were Russia to provoke a NATO state, these actions would be 'game changers' strategically—the interest asymmetry would change and the West would respond with more force and be more willing to take risks.

However, in a normal situation the strong state takes little interest in the weak guerrilla actor. This induces the weak actor to attack the most politically vulnerable parts of the strong actor, for instance Germany in International Security Assistance Force (ISAF). Targeting Germans in kidnappings and suicide bombings is a rational tactical move on the part of the Taliban; as a state actor, Germany represents a weak link in the NATO 'chain' and the German reaction could easily be to withdraw rather than to implement stronger measures. Had the Taliban targeted a state with a larger stake in the conflict and more of a military culture, such as the US, the result may have been the opposite.

Mack applies his thesis to the Vietnam War where the difference in the political interest in winning between the Vietcong and the American public seems to a large extent to explain the unexpected outcome. The US was simply not interested enough in winning, given the cost and risk. However, as Arreguín-Toft points out, there are alternative explanations, and it is also difficult to determine empirically what is to be defined as 'interest' here. An actor that is militarily successful will often neglect political rallying in support of the cause, as this is unnecessary, but if he starts to lose militarily, he will need to mobilize politically. If he suffers losses, he can thus be expected to make an extra effort to point out the security implications of the war.

We can also assume that the 'sunk cost' in being involved in a war matters greatly to a government: once in the fray, the war cannot be discontinued easily. To enter into a war is such a cumbersome and difficult decision for a democracy that once in, it is nearly impossible to reverse this decision as long as one is a member of NATO. Retreating from a NATO operation like ISAF is tantamount to political loss of standing and reputation and also leads to a considerable deterioration of the alliance. The difficulty of exiting means that states have to accept the 'mission creep' that inevitably occurs in any military operation, but which was never explicitly agreed to at the moment of joining the operation. Rather there is a tendency on the part of governments to downplay the risk and possible duration of an operation at that point so that their countries will agree to join. However, if the enemy that has been engaged actually behaves like an enemy, the discrepancy between the real-world development in theatre and the piece of paper that describes the mission, which is always a political compromise, becomes more and more glaring as time passes. The government in each NATO state is subject to factors that pull in opposite directions, from a home public that is eager to withdraw and NATO allies that are eager to contribute more and ensure real military burden-sharing, to the threat of effects from theatre caused by the enemy. For the governments involved, such an operation is more like a three-front war than a peace operation. This is more true for modern wars, which are almost always multinational. But as Arreguín-Toft proposes, an initial lukewarm commitment can often be transformed when the going gets rough simply because the stakes become so high. Thus, there is a counter-argument to Mack: The more critical the military situation, the more likely there will be an increase in political interest in the outcome of the war.

The second work that theorizes the role of democratic politics is Gil Merom's *How Democracies Lose Small Wars*.[7] He discusses the domestic differences inside states with regard to military culture and the willingness to sustain losses, and argues that: 'democracies fail in small wars because they find it extremely difficult to escalate the level of violence and brutality to that which can secure victory'.[8] His argument concerns modern democracies, which he understands to be constrained both in terms of suffering losses and in taking enemy lives. The modern predicament is its view of human life as extremely precious, he argues.

Arreguín-Toft has objections to Merom's arguments, but they are not entirely convincing. First he argues that optional wars may in fact be existentially important for strong states as well as for weak ones: 'one can hardly think of a democratic state launching a small war it did not claim (and its leaders and citizens did not in some measure believe was of vital importance to its survival)'.[9] To this it must be added that the ISAF operation was never presented as an existential war in Germany or in Norway, but rather as assistance to nation-building.

INSURGENCY: THE 'POLITICAL' WAR

Another explanation of 'who wins' is purely tactical. The tactics employed by a strong power in a direct strategy are usually conventional military attacks, whereas weak powers might employ a tactic like barbarism aimed at weakening the will of the enemy. The most common indirect military tactic for the weak is guerrilla warfare, which, in the case of the Taliban, is combined with elements of terrorism. Guerrilla forces depend on bases and support among the people, something the Taliban increasingly enjoys in the Pakistani border areas with Afghanistan. Guerrilla tactics are primarily political and not military: 'The constant-if-incremental loss of soldiers, supplies, and equipment, with little chance of a quick resolution is aimed at the balance of political forces in the stronger actor's homeland.'[10] The desired political effect is to increase resistance in the attacker's home country because there is no 'victory' in sight and no exit date. A modern democracy based on periodic elections is used to seeing political results quickly, and certainly within an electoral cycle. What politician standing for election can ask the electorate to fight a war that might last indefinitely with no clear standard for winning, a risk for losses, and little political interest, even in victory?

An essential element in any war is therefore the *time dimension*. Time is much more important in guerrilla warfare than in conventional war because it is an essential resource for the guerrilla. The COIN operation favoured by ISAF emphasizes the 'hearts and minds' strategy, while the military element is kept as passive as the enemy will allow. The ideal COIN situation in Afghanistan is therefore that the Taliban not fight so that ISAF forces avoid fighting among the people and the often concomitant killing of civilians, so that the population feels increasingly secure and civilian tools can be put to work. The worst situation for ISAF forces was when the Taliban attacks led to fighting among the people and civilian losses, and/or spectacular losses among ISAF forces. The latter lead to major political questioning at home. ISAF fighting—the tactical level—therefore in and of itself could result in important political effects for the states that sent troops, irrespective of military outcomes.

Political 'losses' are also incurred when deaths are barbaric, as when kidnapped civilians are beheaded. The rational insurgent tactic is therefore to ensure maximal civilian casualties for the strong actor and spectacular and/or large losses among Western nationals, soldiers as well as civilians. It is not the military weakening of the insurgent that is the objective, but the political weakening of member states—the more barbaric, the larger the political impact.

There are also problems for postmodern Europeans in waging war in the form of sharp operations. According to the literature surveyed here, the political weaknesses that concern war are part of liberal democracy's make-up, and these are compounded by cultures that demand that warfare, if at all allowed, must be humane in an almost civilian sense. The theses of Mack, Merom, and Arreguín-Toft all point to the importance of political factors: Mack and Merom cite such as direct causal variables for the outcomes of wars, whereas Arreguín-Toft includes them as indirect causes in citing the choice of military tactic as the main explanatory variable. If strong actors take on guerrilla forces in *direct* warfare, the strong actor wins. This is hardly surprising; indeed, engaging in direct warfare is a poor tactic indeed on the guerrilla's part. The point is rather that is it impossible militarily to engage a guerrilla in direct attacks most of the time, and that the strong party therefore must employ an indirect military approach as a matter of necessity. But such an approach is also the smart one, given the political nature of war: as we saw in the Israeli cases, neither the direct attack in 2006 (Southern Lebanon) nor the one in 2008 (Gaza) led to the desired political outcomes for Israel, the militarily strong actor.

Political dynamics can be defined as *patterns of cause and effect that determine outcomes in an issue area*. For instance, if a 'peace logic' prevails in a given country, it is very hard for its politicians to wage a war, even if it is a guerrilla or 'small' war. This is all the more true today when we operate in *political real time* where citizens in Europe know about and even follow warfare developments as they unfold in theatre. There is ultimately only *one* political space, and both sets of actors in the war operation know this full well. The governments of Europe are therefore not able to control their own political space as before. They cannot act as 'gate-keepers' any more. This is a major difference from earlier times where information from battles was very slow in reaching home. The British were informed of the victory at Trafalgar only after an intense six day journey by sail and horseback, something which was very speedy at the time. Today, the internet operates as the instant venue of information. The Western public and politicians are therefore subject to influence by the adversary in a novel manner: The Taliban or another enemy can act directly in achieving influence in European political space, whether by targeting specific nationalities in theatre or directly in a European country. They are also able to recruit from European states. The newer threat posed by Daesh is similar to the threat from al-Qaida and Taliban: asymmetric terrorist methods waged in theatre but also in the extended theatre of the West.

Thus, we face political dynamics that increasingly meet and confront each other between home state and battlefield. Both parties to a conflict will therefore rationally and logically seek to influence each other through strategic thinking that embraces both home and theatre. If we accept that war is about breaking the will of the adversary, we have a situation where the *political dynamics in home country and in the battle field matter to each other*. In former times, the dynamics on the battlefield were key, and politics did not 'intervene' as it does today. Moreover, the government sending troops into battle would rarely have to justify its actions after the battle had begun. The political logic of war was then at work, diametrically opposed to the political logic of peace.

The introduction of COIN in Western combat manuals testifies to the importance that this type of warfare has assumed. The Daesh and greater terrorist threat against the West has by now moved beyond Afghanistan. As a result of the war in Afghanistan over the last 14–15 years, al-Qaida has been greatly weakened. Yet other terrorist actors have emerged, profiting from chaos and ungoverned spaces in the Maghreb and in the Middle East. By 2015, Yemen was also in terrorist hands, and various dangerous groups joined forces, including militias in Libya and Algeria. In addition Somalia's Al-Shabaab and Nigeria's Boko Haram threatened civilians in several African countries and beyond. The guerrillas turned terrorists had a uniting and powerful ideology and could recruit from Europe and train the recruits at their own bases.

The threat from these groups became so great in 2014 that Western states, led by the US, had to address its roots and safe havens, especially as Daesh acquired conventional weapons from the defunct Iraqi army. Their possession of serious weaponry and their unequalled barbarism led to a need to confront this enemy, not only to try to contain it. The interest asymmetry between the West and these guerrilla groups disappeared as the guerrillas managed to be a conventional threat in theatre as well as an asymmetric actor in the West. The guerrilla became a hybrid actor, raising the stakes in the West and demanding a new consideration of strategy. Direct attack became necessary, along indirect methods of containment.

Thus, we see the immediate relevance of the 'hybrid' category for the guerrilla/terrorist actors if they are able to take command of territory and conventional weapons, the two hallmarks of traditional state actors. COIN doctrine is at that point no longer sufficient.

We will now examine the most recent cases of use of force to confront insurgents and terrorists in the MENA region in order to find out which of the states in this study that played leading roles. We start with an analysis of the Libyan case, which is relevant even if not being an anti-terrorist operation for the simple fact that the US did not want to lead in this operation. It is therefore a (rare) case where Europe itself had to lead and thus makes for an interesting test of which actors in Europe took the lead.

Libya, 2011: French Leadership

Libya in 2011 was not an attack on terrorists, but a humanitarian intervention that became a regime change operation. The Mali operation was an anti-terror operation aimed at stopping terrorist groups from taking control of the country. The operation against Daesh in Iraq/Syria had as a goal to deprive Daesh of infrastructure, territory, and training grounds.

'NATO's operation in Libya has rightly been hailed as a model intervention. The alliance responded rapidly to a deteriorating situation that threatened hundreds of thousands of civilians rebelling against an oppressive regime. It succeeded in protecting these civilians.'[11] Such was the verdict after the 7 month air operation against Libya in 2011. The dictator was removed and the regime changed in an operation that has a mandate for humanitarian protection. The R2P—*Responsibility to Protect*—principle had been vindicated in a unique UN mandate and NATO had carried out an operation where civilians were protected from the massacres promised by Gaddafi.

CONFRONTING TERRORISM AND INSURGENCY   135

The decision to start the operation was taken in less than 100 hours from the time the mandate was given, a record in strategic action, it would seem. Two major actors and two smaller ones were key in the confrontation: France and Britain, Norway and Denmark.

The Libyan conflict started in February 2011 with opposition in the North, in Benghazi, Misrata og Zawiyah, turning against Gaddafi. In a week these towns were taken by insurgents. Two days later the UNSC adopted resolution 1970 which contained sanctions of the Gaddafi family, freezing assets abroad. The international criminal court (ICC) issued a statement that it might charge Gaddafi with crimes against humanity on the 3 March. On 27 June the International Criminal Court (ICC) issued a court order for the arrest of Gaddafi, his son Saif, and his security chief Abdullah al-Senussi.

On 6 March the government forces of Gaddafi started a counter-offensive and retook Ras Lanuf and Brega. AWACS (Airborne Warning And Control System) planes from NATO were deployed on 8 March. France acknowledged the opposition as the legal government of Libya on 10 March, now called the 'The National Transition Council' (NTC). The African Union (AU) tried negotiations while the Arab League (AL) voted for the UN-mandated 'no fly' zone on 12 March. As soon as 17 March R2P-resolution 1973 was adopted, containing the words 'all necessary means', which means military force mandated to stop attacks on civilians. The resolution had a number of important abstentions: China, Russia, Germany, Brazil, and India. Even Germany abstained, something which became a major political issue among allies, especially as the Libya operation quickly became a NATO operation.

The Western attacks started on 19 March by French, British, and American fighter planes. The Libyan air defences were the first object of attack. Operation *Odyssey Dawn* under American command (US Africom) had started. Some days later, on 23 March, NATO assumed command of the operation, henceforth named *Unified Protector.*

On 27 June Britain also recognized the NTC as the legal government and Gaddafi's diplomats were expelled from the country. On 20 August opposition forces broke through the defences of Tripoli and the city fell on the 23rd. On 1 September Russia also recognized the NTC. The mandate for *Unified Protector* was prolonged for 90 days as fighting continued in Sirte, the hometown of Gaddafi, and he was killed on 20 October while fleeing. On 31 October the operation was finished, and the UN secretary general adjudged that it had been a success.

There can be no doubt that there was political will and plans for military intervention when the mandate was proposed to the UNSC.[12] The time span between the first (1970) and second resolution (1973) was only three weeks and the attack on Libya started only two days after the second resolution was adopted, the dates being the 17 March and the 19 March respectively. A military operation needs considerable time for planning and preparation, and this short time frame implies that the planning was finished well in advance of the mandate. Usually the situation is the opposite: the UNSC adopts various resolutions and there is considerable political back-and-forth negotiation before a decision to use force may come. In the Libyan case the evidence points to *French leadership in all phases*, from agenda-setting to the starting the first bombing sortie. The French recognition of the new government came only 14 days after the first resolution, before the fighting was over. This is exceptional and it has the unfortunate effect of foreclosing negotiations with the enemy. Gaddafi had no chance of agreeing to a truce and subsequent solution after having been replaced by another 'government'. It must also be said that he had no will to negotiate at the outset of the operation, this having been tried by the AU.

The fighting itself lasted for seven months only, with special operations forces (SOFs) on the ground, the locals as the 'land army', and allies in the air and from sea. American cruise missiles, attack helicopters, and other equipment that allies lacked was combined with major combat roles for France, Britain, Norway, and Denmark. As stated, the swift deployment and early recognition of a new government are strong indicators of early strategic planning for the whole operation. This was not a situation where force was used when this could no longer be avoided; on the contrary, there was little or no scope for a negotiated solution. Also, why was Libya all of a sudden important when Gaddafi had been a 'friend' of European states for a long time? The answer lies in France and French strategic interest in the Maghreb. At this time it was important to be with the progressive forces of the so-called Arab Spring, and France had unfortunately supported the Tunisian President Ben Ali for too long.

After the operation was finished, Russia criticized NATO for going far beyond the mandate, from protecting civilians to regime change. Although it is difficult to distinguish between the two in this case, they have a point. It is probably true that regime change was an unavoidable consequence of this war since there was no scope for negotiation with Gaddafi and since he was not offered free passage to any other African or Arab state, but it is as said highly irregular for a state to recognize an opposition group as the new government while a civil war is going on. It smacks of a pre-planned *fait accompli*.

This leads us again to the issue of strategic leadership. This operation was conceived by France and President Sarkozy, and he got Prime Minister Cameron onboard early despite the fact that his military and civilian advisers in the Ministry of Defence were against it.[13]

The two countries have close cooperation in security and defence policy, both in the EU and bilaterally.[14] In 2010 they agreed formally to develop procurement, research, and maintenance together, also with regard to some aspects of nuclear weapon cost-cutting on maintenance. The two states will also develop a joint brigade for expeditionary operations by 2018.[15] The Libya operation should be seen as one more aspect of this cooperation, as a chance for both political leaders to play a role as commanders-in-chief of military operations, and this was also a way to find the right political balance regarding 'The Arab Spring'. Here France had a problem at that time; it was seen as lingering on the side of autocrats for too long.

France is the leading Western actor on Africa and strategic realism characterizes its approach.[16] Catherine Gegout argues that all French interventions in Africa have had an interests-based reason behind them: 'Military interventions in Africa enhanced the *rang international* and the *rayonnement de la France* vis-à-vis the international community.'[17] The status and role of France in the world is key. Prestige and rank matter. Davidson analysed why France, Britain, and Italy contributed in Lebanon 1982, the first Gulf War in 1999, Somalia 1992, Kosovo 1999, Afghanistan 2001, and Iraq 2003. Relying on an unprecedented number of elite interviews, he concluded that 'the cases demonstrate that alliance value is significantly less important than threat and prestige. [...] Strong evidence supported threat and prestige in twice as many cases as alliance value'.[18] He continued: 'Strong evidence supported the claim that prestige was among the most important factors in government decisions in 11 of 21 cases'.[19] In the case of France he found that the contribution to *Operation Enduring Freedom* in 2001 was based on prestige: 'the Chirac/Jospin government made a military contribution primarily to defend France's prestige'.[20] The same was true of Kosovo, he finds, when Britain and Germany participated, 'we had no choice. The alternative was to go down in splendid isolation', as one central actor put it.[21] In Somalia in 1992—a humanitarian intervention that seems to be like Libya—he found similar reasons:

There is a significant amount of evidence that prestige concerns spurred the Mitterrand government to contribute to UNITAF. [...] France's prestige was implicated in Somalia primarily because of France's special role and status in Africa. [...] today Africa remains the only area of the world where France retains enough power and influence to support its claim to medium power status in the international system.[22]

Concerning Libya 2011, France was associated with the regime of President Ben Ali and Hosni Mubarak for too long. In Tunisia the then French Foreign Minister Michèle Alliot-Marie enjoyed a vacation as the guest of Ben Ali at Christmas time right before the insurgency and protest movement started; she later had to leave office because of this. But also other French members of *la classe politique* maintained close ties with the Ben Ali government when it was toppled in February 2011. It was imperative for France to re-establish close ties with the new regimes of the Maghreb as soon as possible. Without such, French Africa-policy would be at risk. Therefore, 're-establishing France's credentials in the region demanded a demonstrable engagement: it came with France's support of the budding Libyan revolution'.[23]

Also President Obama re-oriented himself away from supporting old regimes: he abandoned support for Mubarak for the opposition, yet only when it became clear that the president would have to leave did he and other Western leaders turn away from supporting him. The Libyan case thus became a kind of litmus test for Western powers, but Obama was in much doubt about whether to support it.[24] Tongue-in-cheek it is said that women by the name of (Samantha) *Power* and (Anne-Marie) *Slaughter* put pressure on him, seconded by Susan Rice and Hilary Clinton. An added element was the importance of coming down on the right side of the R2P-principle which was so prominent in the resolution.

The French desire to 're-balance' its Maghreb policy must be seen against this background. But can it explain the French initiative in the first place? President Sarkozy had a meeting already on 27 February with the opposition in Benghazi, brought to Paris by the very engaged French intellectual Bernard-Henri Lévy. After some meetings with leading French politicians this group was as said recognized diplomatically, and the British were kept informed of this and followed suit in this recognition later.[25] It remains unclear how much Lévy influenced Sarkozy, but the contact between them was close and Levy appears to have acted like some kind of 'private' foreign minister, reporting directly from Libya to Sarkozy.[26]

Sarkozy brought Hilary Clinton into the loop when she met the opposition leader during a visit to Paris, and the next morning Sarkozy informed Lévy that 'the American position is shifting'. According to Lévy the latter said that he would work for a UN resolution, but intervene should it not materialize.[27] The process now involves both Prime Minister Cameron and the Americans.

The military tool is central to French foreign policy. Long-term French UN ambassador Jean-David Levitte stated, 'If you don't have the military means to act, you don't have a foreign policy'.[28] Both the Libya operation and the operation in Mali in 2013 had much support in French public opinion. More than 66 per cent supported the Libya operation, while the Mali operation has more than 75 per cent support.[29] France is a great power with a strong military posture and strategic culture and the ideological colour of the president—Sarkozy in Libya and Hollande in Mali—did not matter.

As mentioned, British officers and civil servants did not support the Libya intervention The British doctrine—the *National Security Strategy* (NSS)—has 15 criteria for the use of force and Libya did not meet any of these, it was pointed out.[30] There were no national British interests at stake. In addition, the government had decided that Tony Blair's 'liberal interventionism' would change in the direction of strategic security policy. The proposal of participation in the Libyan intervention 'was not how national strategic decision-making was supposed to work',[31] but the decision was made by Prime Minister Cameron himself. Then Minister of Defence Liam Fox, a sceptic, 'was effectively overruled by Downing Street and then became hawkish about the operation once the die was cast'.[32] The Chief of Defence Staff (CHOD), General Sir David Richards, was also against British participation and saw regime change as a looming threat and problem. He said publicly that the resolution did not mandate regime change.[33] The entire British top brass was deeply sceptical, as was the American Defence Secretary Robert Gates. British commentators point out that Cameron agreed to the intervention almost alone, against the advice from his own, and before the Americans were onboard.[34]

It is however clear that the real leadership in this case was French. The bombing sorties started right after a lunch at the *Elysee* with the coalition of willing contributors, and France was in all news channels: '[…] France's intervention in Libya is considered with a great deal of satisfaction by its political and military establishment, (and is) largely seen as a validation of the strategic orientations taken by France's last 2008 defence white paper'.[35] The priorities of the French are in the South, as discussed in Chap. 8 below.

The French also tested their new bilateral relationship with the British through this operation. Also the British prime minister got a lot of attention, and a meeting with the coalition partners was held some days later in London so that Cameron could show that he shared in the leading function. It was only when the US entered with some weight that the French had to allow NATO to take over the command function, and it became a NATO operation.

Germany was on 'the wrong side' in this case '[...] the country's abstention in the UN vote on military action in Libya has done lasting damage to its reputation'.[36] In Germany 88 per cent were against the operation, but 56 per cent wanted a 'no fly' zone over Libya as a preliminary measure. But few wanted Germany to join in.[37] Only 29 per cent supported German participation.[38]

Some thought that there were no reasons why Germany should spend energy and money on such an operation,[39] while others pointed to domestic elections. The German abstention on the mandate led to massive US and NATO criticism of Germany.[40] Robert Gates said Poland and Germany did not carry their share of the burden in NATO.[41] Among the French, 'top officials were furious at Germany's abstention on UNSC resolution 1973 and the subsequent decision to withdraw German crew members from AWACS aircraft assigned to Operation Unified Protector'.[42] Also in German domestic politics there were strong reactions: '[...] the German diplomatic community has reacted with indignation to the government's behaviour'.[43]

Yet when it comes to strategy, there was none. What should the political end state be like? The mandate stipulated that civilians were to be protected by the intervening forces, but what exactly did this mean? Britain and France opted for regime change early in the military campaign, precluding effective coercion, but allowing for effective military coercion. There was disagreement on whether regime change was the strategic aim all along, and this translated into a lack of political direction of the war.

The Libyan war did not have a political strategy,[44] and the military actor, NATO, withdrew as soon as its mandate was over. Nothing came in its stead. Post-Gaddafi Libya has become a free haven for all sorts of militias, even terrorist groups. The clear aim was to avoid so-called nation-building and ground troops. This war was, like the one in Kosovo in 1999, fought from the air alone to avoid risk, and there was no political will to

CONFRONTING TERRORISM AND INSURGENCY   141

'own' the problem of post-war reconstruction, also politically. This was a war that was successful militarily, but military victory was not political victory.

It was undoubtedly France which led the policy process towards the operation, with Britain as a follower. Germany made a major political blunder in not voting for the resolution on Libya, putting itself outside the company of allies; in the company of Russia and China. This mistake was later sought rectified through a real contribution to the anti-Daesh campaign, when Germany decided to equip a whole brigade of Iraqi soldiers. The US tried to avoid being involved in the Libya war, but was unable to stay out. It had to 'lead from behind' as it was called, providing key military capacities.

As said, Norway played a key role in the Libya operation, flying as many sorties as the great powers. Also Denmark played such a role. In sum, these two small NATO states and the two major great powers in Europe, France and Britain, made up the coalition of the willing and able in this case, strongly backed by the US. Germany put itself on the outside by its abstention in the UNSC and even withdrew crew from the AWACS planes once the operation came under NATO command.

The Sahel, 2013–17: More French Leadership

In Mali and the other African states where terrorists are fought, France is the leading state in decisions to confront and in the execution of operations. Indeed, the Maghreb and Africa, as well as the Middle East are the key French strategic priorities. The French have borne the brunt of the fighting in these places, seconded by the British while the rest of Europe has largely confined their support to the political and rhetorical levels. In Mali France is the leading actor in fighting terrorists in the North and it is also leading in other operations in Africa, as will be discussed in Chap. 8 on France as a strategic actor. The French had more than 7000 soldiers in Africa in 2015 and most of these were in the Sahel.

When Islamists—largely enabled by the defeat of Gaddafi—attacked Northern Mali in 2012, then French President Hollande intervened in an operation named *Serval*. Under French leadership also the EU seconded with a small mission entitled, EU Training Mission (EUTM) Mali, and a larger UN operation, mission multidimensionelle integree des Nations Unis a Mali (MINUSMA), is also in place. Operation *Serval* was later replaced by a larger operation covering all of the Sahel by the name of *Barkhane* with headquarters in Chad and a large regional contingent in

142   J. H. MATLARY

Mali. This operation, which is a military confrontation with Islamist terrorists, extends to five former French colonies in the Sahel—Burkina Faso, Chad, Mali, Niger, and Mauretania. A RAND study of the French military doctrine and leadership in operation Serval concluded that the 'French Army operations in Mali in 2013 provide a model for designing and operating an expeditionary force, one that has a number of attributes and competencies that United States Army Chief of Staff General Raymond Odierno has indicated to be requirements for the Army'.[45]

Syria and Iraq, 2014–17: Americans, Russians, and the French in the Lead

When Daesh became a territorial actor with conventional weapons and started to perform their barbaric acts of executions and massacres, the US took the lead in confronting them militarily, but France was all the time a key actor.[46] Russia, also the object of terrorist attack, also took a leading role in fighting terrorists in Iraq and Northern Syria.

The US continued to lead the Western coalition, despite much domestic criticism of Obama's leadership.[47] Europe beyond France and to some extent, Britain, has been reluctant to commit troops. Here the German military aid to the Iraqis can be seen as 'repairing' the relationship to allies in NATO. France was willing to lead in the Daesh campaign after it was attacked severely in November 2015, but Britain was conspicuous in its limited contribution. The sheer horror of the enemy's actions and the growing terror threat in Europe made this a case where burden-sharing seemed reasonable indeed. There was not much interest in real and risky contributions. The key American ally, the British, came under fire from domestic opposition about the size of the British contribution: The prime minister is demeaning himself with a 'flaccid' contribution to the Daesh campaign, wrote General Sir Richard Shirreff.[48] Some months later the House of Commons Select Committee on Defence came to the same conclusion: The rhetoric on the British contribution was impressive; the military contribution was not: Only one combat sortie per day, only some few troops, and it was 'very surprising that the UK government is doing so little'.[49] *The Times* reported on how British generals say that the government is just 'posturing' over Iraq, speaking very loudly, almost hysterically, but doing nothing.[50] In the same article one general is quoted as saying that 'no one takes the UK seriously anymore'.[51] The Iraq involvement is 'beyond parody', wrote the Independent commentator Cockburn, there are no British officers on the ground, no intelligence, and no policy or strategy. The committee itself was said to be shocked by its own findings.[52] In response to this the defence secretary promised 'hundreds more troops to Iraq'.[53]

There was very fierce criticism of the lack of serious British involvement. It included air strikes,[54] but this alone would not do much, said officers.[55] The verdict among the professionals in security and defence seemed to be that 'posturing is no substitute for foreign policy'.[56] General Dannatt, former CHOD, was very critical and demanded that Britain do something to stop the massive persecution of the Yazidis and Christians in the summer of 2014. We are 'watching in horror',[57] he said, while the prime minister was on vacation and parliament in recess. He added that 'we know the dangers of inaction' in a strong plea to intervene properly and quickly.[58] Other calls for humanitarian intervention and counterterrorism intervention were heard—here was in fact a case where both types of security merged.[59] Yet there was little willingness in terms of contributions.

Even the Holy See called for military intervention, calling it a just war.[60] This rare instance of accepting the use of force was significant indeed. The Germans surprised everyone in deciding to arm a full brigade of Iraqi forces,[61] but the government there was also under heavy criticism for inaction: 'Die Welt brennt und Europa macht Urlaub' (the world burns and the world is on vacation), Theo Sommer wrote.[62]

This was a 'hollow coalition' consisting of 62 states of which only 11 had conducted offensive operations by November, 2015.[63] In this case the leader was the US, seconded by the French.

In sum, the role of France is the key one in the Maghreb, seconded by the US and Britain, in particular in the Middle East. In fighting terrorism through military confrontation, all three states have been actors, but it is obvious that the states affected the most are the ones most active. France, like the US, declared war against Islamist terrorists when attacked in Paris on 13 November 2015. *Nous sommes en guerre*, President Hollande stated, just like President Bush had done in 2001. The interest that the affected states take in fighting terrorism is therefore a major one: the more targeted, the more interested in fighting against Daesh and other groups. But also the risk posed by these groups when they acquire territory and training grounds as well as civilian infrastructure explains the willingness on the part of Western states to fights them militarily.

Conclusions: Optimal Strategy for Fighting Terrorism

In sum, in terms of fighting—the strategic choice of confrontation—we have noticed that ISAF and before that, "Enduring Freedom" in Afghanistan, led to major engagements over many years on the part of European states. Elsewhere we have noticed that ISAF represented a turning point in the strategic culture of Europe: the British contributed greatly and suffered great losses, while France was less engaged and the Germans were almost pacifistic in their many caveats in theatre.

In the cases analysed in this chapter—after Afghanistan—France stands out as a leader in the use of force in Europe. Britain has become less willing to lead, it seems, although we cannot judge from so few cases. What seems clear, however, is that France will act decisively it its strategic interests, anti-terrorism and otherwise—are involved. This is also made clear in the *Livre blanc* of 2013 where Northern Africa remains a key priority, followed by the Middle East. Russia and Northern Europe are not very important to France, and Russia has traditionally been a strategic partner, sharing a common vision of multipolarity and a long history of French influence in imperial times.[64]

In this chapter we have seen that Europe cannot escape from confronting insurgents, and we have argued that sometimes this is the best strategy. When insurgents-*cum*-terrorists pose a direct threat to Europe they must be deprived of safe havens and training grounds. When the risk is lower, they can be fought at home in Europe with intelligence and police tools. The risk factor—how great the risk is—is the major factor in deciding whether to confront militarily or not.

Terrorism originating in the MENA continues to pose a major threat to all of Europe, but only few states take active part in the risky operations fighting such groups. One explanation is that states vary in their political interest in doing so, that is, interest asymmetry. Germany is as affected as is Britain, yet their contributions to operations in the MENA differ significantly. As we will see in Part II, there are major differences between states in terms of strategic culture that account for this. Yet the conclusion remains that at a certain level of risk, insurgents that are also terrorists, must be confronted and fought militarily.

CONFRONTING TERRORISM AND INSURGENCY   145

NOTES

1. Bjørgo, T. (2005) (ed.) *The Root Causes of Terrorism: Myths, Reality and Ways Forward*, Routledge, London and New York, p. 251 from Bjørgo's chapter 'Conclusions'.
2. Arreguín-Toft, I. (2005) *How the Weak Win Wars: A Theory of Asymmetric Conflict*. Cambridge, UK.
3. The data he uses are from the Correlates of War project and comprise 202 cases from 1809 to 2003.
4. Arreguín-Toft states that 'few international relations scholars have advanced explanations focused specifically on the subject of asymmetric conflict, and with the exception of my own work and Mack's, none has advanced a general explanation of asymmetric conflict outcomes' (ibid., s. 6).
5. Mack, A (1975) 'Why Big Nations Lose Small Wars: The Politics of Asymmetric Conflict', *World Politics*, January, volume 27, issue 2, pp. 175–200.
6. Merom, G. (2003) *How Democracies Lose Small Wars State, Society, and the Failures of France in Algeria, Israel in Lebanon, and the United States in Vietnam*, Cambridge University Press.
7. Op.cit. see note 6.
8. Merom, cited in Arreguín-Toft, p. 15.
9. Arreguín-Toft, op.cit., p. 16.
10. Ibid., p. 34.
11. I. Daalder and I, Stavridis, 'NATO's victory in Libya: the right way to run an intervention', *Foreign policy*, March/April 2012, s. 2.
12. UN Pact Chapter VII.
13. M. Clarke 'The making of Britain's Libya Strategy', p. 9: '... there was a distinct difference of emphasis, if not explicit disagreement, between the prime minister's own view and the military advice he was receiving ... but prime ministers can decide, and this one did.'
    Short War, Long Shadow. The political and military legacies of the 20122 Libya campaign, RUSI report no. 1, 2012.
14. Matlary, J. (2009) *European Union Security Dynamics: In the New National Interest*, Palgrave Macmillan, UK.
15. Michel, L (2012) *French report.*
16. Dokken, Karin (2000) 'Frankrike og Afrika ved tusenårsskiftet', Internasjonal politikk, 58, 2, s. 233–250.
17. Gegout, Catherine, 'Explaining European Military Intervention in Africa: A Realist Perspective', p. 10, unpublished paper, 2003.
18. Jason W. Davidson. (2011). *America's Allies and War: Kosovo, Afghanistan, and Iraq*, Palgrave Macmillan, UK, s. 175.
19. Ibid., s. 176.

20. Ibid., s. 130.
21. Ibid., s. 89.
22. Ibid., s. 67–68.
23. A. Cameron, 'The Channel Axis: France, the UK and NATO', i RUSI, op.cit., s. 15.
24. Dette stadfestes av sentrale norske aktører.
25. 'Thinker led president to war', IHT, 3.4.2011.
26. Ibid., Det var en rekke besøk fra Lévy i Libya og mye aktivitet for en intervensjon fra hans side i fransk offentlig debatt.
27. Ibid.
28. 'The French Way of War', *New York Times*, 19 January 2013.
29. Ibid.
30. Clarke, op.cit., s. 6.
31. Ibid., s. 8.
32. Ibid.
33. Ibid., s. 9.
34. Bagehot, 'The Ghost of Tony', *The Economist*, 26.3.2011.
35. Cameron, op.cit., p. 16. Det strategiske dokumentet som refereres til er '*Livre blanc sur la defense et la security nationale*'.
36. 'Germany's reputation in NATO has hit rock bottom', Spiegel Online, 17.5.2012.
37. 'Umfrage zu Unruhen in Libyen: Deutsche wollen sich nicht einmischen', 16.3.2011, *Stern* Online, 1008 spurte, representativt utvalg.
38. Die Welt, online, '62% der deutschen für Militärschlag', 20.3.2011.
39. Maull, H. 'Der überförderte Hegemon: Ziele und Grenzen deutscher Macht' *Atlantische Initiativen*, 24.2.2012.
40. Se note 6, i samme artikkel intervjues en amerikansk diplomat som sier at dette ikke vil bli glemt på lang tid og at man ikke lenger kan stole på Tyskland.
41. 'Gates accuses NATO members of failing to act in Libya air war', *Financial Times*, front page headline, 9.6.2011.
42. 'Cross-currents in French Defense and US Interests', Leo G. Michel, National Defense University Press, Strategic Perspectives, April 2012, s. 11.
43. 'Libya Crisis Leaves Berlin isolated', *Spiegel Online*, 28.3.2011, 'Westerwelle ist eine Desaster', *Spiegel Online*, 27.3.2011, Cameron Abai, 'Stage fright', *Foreign Policy*, 25.3.2011, 'Germany steps away from European Unity', *New York Times*, 23.3.2011.
44. *The NATO Intervention in Libya: lessons learned from the campaign*, Engelbrekt, K. et al., (eds.) Routledge, UK, 2014.

CONFRONTING TERRORISM AND INSURGENCY **147**

45. *France's War in Mali: Lessons for an Expeditionary Army*, Michael Shurkin, RAND Corporation, California, 2014.
46. 'A War strategy takes shape', *The Washington Post*, 25 September 2015, online, 'Clashing Goals in Syria Strikes Bedevil Obama', *NYT*, 26 September 2015.
47. 'US allies abandon hope of Obama leadership', *The Washington Post*, 27 August 2014, online, 'Obama's Foreign Policy Record', Stratfor, 13 August 2014; 'What if the US had a Middle East Strategy?', Rothkopf, D., *Foreign Policy*, online, 14 August 2014, 'Clinton faults Obama on foreign policy', 13 August 2014.
48. 'Top general blasts Cameron's weakness on Islamic state', *The Telegraph*, 1 September 2014, online.
49. The Daily Mail, 5 February 2015.
50. The Times, 8 February 2015, 'Generals berate PM's "posturing" over Iraq', online.
51. Ibid.
52. *The Independent*, Patrick Cockburn, 'Isis in Iraq', 11 February 2015, online.
53. *The Guardian*, 'Britain to send hundreds more troops to Iraq', 3 February, 2015, online.
54. 'Britain votes to join airstrikes', *NYR*, online, 27 September 2014, 'British options in Iraq', RUSI, 14 August 2014, online.
55. 'Bombing jihadis is futile, says top British general', *The Sunday Times*, 29 September 2014, online.
56. *The Times*, same title, online, 27 August 2014.
57. 'Iraq crisis: David Cameron refuses to recall parliament despite growing calls from own MPS', *The Telegraph*, online, 12 August 2014.
58. 'We know the dangers of inaction', *The Telegraph*, online, 13 August 2014.
59. 'Beating the barbarians', *The Times*, editorial, 12 August 2014, online.
60. 'More US military advisors to Iraq as Vatican supports airstrikes', *The Times*, online, 13 August 2014, 'Vatican calls on Muslim leaders to condemn Christian persecution in Iraq', *The Guardian*, online, 13 August 2014.
61. 'Deutschlands Hife für Nordirak: Plötzlich einsatzbereit', *Spiegel online*, 13 August 2014.
62. *Die Zeit*, same title, online, 13 August 2014.
63. 'The Hollow Coalition', R. Cohen and G. Scheinmann, *Foreign Affairs*, 5 November 2014.
64. 'France's Russian Policy: Balancing Interests and Values', Thomas Gomart, *The Washington Quarterly*, 30:2, pp. 147–155, 2007.

148   J. H. MATLARY

REFERENCES

Arreguín-Toft, I. (2005). *How the Weak Win Wars: A Theory of Asymmetric Conflict*. Cambridge: Cambridge University Press.

Bjørgo, T. (Ed.). (2005). *The Root Causes of Terrorism: Myths, Reality and Ways Forward*. London/New York: Routledge.

Clarke, M. (2012). The Making of Britain's Libya Strategy. In *Short War, Long Shadow. The Political and Military Legacies of the 20122 Libya Campaign* (RUSI Report No. 1). London: RUSI.

Daalder, I., & Stavridis, I. (2012, March/April). NATO's Victory in Libya: The Right Way to Run an Intervention. *Foreign Policy*.

Davidson, J. W. (2011). *America's Allies and War: Kosovo, Afghanistan, and Iraq*. New York: Palgrave Macmillan.

Dokken, K. (2000). Frankrike og Afrika ved tusenårsskiftet. Internasjonal politikk, 58.

Engelbrekt, K., et al. (Eds.). (2014). *The NATO Intervention in Libya: Lessons Learned from the Campaign*. New York/London: Routledge.

Gegout, C. (2003). *Explaining European Military Intervention in Africa: A Realist Perspective* (Unpublished Paper).

Mack, A. (1975). Why Big Nations Lose Small Wars: The Politics of Asymmetric Conflict. *World Politics, 27*(2), 175–200.

Matlary, J. (2009). *European Union Security Dynamics: In the New National Interest*. Basingstoke: Palgrave Macmillan.

Maull, H. (2012). 'Der überförderte Hegemon: Ziele und Grenzen deutscher Macht', *Atlantische Initiativen, 24.2.2012*.

Merom, G. (2003). *How Democracies Lose Small Wars State, Society, and the Failures of France in Algeria, Israel in Lebanon, and the United States in Vietnam*. Cambridge/New York: Cambridge University Press.

Shurkin, M. (2014). *France's War in Mali: Lessons for an Expeditionary Army*. Santa Monica: RAND Corporation.

PART II

Strategic Action?

In Part II of the book I devote one chapter to each actor in Europe, starting with Germany, followed by chapters on Britain and France. These chapters start with a general analysis of whether the state in question has a strategic culture and proceeds with an analysis of the three cases presented in Part I, asking whether the state in question acted strategically in its political response to these cases.

CHAPTER 6

Germany

In this book the central question is the exercise of strategic leadership. The European great powers are France, Britain, and Germany, although Germany is not usually termed a strategic power. Despite being the richest, largest, and most populous state in Europe, Germany is marred by a culture of military self-restraint that borders on pacifism even more than 70 years after WWII.[1] Germany has notably moved in the direction of normalization in this area, but as we shall see below, its self-styled identity as a nation of peace that uses soft power tools almost exclusively makes for very different policy responses than France and Britain to the three challenges analysed in this book.

The latter two states have played traditional great power roles and have a tradition of using force globally. They both have strong strategic cultures and maintain the most important militaries in Europe. They have also developed a close bilateral relationship in military affairs, and have led the work in the EU to develop battlegroups and the European Defence Agency (EDA) from about 2003 onwards.[2] The two states maintain close ties between their respective Ministries of Defence (MODs), as well as with Washington, and are undoubtedly the key military actors in Europe, participating with sharp fighting ability in operations under NATO or coalition

---

The generic description and analysis of German strategic culture draws somewhat on my previous work: Matlary, J. H. (2009, 2013) *European Union Security Dynamics: In the New National Interest,* Palgrave Macmillan, UK.

© The Author(s) 2018   151
J. H. Matlary, *Hard Power in Hard Times,*
https://doi.org/10.1007/978-3-319-76514-3_6

command. They also cooperate closely in African conflicts and former colonies and have troops stationed in those regions. Indeed, they were the only key actors in operations in Africa and in deployment of EU battlegroups.

In France, the president effectively decides on the use of force in his 'nuclear monarchy'. The Fifth Republic has concentrated power in the presidency's *domaine réservé*, or reserved domain, which means that the president alone takes decisions on the use of force.[3] In Britain, the same power traditionally applies to the prime minister. The defence budget is only summarily examined by the Select Committee of the House of Commons, and foreign policy is formally still under the royal prerogative, which has been defined as 'the residue of discretionary or arbitrary authority which at any time is legally left in the hands of the Crown'.[4] In addition, foreign and security policy are usually not of much interest to the British public, 'except in moments of extreme crisis'. But in Germany it is the *Bundestag* that takes these decisions, often laboriously, as we will see below. The use of force still remains a taboo in Germany, where public opinion matters much more in such decisions than it does in the other two countries.

However, with the Iraq war, the French and the British publics—the latter belatedly—also became active on the question of deployment of national forces. Thus, although the institutional set-up for deciding on deployment still follows a foreign policy prerogative (FPP) model, meaning that the government decides, publics in especially Britain and France are now more concerned about the issue. Thus, strategic culture could be said to consist of two elements: decision-making rules for the use of force and the role of public opinion regarding the same. How these relate to one another is not altogether clear.

A survey of attitudes to the use of force from 2005[5] illustrates the major differences between these states:

The question 'Are you proud of your country?' yielded 51 per cent in Britain, 40 per cent in France, and a meagre 17 per cent in Germany. Asking 'Are you willing to fight in a war for your country?', the survey found that in Britain a high 75 per cent answered affirmatively. Positive response was also high in France, with 66 per cent answering in the affirmative, whereas the lowest percentage of positive responses once again was in Germany, where 53 per cent responded in the affirmative. When looking at attitudes towards the use of force for various causes, we see that the more 'benign' the cause, the more support there is for it; but there are still major differences between Germany and the other two states in terms of level of support. Support for the use of force for regime change is at 40 per cent among the French and British, but only 28 per cent among Germans.[6] Responses to the question 'Is NATO essential to my country's security?' revealed a marked negative development from 2002 to 2005 for Germany, from 74 to 59 per cent.

These are but illustrative examples, yet interesting as such. It is common knowledge that Germany's lack of a military and strategic culture stands out in comparison with France and Britain. This is well documented and widely acknowledged, and is visible in such areas as the rules of engagement (ROEs) for deployed troops (little, if any, risk-taking and war-fighting); in the reception of war heroes,[7] who are not accepted as such, but rather treated as civilian workers; and in the role that public opinion and the Bundestag play in decision-making in this area.

STRATEGIC CULTURE

The importance of strategic culture, or the lack of it, can hardly be overstated The concept has been defined in various ways in the literature, but here I adopt Britz et al.'s conception of strategic culture as representative of 'the normative and institutional setting within which political decisions are shaped, made, and justified'.[8] The *normative* setting is national culture and identity. Decision-making rules are a reflection of the general political culture of a country: in states with considerable public engagement on the use of force—in other words, where public opinion matters very much—parliaments naturally tend to be involved much more than in states with the FPP. France has the most 'insulated' decision-making process of all European states when it comes to the use of force—decisions are made without any public or parliamentary debate, mostly in secret. However, the French public is generally very supportive of the use of force. Britain can be said to resemble France, but in recent years there has been a shift towards more public debate and involvement as well as more consultation and decision-making by Parliament. In his study *The Imperial Premiership*,[9] Goodman concludes that 'over the last few years we have seen the emergence of an informal convention that Parliament should be consulted and able to vote on military action'.[10] In the case of Syrian use of chemical weapons in 2013, President Obama, who had issued an ultimatum that the US would punish such use, asked Congress to decide for him whether or not to respond with force and got a no—an unprecedented departure from the FPP by the US president. In Britain, Prime Minister Cameron

154   J. H. MATLARY

similarly opted to consult Parliament, even asking them to decide for him. Goodman regrets this development, arguing that 'there is a need for formal parameters establishing Parliament's role and a mechanism for the PM to react rapidly to world events without having to wait for prior approval'.[11]

Thus, the three states studied here vary very much in terms of the importance of domestic politics for hard power decisions. The French president essentially acts alone, and can therefore act fast, use the element of surprise, and keep decision-making secret. This fulfils the requirement of strategic action, or at least enables it. The British are moving away from this kind of traditional FPP towards more Parliamentary participation and a larger role for public opinion. In Germany, as we shall see below, both parliament and public opinion play essential roles in decision-making, hindering strategic action.

Britz et al.[12] make the point that in states such as Germany it is almost impossible to uphold the distinction between the military profession and civilian life. The idea that war and peace are very different and that there is in fact a separate military sphere and a military profession has become quite foreign. In order to be legitimate in such a society, the military must be as civilian as possible. As Dahl-Martinsen showed in his study of funerals for the fallen in Afghanistan, in Britain and Denmark, two states with a military culture, the fallen were welcomed as national heroes in public ceremonies, whereas in Germany they were treated like civilians who died on the job and buried in private.[13] This is a telling empirical 'indicator' of the variance in social reality between states, and these differences show themselves in how the use of military force is legitimized and therefore accepted or not. Studies of the NATO-led International Security Assistance Force (ISAF) in Afghanistan show that while many European states legitimized their contributions as a 'force for good', some leaders, notably Britain's then Prime Minister Gordon Brown reiterated that Helmand [province] was 'the front line', implying that Britain was indeed fighting a war there. The Germans, on the contrary, refused to term it war-fighting, even though Britain and France were engaged in just that, calling it war and war-fighting.

I emphasize the importance of military strategic culture so much because the lack, or presence, of such a culture explains a great deal about a state's strategic action or lack of such. If a state cannot take quick and unitary action, it cannot act strategically. It also needs some measure of discretion and secrecy in its decision-making. Adversaries should not be able to know everything that goes into a decision or to follow every

GERMANY 155

argument made. There should be some uncertainty involved; outsiders should not necessarily know whether the information they have is comprehensive or correct. The old term *Kriegslist*—cunning—comes to mind. Cunning is allowed, and indeed encouraged, among soldiers.[14] Strategy has an inherent element of cunning and deception when it comes to intentions, willpower, and planned moves, just like a chess game. Clearly this makes it difficult for a liberal democracy to engage in strategic action, but that is precisely why the FPP is there. It is an exception to normal peacetime, transparent decision-making because there is a need for strategic ability when using force and other hard power that entails risk.

STRATEGIC CULTURE IN GERMANY?

Germany's unwillingness to deploy in sharp operations is clear and consistent throughout its modern military history. I analyse this in detail in my book on EU security dynamics from 2009 where the case of Germany stands out, having to do with its history of both world wars and an almost pacifist public opinion.[15] Germany prefers peacekeeping and peace operations with the goal of stabilization only, based on legitimacy in the form of a Security Council mandate. Germany has yet to deploy soldiers in African operations and has been a reluctant ally in NATO's history. It was allowed to join NATO in 1955, but not to recreate a general staff (*Generalstab*). Thus, the German army is not only a parliamentary army, *ein Parlamentsheer*, but also a NATO army, always under the command of its allies.

As shown at the beginning of this chapter, German public opinion differs from public opinion in other European states. Moreover, a recent poll shows that a majority of Germans refuse to assist the Baltic states militarily in case of a Russian attack: 53 per cent say no, according to a poll by Pew.[16] When asking women only, as many as 62 per cent agree—thus making German women extremely reluctant to fulfil the NATO solidarity obligation which forms the very backbone of the alliance. Comparing these results to those of other NATO states, we find that those who would refuse to assist allies stand at 23 per cent among the Dutch, 26 per cent among the Poles, 31 per cent in the US and Canada, but in both France and Britain the percentage is 43 per cent.[17]

The normal vocabulary of war and war-fighting is not found in the public debate; the German chief of defence is called a 'general inspector' (*Generalinspekteur*), and discipline in the curriculum in the officer's education is known as *Innere Führung*, which translates into military and civic leadership. The lack of realistic and military terminology leads to excessive political correctness in public debate.[18]

Germany has had to react to external pressures for troop contributions and NATO policy, however. As a NATO member, it must act as a responsible ally, although it spends very little on defence compared to France and Britain. The Germans are very far from the 2 per cent of GDP goal. In 2015 defence spending stood at 2 per cent of GDP for Britain, making for US $55.8 billion, and at 1.80 per cent for France, amounting to almost US $50 billion. But Germany, the richest and biggest country, spent only 1.18 per cent, which was also the smallest amount of the three, US $43.8 billion.[19] Moreover, there were reports of the German army having very outdated equipment and thus not being in a fit state to fight.

In the EU, Germany has a battle group on rotation like France and Britain, but when it was to be deployed to Kinshasa to secure an election in 2006, the German government ran into domestic trouble. The thought of deploying soldiers to Africa was not acceptable to the German public. In the end, the battle group was manned by France while Germany saved face by having the pro forma command of the operation from their headquarters in Potsdam.[20] This is a clear example of how parliament and public opinion can intervene to make it impossible for the government to keep to its international obligations.

The problems related to German participation in the ISAF were the exceptionally circumscribed rules of engagement (ROEs), something which meant that the German contribution could be legitimized as some sort of peacekeeping. When the humanitarian intervention in Libya took place in 2011, Germany abstained from voting on the mandate in the UNSC, placing it in the company of Russia and China against the US, France, and Britain, its NATO allies.[21] This elicited strong criticism from then US Secretary of Defence Robert Gates who called out Poland and Germany for opting out of what became a NATO operation in Libya.[22] How this German vote came to pass is unclear, but it is not possible to vote in the UNSC on such an important matter by default. It must have been a decision made in Berlin and not in New York. Bergstrand and Engelbrekt find that 'the FDP party leader and foreign minister Guido Westerwelle and his staff exerted considerable influence over the German decision to withhold endorsement'.[23] Indeed, the Foreign Ministry, which has to accept such decisions, declined to do so. This led to major criticism

GERMANY 157

in NATO—here was proof that Germany was not a reliable ally, not even in the case of a UN-mandated humanitarian intervention.

Partly as a compensation for this refusal and to show that it was a serious military actor, Germany announced at the 2014 NATO Wales Summit that it would be the leader of the so-called Framework Nation Concept in NATO.[24] The German President and Defence Minister von der Leyden had given speeches at the Munich security conference earlier that year about Germany's intention to take on a leading role,[25] and this was the manifestation of this new role. Germany offered to lead the Interim Very High Readiness Joint Task Force which was agreed at the Wales summit. This force was to be able to reinforce threatened allies 'within a few days'.[26] Germany, the Netherlands, and Norway supplied an interim force in 2015 with Germany as contributing the most troops.[27]

Moreover, Germany opted to supply the Kurdish Peshmerga force in Iraq with arms, up to a small brigade size, a decision which then Foreign Minister Sigmar Gabriel, a Social Democrat, found to be the hardest of his career.[28] Germany did not, however, supply fighter aircraft to the battle against Daesh, as France and Britain did. When France called for help from its allies under Article 42(6) of the Lisbon Treaty following the terrorist attacks in Paris on Friday, 13 November 2015, Germany agreed to supply the fighting forces with Tornado reconnaissance aircraft, but not fighter planes. This shows a certain logical consistency: Germany supports sharp military operations, but does not lead or even fight.

It still remains 'the reluctant ally', as Shreer puts it.[29] Bergstrand and Engelbrekt conclude that Germany 'is perhaps best described as an ambivalent country'[30] when it comes to the use of force, but they note that actual participation in international operations leads to experienced forces and a change of public opinion, albeit slowly. The turn away from major international operations towards defence of the transatlantic region—the original goal of NATO—means that Germany can more easily justify the use of force for deterrence in defence of the state. This may lead to more of a normalization of German views on the use of force.

Yet commentators are not impressed by the political signals that Germany will 'normalize' its strategic culture. '*Deutsche Sicherheitspolitik, ziellos und unkoordiniert*',[31] writes one, German security and defence policy is without direction and not coordinated. The White Book on Defence adopted in 2016 presents a more strategic and robust defence, and allows for participation in so-called coalitions of the willing, that is, groups of state outside formal organizations like the EU, NATO, or the UN. The reality of the growing importance of such is recognized: '*ad hoc* cooperation will continue to gain significance as an instrument of international crisis and conflict management'.[32] Others are less impressed that any real change is happening: 'Germany's least menacing military build-up ever',[33] writes *The American Interest* in a comment, pointing out that even if Germany adds 7000 positions in their military by 2023 and plans to spend US $150 billion on investment in the next 15 years, this still amounts to only a little more than 1 per cent of GDP.[34] There is also the disconcerting background to this that can be termed old-fashioned anti-Americanism, something that has a strong tradition in German public opinion. The election of President Trump led to major worry in Germany and to open criticism from chancellor Merkel, and a debate about becoming more autonomous ensued: 'Since Trump's victory, however, German politicians, pundits, and media have agonized over the issue, with more and louder voices calling for a stronger military.'[35] Yet independence from the US in terms of deterrence would mean the German or at least European ability to deter also with nuclear weapons, a theme far from popular or even viable in the German debate. A group of prominent intellectuals warned against a new round of anti-Americanism for this reason, publishing a manifesto to this end entitled 'In spite of it all, America',[36] where they pointed out that Germany remains dependent on US extended deterrence. The signatories fear the Social Democratic Party (SPD) criticism of Merkel's Christian-democratic Union (CDU) and the former's rejection of the 2 per cent GDP goal of NATO.[37] The SPD's candidate for chancellor, Martin Schulz, used this theme in the national election campaign, something which is usually never done—national politicians who favour NATO membership do not depart from government policy in this sensitive field in a national election campaign. The fact that Schulz did so shows that German strategic culture is quite fluid, as criticizing NATO commitments is one of the things that is simply not done by responsible parties in member states. Yet the present Social Democratic Foreign Minister Sigmar Gabriel echoed his party's line in a meeting with US Secretary of State Tillerson when he said that he knows no German politician who thinks that the 2 per cent goal is reachable or indeed should be reached.[38] This kind of statement from a sitting foreign minister confronts the important NATO policy of reaching 2 per cent and is wholly counter-productive, creating unnecessary conflict between allies. It also makes the position of Germany even more difficult within NATO where its 'reputation has hit rock bottom.'[39] But in Germany this kind of opportunism is apparently possible. Also, the Social Democrat

Steinmeier when he was foreign minister (now German president) took the liberty to criticize NATO exercises in the Baltic region as 'sabre-rattling', as mentioned before.

Summing up, Germany is far from having a 'normal' strategic and military culture and deviates from the other two great powers in this study in its inconsistency and lack of principles in security and defence policy. It debates major NATO policy domestically after NATO has adopted these policies, such as the 2 per cent goal, and public opinion is by a majority actually opposing the solidarity obligation of the alliance. The latter is a major blow to serious NATO participation for Germany. It remains a reluctant ally.

The German Reaction to Russian Revisionism

Considering the country's anti-militaristic stance, it perhaps comes as a surprise that Germany is in the leading role in Europe with regard to diplomacy with Russia. A major survey by the think tank European Council of Foreign Relations found that Germany now ranks as the leader in Europe, above both Britain and France: 'Deutschland gilt als besonders vorbildlich im Hinblick auf der Entwicklung von Sanktionen gegenüber Russland' (Germany ranks as the model on how to deal with Russia now).[40] While this survey may not be entirely scientific, the suggestion that Germany is a leader in foreign policy represents a major change.

We have noted the discrepancy between Germany's political role as the European leader vis-à-vis Russia and its almost pacifist military culture. Given that military power is Russia's 'weapon of choice', this presents a problem. Can Germany put weight behind its diplomacy with economic power alone?

The House of Lords report mentioned earlier in this chapter concludes that Germany has a key role because of its particular historical relationship with Russia and its important trade ties. Despite these ties, however, it notes, contact between Germany and Russia (namely between Merkel and Putin) had decreased towards the end of 2014 and into 2015.[41] The Minsk II negotiations in early 2015 were seen by many as a last and almost desperate attempt to find a diplomatic solution.

Yet it was not Germany that took the lead at first when Putin started to act on Ukraine. Germany has had a tradition of *Ostpolitik*, first implemented by the Social Democrats under Willy Brandt, whereby it has sought dialogue and understanding with Russia. Military power had no place in this foreign policy, and still does not in Germany's policy towards Russia and Ukraine. This is one of the paradoxes and possible problems in the strategic interaction—Germany per se opposes arming Ukraine or paying much attention to deterrence. Using the military tool as a tool of statecraft is still largely foreign to Germany, a fact that might result in impotence when trying to put pressure on an adversary who prefers using military power in its various forms.

Germany carries on extensive trade with Russia, and this plays a key role in determining what foreign policy is possible. Stephen Szabo calls this 'commercial realism' and argues that 'future economic sanctions will go as far as Berlin permits'.[42] Commercial realism refers to the reality that the type of hard power that is usable is economic power, and also that the use of economic power as a tool of statecraft is constrained by interdependence and national actors that stand to lose in conflicts.

Szabo argues that 'this type of power has caused a tectonic shift in German foreign policy and has important implications ... it cedes overall grand strategy to business interests ... and reduces the role of political and administrative leaders in government'.[43] This means that military power is no longer seen as a usable tool of statecraft and it is therefore not given status or subsidies: 'Russia is not regarded as a threat by Germany's public or policy makers.'[44] While Germany is one of the world's largest arms exporters,[45] German use of force seems a foreign idea unless it is a 'force for good' in UN operations.[46]

Russian-German trade involves many companies—more than 6000 of which are located in Russia—and is worth more than €75 billion per year. This is five times more than the value of German-American trade.[47] In all, more than 200,000 German jobs depend on Russian trade. Germany relies on gas imports from Russia to meet more than one third of German demand, and this dependence is very direct: gas flows to households as well as to industry. These figures tell us that it is imperative for any German government to manage the relationship with Russia well. They also explain why we find major opposition to the new German policy on Russia that Chancellor Merkel developed after the downing of the Malaysian airliner in Ukraine in July 2015.

Before Merkel's new tougher stance, Germany played a key role in negotiating the deal between Ukraine and the EU, and German NGOs had close ties with the Maidan demonstrators. There is a strong normative element in German foreign policy in addition to the emphasis on trade—the spreading of democratic norms is important.[48] This strong role, both

GERMANY 161

in trade and in normative politics, became problematic once the military tool played a role in the conflict. As Friedman writes, 'as the Germans came to realize that this affair would ... take on a military flavour, they began to back away from a major role'.[49] Germany's unwillingness to arm Ukraine, no matter what happens, creates the problem of how to apply pressure without having the major 'stick' provided by the military tool, if needed. Germany is 'disarming' itself by putting military force inside a 'locked room' politically, leaving itself only economic force to play with. Other European states have not ruled out military force in every circumstance, conveying instead only that arming Ukraine is not an option for the time being, and the US has stated that 'all options are at the table'; neither of these stances rules out arming Ukraine forever. Germany, however, seems to have to ruled out any use of force on principle.

Keeping open the option of arming Ukraine is a major part of the strategic game of putting pressure on Putin, but Germany does not accept this and seems to be willing to forego the power implicit in uncertainty. Instead, both the chancellor and the defence minister keep repeating that there is no military solution in Ukraine, like a mantra.[50] It is interesting to note that the defence minister talked about weapons as if they were a danger in and of themselves: 'there are already far too many weapons in Ukraine', she said, and 'they can ignite a fire and remove us farther from a solution'.[51]

This quote betrays a view of military force as a problem rather than a tool that can have useful effects: If there are no weapons, diplomacy can work. This view is simplistic and wrong; weapons serve a political function, just like economic tools. There are never military solutions to anything, only political ones; wars and armed conflicts end with some political solution, and the use of military force or the threat of force have major political effects, as they probably have in this case.

Friedman writes that Germany has 'disproportionate strength overlying genuine weakness',[52] because its *economic power cannot substitute for military power* in situations where the adversary is prepared to use military power. Ukraine is a good example: no actor can 'win' in a confrontation with Putin there as long as he is the only actor who is willing to use military force. He may be effectively put under pressure and choose to back off, but if the issue is confined to a game over who prevails in Ukraine and one actor is willing to use force, he can dictate the outcome—the political endgame. The common rule in endgame negotiations is exactly this: the actor with the greatest territorial gains will get the most out of the result, as Milosevic did in Bosnia at Dayton, and as in the Minsk II agreement where some sort of autonomy is granted to the Donbas. Facts on the ground cannot be ignored, and that is why military force is unsurpassed as a tool of statecraft. It is the ultimate tool when the stakes are very high; the power of economic might presupposes some degree of order and some existential security.

Germany, therefore, is leading Europe in the conflict with Russia with one hand tied behind its back, as it were. Its lack of a normal strategic or military culture has become an obstacle to developing leadership and statesmanship. Germany is being driven by the actions of an adversary, as indeed was finally realized in Berlin in 2015 when the defence minister announced that a new White Paper on Defence would be written, replacing the one from 2006 in which Russia was included as a partner. The aim of Germany's new posture is to bolster national defence and develop deterrence.[53]

A good analysis of the fateful year 2014 in German politics can be found in Seibel's article chronicling the turn from *Ostpolitik* to strategic interaction with Putin as an adversary.[54] His point of departure is public opinion: 61 per cent of Germans did not want NATO to respond to the crisis with any deployments in Poland or the Baltics. He recounts how important German Social Democrats like Schröder and Platzeck pleaded for a 'middle way', a third way of dialogue between Germany and Russia, and how the Foreign Minister Walter Steinmeier tried to keep this as the main option until Merkel forced him to get behind her policy line late in 2014.

The crisis in Ukraine acted as an external shock for Germany, whose beliefs about Russian modernization and democratization served as the basis for its *Ostpolitik*. It was 'only after the annexation of Crimea ... that the German government substantially changed course'.[55] There were tensions between the chancellor's office and Steinmeier's Foreign Office up to the very end of the year, Seibel claims, and this is corroborated by international news and new analyses. Steinmeier, for example, did not criticize Russia publicly and even visited Moscow in November 2014.[56] A conflict was looming in Berlin: 'A rift may now be growing between chancellor Merkel and her foreign minister', announced *Der Spiegel*.[57] 'Steinmeier [wanted] to avoid provoking the Russians', while Merkel demanded a united front,[58] with all politicians in the coalition behind her.[59]

This was no small matter. As prominent a politician as Matthias Platzeck wanted to formally acknowledge Russia's annexation of Crimea[60] and 39 per cent of the German public was behind him.[61] 'Putin must not be demonized', he insisted.[62] These ideas were not at all uncommon in business circles and on the political left; in fact, 'sanctions against Russia had been anathema to the Federal Government and the German political class in general until the annexation of Crimea and the same was true for a stronger presence of NATO in Eastern Europe through the deployment of combat troops'.[63] In fact, Seibel points out, it was German opposition in Cardiff that hindered NATO efforts to deploy more troops to the Baltics and Poland: 'At the Wales summit the German proposal ... prevailed over Poland and [the] Baltic states' demand ... Germany insisted on keeping the NATO-Russia Founding Act of 1997 intact.'[64] Thus, even though Russia clearly violated the agreement in deploying forces in and outside Ukraine, NATO ended up still respecting it.

It would thus appear that Germany tries to avoid all thinking about deterrence and coercion with the military tool. Moreover, problems with its own military have come to the fore in recent years: its air force was unable to deploy military trainers to Iraq and had to land in Bulgaria,[65] and Poland expressed concern about the German 'Truppenzustand'.[66] International media reported on a 'ramshackle military at odds with global aspirations'.[67]

Germany also acted conservatively with regard to the EU sanctions. At the meeting of EU heads of state on 27 June 2014, 'it was due to decisive German influence that no further sanctions were declared at the summit itself',[68] but the downing of the Malaysian Airlines flight was yet another external shock and acted as a game changer. As Seibel points out, 'For the first time the German government openly supported sectoral economic sanctions against Russia in accordance with phase III' of the EU sanctions.[69] Both German and American intelligence attributed the attack to Russian separatists using Russian weapons.[70]

In the aftermath of this event, Chancellor Merkel united her political coalition and demanded support for a tougher line of keeping up sanctions and increasing them if necessary. Steinmeier continued to lapse from time to time—saying, for example, that Ukraine should not be able to join NATO—but it was Merkel who was the actor from then on. Seibel discusses in detail the many counter-productive statements that have been made by various German politicians, undermining Merkel's message and attempts to apply coercive pressure; he attributes these to a lack of practice in and understanding of how coercion as a foreign policy tool should work. 'Berlin sent mixed messages and exposed intra-governmental fault lines'— while Merkel insisted on sanctions, Steinmeier was publicly worried that sanctions would have an adverse effect on the Russian economy.[71]

The fact that Merkel is the only Western politician who can talk easily with Putin—in Russian or in German[72]—does not alter the fact that her platform is rather weak. Germany does not have a strategic culture and it will take decades to develop one. The military tool as a deterrent, threat, or coercive instrument is therefore largely non-existent. The control question of deterrence is the fear factor: Are you scared? Do you fear us?

Putin does not fear German military force. Germany's lack of a military tool in this strategic interaction is therefore a major handicap. Inside Germany, the forced consensus on Russian sanctions remains, imposed by external shocks, but we cannot expect this to last very long. The united front behind Merkel is a direct result of the emergency situation that existed at the time and *does not represent a change in German foreign-policy thinking*. It is a superficial change, not a deep one. Large parts of the political spectrum prefer the old middle way of *Ostpolitik*. This is also the preference of the business community, whose importance in foreign policy generally is much higher than in France or Britain: 'In 2014, exports from Germany to Russia dropped by 18 per cent' and they have continued to drop after that.[73]

All forces on the domestic scene therefore point in the direction of a return to normal diplomatic and economic ties between the two states. Although, as Hans Kundnani points out, 'Russia's annexation of Crimea … was a strategic shock for Germany'. The major trend had been a 'long-term weakening of the so-called *Westbindung*'.[74] As we recall, Germany made the major mistake of weakening the resolution on Libya in 2011, undermining the Western NATO coalition. While this seems at first like a strange position for Germany to have taken, against the backdrop of an analysis of a country 'in the middle' where NATO is no longer so important, it makes more sense. Thus, Anne Applebaum may have a point when she warns against 'the risks of putting Germany front and center in Europe's crises'.[75]

During 2017 the Enhanced Forward Presence (EFP), a force consisting of four battalions, was deployed in the Baltics. The Germans agreed to send a battalion to Lithuania, but only after moving slowly in this direction.[76] At Cardiff, Germany still argued that the 1997 Russia-NATO Founding Act should be respected. In that agreement both parties promised not to station troops in East-Central Europe. Russia had clearly violated this agreement in Ukraine and Crimea, but still Germany insisted on respecting it.[77] When, finally, Germany agreed to deploy in the Baltics, it was with reluctance, and then Foreign Minister Franz-Walter Steinmeier

GERMANY 165

criticized Western exercises in the region as 'sabre-rattling'.[78] This is rather extraordinary, given that Germany is a member of NATO.

There is and has traditionally been a more anti-American and anti-NATO attitude in the Social Democratic party than in the Christian Democratic Party, and the reflex in the former is dialogue and diplomacy rather than deterrence. The prospect of having to deter Russia was not at all welcome in German politics, and the main drivers for such deterrence were Poland, the Baltic states, Britain, and, of course, the US. A large percentage of Germans also do not want to defend the allies against Russia, a Pew survey found.[79]

There has been no progress in the Minsk process in 2017, and the relationship with Russia has remained very frosty. War-fighting in the Donbas has continued and there has been little Western attempt to do anything about the situation. EU sanctions are still in place, as are US sanctions, which have been tightened by the US Congress. Germany plays no particular role in relation to Russia as there is no diplomatic process that is ongoing.

In sum, Germany led by Chancellor Merkel was pivotal in the diplomatic process with Russia from the summer of 2015, after the downing of the Malaysia Airlines plane, both bilaterally and in the EU where it led the work on getting agreement on sanctions. But Germany has been reluctant to see sanctions (coercion) in connection with military deterrence, and the sanctions are not very clear in their conditionality, as discussed below in Chap. 9. The preference has been to preserve as much as possible of the traditional *Ostpolitik* with dialogue and diplomacy as the only means of interaction. Energy cooperation with Russia has also continued through the Nord Stream 2 project.

In German domestic politics, the sanctions continue to split, and 'Germany struggles to find united stance on Russia'.[80] Within NATO, Germany was sceptical of all talk of deterrence and preferred the term 'reassurance', and it even considers its own deployment of a battalion in the EFP a 'presence' and not a military operation. The deployment there constitutes 'Berührungspillen gegen die Putin-Phobie', writes *der Spiegel*[81]—pills against the Putin-phobia, as then Foreign Minister Steinmeier's attitude was described. The same Steinmeier, now president of Germany, travelled to Moscow on 25 October 2017, on what was named a 'working visit',[82] not an official visit, the latter which would have been impossible, given the sanctions.

THE GERMAN REACTION TO MIGRATION SHOCK AND TERRORISM

Germany also played a leading role in confronting the 2015 migration crisis, albeit a much more controversial one than in dealing with Russia. As recounted in Chap. 4, chancellor Merkel opted to keep the German border open as more than 1.2 million migrants and refugees descended on Europe in the summer and autumn of 2015. The declaration that Germany was up to the task—'*wir schaffen dass*', or 'we can do it'—sounded like the right response ethically, but the country's open door policy soon became a major problem as ever more migrants arrived in Germany. EU-level policy failed despite German insistence that a system of burden-sharing be established; although such a system was adopted by majority voting, it was never implemented.

Merkel became increasingly unpopular at home as the influx showed no signs of stopping and other states on the route from Greece simply let migrants pass through, from Greece to Hungary to Serbia. Local communities made an uproar, as for example, Cottbus which declared that it will not take in more migrants and refugees because of crimes committed by those who came in 2015.[83] This is a very unusual statement to make for a city; in defiance of national policy, and should be seen as a *cri de coeur* as a local 15 year old girl was stabbed to death by a Syrian refugee of the same age.

In 2015 there were 890,000 asylum seekers in Germany, but in 2016 the number was only 280,000, and in 2017 186,664.[84] Thus, chancellor Merkel's Turkey deal made a very big difference, yet the deal depends entirely on the will of President Erdoğan. There was also a new realism in German policy statements on this: The Interior Minister Thomas de Maizière said that the numbers are too high still, and that 'it is still the case that the people who decided whether someone comes to Germany or Europe are criminal smugglers'.[85]

Merkel's *Willkommenheitskultur* effectively abolished the Dublin system by allowing migrants to move to Germany through other EU states and by refusing to return them to the country of first arrival. It also acted as a major pull factor, making for more arrivals. It is interesting that Merkel

GERMANY 167

never agreed to an upper limit for refugees into Germany until a coalition government with the SPD depended on their insistence of such a limit, discussed in Chap. 4. The annual quota of refugees, a normal policy of any state, is based on the number of people that can be integrated meaningfully in a year, usually some few thousand administered through the selection process of the UNHCR.

Merkel's refusal to define an upper limit for the annual German intake of refugees posed a major problem in the negotiations over a coalition government after the elections in 2017 which yielded a large parliamentary group for the anti-migration party Alternative für Deutschland (AfD), something directly related to Merkel migration stance. The party won 12.7 per cent in the elections, gaining 94 representatives in parliament.

The challenge for Merkel's government was how to control or stop migration while keeping German borders and the outer Schengen border open. Robin Alexander, a journalist who has investigated the decision-making process that led to the continuation of the open border policy, argues that it was the prospect of media coverage of German police shutting out migrants and refugees that led Merkel to opt for maintaining open borders.[86] No doubt the Germans are more reluctant than most other Europeans to be seen as 'hard'; and German public opinion was in fact positive for a long time. However, an investigation into German press coverage showed that the mainstream press repeated Merkel's arguments about the necessity of being generous and welcoming people in need, as discussed in Chap. 4. Those critical of this policy were seen as illegitimate and as immoral.

This one-sidedness did not last very long. The sexual assault of women in Cologne by migrants on New Year's Eve 2016 was initially underreported in the press, and it was later disclosed that the police had been afraid to report the facts. People were shocked and outraged, and called for Merkel to implement a more muscular immigration policy. The dilemma was clear: migration had to be halted somehow, but what was to be done if borders could not be closed nor national quotas defined?

The solution was to outsource the problem, as described in Chap. 4. Merkel's advisors brokered a deal between the EU and Turkey, and Merkel herself travelled to meet President Erdoğan several times, shaking hands in photo sessions and assuring the EU that this was a 'win-win' deal. All concerns over human rights issues were brushed aside, and the key elements of the deal were payment to Turkey, visa-free travel for Turkish citizens into Europe, and accelerated negotiations for Turkish EU membership.

The deal with Turkey has worked in terms of stopping migration into Greece, and from there up to Germany and other states, but it has come at a high price, ethically speaking. One issue is the lack of willingness to face the problems at home, both in Europe and in Germany: The less ethical solution is to pay someone else to solve one's own problems, especially as this solution also entails large dependency and therefore vulnerability.

Despite these ethical concerns, Merkel's choice, on behalf of the EU, was to outsource immigration problems to Turkey. Since the attempted military coup in the latter country in June 2016, the relationship between Turkey and Germany has gone from frosty to hateful. Germany, like several other NATO states, has granted political asylum to Turkish officers and diplomats, and German human rights advocates and journalists in Turkey have been arrested on trumped-up charges. German politicians have been denied the right to visit German soldiers at Incirlik Air Base, and Merkel has gone so far as to state that Turkey should no longer be a candidate for EU membership. Visa freedom for Turks is as far from realization as possible, and President Erdoğan and his ministers habitually issue threats to Europe and Germany. Where this will all end is unclear, but it is certain that Germany and the EU remain vulnerable to a new massive influx of migrants in the future. This shows how unstrategic this policy really is.

As discussed in Chap. 5, the only remedy for economic and political migration is to improve conditions in the countries of origin, combined with border controls and even border closures into Europe. This means improving conditions in the whole MENA region, which also involves anti-terrorism operations. The problem of terrorism in Europe, be it the work of Daesh, the Nusra Front, or other groups, largely originates in this region.

The remedies range from conditionality in development aid to military action against terrorist strongholds like Raqqa, Mosul, and so on. In the fight against Daesh, we have seen the same German reticence as in other military operations, and perhaps even more so. While France and Britain engaged in sharp air operations, Germany offered only reconnaissance flights and mentoring on a small scale. Some 150 trainers were in Iraq by 2016, and Germany even armed a small Peshmerga brigade, which was a first, as mentioned above. But Germany did not actually fight Daesh. This fits with the general picture we have drawn above: Germany avoids sharp operations and opts for a supporting role it if must have one. Thus, in terms of actually fighting terrorism, Germany relies on intelligence at home and hopes that allies, with France in the lead, will undertake operations in the MENA region.

In sum, Germany's supposed leadership role with regard to Russia is not a solid one, and does not encompass deterrence and coercion. On migration, the German government must be said to have ducked the issue altogether, refusing to deal with the physical challenge of border controls and migration numbers. Being in denial of the facts, the German refusal to act led to a total break-down of the Dublin regime of the EU. Finally, on terrorism, Germany played a 'safe' role far away from the risks of war in theatre, but provided defence equipment for a Peshmerga brigade.

NOTES

1. See for example, Thomas U. Berger, *Cultures of Antimilitarism: National Security in Germany and Japan* (Baltimore, MD; London: The Johns Hopkins University Press, 1998). Kerry Longhurst, *Germany and the use of force: The evolution of German security policy 1990–2003* (Manchester: Manchester University Press, 2004). Anja Dalgaard-Nielsen, *Germany, pacifism and peace enforcement* (Manchester: Manchester University Press, 2006).
2. See Matlary, J. H. (2009, 2013) *European Union Security Dynamics: In the New National Interest,* Palgrave Macmillan, UK, for an analysis of this. Germany was only included after the policies had been agreed between the two powers.
3. Hellmann, M. (2016) 'Assuming great power responsibility: French strategic culture and international military operations', in Britz, M. (ed.) *European Participation in International Operations,* Palgrave Macmillan, 2016.
4. Britz, op.cit., p. 171.
5. Transatlantic trends, 2005.
6. Ibid.
7. Kåre Dahl-Martinsen.
8. Britz, Malena (ed.) *European Participation in International Operations: The Role of Strategic Culture,* Palgrave Macmillan, UK, 2016: 2.
9. Sam Goodman, *The Imperial Premiership: The Role of the Modern Prime Minister in Foreign Policy Making, 1964–2015,* Manchester University Press.
10. Ibid., p. 310.
11. Ibid.
12. Op.cit.
13. See note 1 above.

170   J. H. MATLARY

14. The ROEs for Norwegian soldiers specify that cunning is allowed: 'Du kan bekjempe fienden ved å benytte krigslist (misvisende opplysninger, kamuflasje, etc.)' [You may fight the enemy using cunning, such as false information, camouflage, etc.]. The Chief of Defence's Soldier Rules, 14.9.2005.
15. See note 1 above.
16. Pew poll cited in 'deutche würden östliche NATO-partner bei Angriff alleinlassen', Die Welt, 24 May 2017.
17. Ibid.
18. Bid to restore the Iron Cross awakens Germany's Angst. (20 March 2008). *International Herald Tribune*, p. 1.
19. The Military Balance 2017.
20. See Matlary, 2010.
21. Resolution 1973/11.
22. Damon M. Wilson, and Jeff Lightfoot, *Anchoring the Alliance* (Washington, D.C.: Atlantic Council, 2012). vi, 4–5.
23. Bergstrand, A. and Engelbrekt, L., 'To deploy or not deploy a parliamentary army? German strategic culture and international military operations', p. 66, in Britz, M., op.cit, 2016.
24. German Federal Ministry of Defence, *Food for Thought. Framework Nations Concept* (Berlin: German MoD, 2013). See also Claudia Major and Christian Mölling, *The Framework Nations Concept*, SWP Comments 52 (Berlin: Stiftung Wissenschaft und Politik, December 2014). 2.
25. Joachim Gauck, 'Deutschlands Rolle in der Welt: Anmerkungen zu Verantwortung, Normen und Bündnissen' [Germany's role in the world: Reflections on responsibility, norms and alliances]. Speech by Federal President Joachim Gauck at the opening of the Munich Security Conference on 31 January 2014 in Munich, (Berlin: Office of the Federal President, 31 January 2014).
26. NATO Heads of State and Government, *Wales Summit Declaration* (Brussels: NATO, 2014). paragraph 8.
27. Claudia Major, *NATO's Strategic Adaptation: Germany Is the Backbone for the Alliance's Military Reorganisation*, SWP Comments 16 (Berlin: Stiftung Wissenschaft und Politik, March 2015). p. 2–3. Note that the three countries had already been slated to provide the 2015 NATO Reponses Force (NRF) since 2013.
28. Saxi, H. L., 'British-German defence and security relations after Brexit: *Quo vadis* the "Silent Alliance"?' In Matlary, J.H. and Johnson, R., *Britain's Defence Role*, forthcoming.
29. Schreer, B. (2013) 'The Reluctant Ally? Germany, NATO and the Use of Force', in Matlary, J.H. and Petersson, M., op.cit.
30. Bergstrand and Engelbrekt, op.cit., p. 69.

GERMANY 171

31. *Die Welt*, article by same name as cited by Thorsten Jungholt, 5 June 2017.
32. Cited in article entitled 'Germany embraces *Realpolitik* once more', *War on the Rocks*, 19 September 2016.
33. Article by same title published on 7 June 2016.
34. There is also pressure on Merkel to abandon the 2 per cent goal, see 'Left lashes Angela Merkel over defence spending', *The Sunday Times*, 2 April 2017.
35. 'In the era of Donald Trump, Germans debate a military build-up', *The Washington Post*, 8 March 2017.
36. Discussed in 'German Foreign Policy Experts warn against Anti-Americanism', NYT, 13 October 2017.
37. 'Schulz will Zwei-Prozent Ziel der NATO kippen', *Spiegel Online*, 1 June 2017.
38. 'Gabriel sucht die Konfrontation', FAZ, 3 March 2017.
39. 'Germany's reputation in NATO has hit rock bottom', *Speigel Online*, 29 May 2012.
40. 'Denkfabrik hält Deutschland für Europeas Führungsmacht', *Spiegel Online*, 30 January 2015.
41. Lords Report, hsd en p. 30, item 87.
42. 'Germany's Commercial Realism and the Russia Problem', Stephen Szabo, *Survival*, 25 September 2014, vol. 56, no. 5, pp. 117–128.
43. Ibid., p. 119.
44. Ibid.
45. http://www.bbc.com/news/technology-31901493.
46. See Matlary, 2009 and 2013, *European Union*.
47. Szabo, op.cit, p. 121.
48. Friedman, George, 'Germany emerges', *Geopolitical Weekly*, Stratfor, 10 February 2015, online.
49. Ibid., p. 2.
50. 'Von der Leyden warnt vor Waffenlieferungen an due Ukraine', 6 February 2015, *Spiegel online*.
51. Ibid., my translation.
52. Ibid., p. 4.
53. The American Interest, 'Germans shift defense Posture against Russia', 19 February 2015, online.
54. 'Arduous Learning or New Uncertainties? German Diplomacy and the Ukrainian crisis', Wolfgang Seibel, forthcoming *Global Policy*, 2015. This article was published online in June 2015.
55. Ibid., p. 18, draft.
56. Stratfor, 'Competing Ties Force Germany to Mediate in Ukraine', 21 November 2014, online, *NYT*, 'Germanys' man in the Middle', 20 November 2014.

172   J. H. MATLARY

57. *Spiegel online*, 'Cracks form in Berlin over Russia Stance', 26 November 2014.
58. *Zeit* online, 'Alle auf Linie', 26 November 2014.
59. Ibid.
60. *Zeit* online, 'Platzeck halt es nicht mer aus', 26 November 2014.
61. Zeit online, '39 Prozent der Deutschen für Anerkennung der Krim-Annexion', 26 November 2014.
62. Ibid.
63. Seibel, op.cit., p. 19, draft.
64. Ibid., p. 25, draft.
65. *NYT*, 'Seeking Global Role, German Military Stumbles', online, 2 October 2014.
66. *Zeit* online, 'Die marode Bundeswehr ängstigt Polen – ausgerechnet', 8 October 2014.
67. *Spiegel* online, same title, 2 October 2014.
68. Ibid., p. 29, draft.
69. Ibid., p. 33.
70. *Spiegel* online, 'German intelligence claims pro-Russian separatists downed MH17', online, 19 October, 2014.
71. Seibel, op.cit, p. 38.
72. These meetings have been very difficult. Putin has treated Merkel without respect on several occasions: In Rome, he let her wait for several hours; in Brisbane, the meeting lasted for four hours and Merkel was furious when she finished. Yet the number of phone calls she has had with him (33 in 2014) far outnumbers that of Obama (10), Hollande (15), and Cameron (6). *Zeit* online, 'Merkels Wort hat bei Putin das stärkste Gewicht', 26 August 2014, *The Times*, online, 'Putin risks damaging rift with Merkel over Ukraine', 24 November 2014.
73. 'German political leaders divided on approach to Russia', *Der Spiegel*, 26 October 2016.
74. Hans Kundnani, 'Leaving the West Behind', *Foreign Affairs*, January/February 2015, online.
75. *The Washington Post*, same title, 20 February 2015, online.
76. 'Deutsche Leopard-Panzer warden an russischen Grenze verlegt', *Die Welt*, 27 October 2016.
77. 'No permanent NATO troop presence in Eastern Europe, Merkel says, ' *Deutsche Welle*, 3 September 2014.
78. FAZ, 'Steinmeier kritisiert Nato-Manöver in Osteuropa', *Frankfurter Allgemeine Zeitung*, 18 June 2016.
79. Katie Simmons, Bruce Stokes, and Jacob Poushter, *NATO Publics Blame Russia for Ukrainian Crisis, but Reluctant to Provide Military Aid* (Washington, D.C.: Pew Research Center, 10 June 2015). 5.

GERMANY   173

80. Article with same title, *der Spiegel*, 26 October 2016.
81. These are the words used to describe Foreign Minister Steinmeier's attitude during a visit to the Baltic states; see article by same name, *Der Spiegel*, 30 May 2016.
82. 'Steinmeier reist nach Russland', *Der Spiegel*, 17 October 2017.
83. 'Cottbus word keine weitere Flüchtlinge aufnehmen', *Die Welt*, 20 January 2018.
84. 'Arrivals to Germany last year were a fifth of 890000 tally for 2015', *The Times*, 17 January 2018.
85. Ibid.
86. Alexander, R (2017) *Die Getriebenen: Merkel und die Flüchtlingspolitik: Report aus dem Innern der Macht*, Siedler Verlag.

REFERENCES

Alexander, R. (2017). *Die Getriebenen: Merkel und die Flüchtlingspolitik: Report aus dem Innern der Macht*. Siedler Verlag.

Berger, T. (1998). *Cultures of Antimilitarism: National Security in Germany and Japan*. Baltimore/London: The Johns Hopkins University Press.

Bergstrand, A., & Engelbrekt, L. (2016). To Deploy or Not Deploy a Parliamentary Army? German Strategic Culture and International Military Operations. In M. Britz, op.cit.

Britz, M. (Ed.). (2016). *European Participation in International Operations. The Role of Strategic Culture*. London: Palgrave Macmillan.

Dalgaard-Nielsen, A. (2006). *Germany, Pacifism and Peace Enforcement*. Manchester: Manchester University Press.

Longhurst, K. (2004). *Germany and the Use of Force: The Evolution of German Security Policy 1990–2003*. Manchester: Manchester University Press.

Major, C. (2015, March). *NATO's Strategic Adaptation: Germany Is the Backbone for the Alliance's Military Reorganisation* (SWP Comments 16). Berlin: Stiftung Wissenschaft und Politik.

Saxi, H. L. (forthcoming). British-German Defence and Security Relations After Brexit: *Quo vadis* the 'Silent Alliance?' In J. H. Matlary & R. Johnson (Eds.), *Britain's Defence Role*.

Simmons, K., et al. (2015). *NATO Publics Blame Russia for Ukrainian Crisis, but Reluctant to Provide Military Aid*. Washington, DC: Pew Research Center.

CHAPTER 7

Britain

Britain and France are the major military and strategic powers in Europe and beyond. They both have a global force posture, nuclear deterrent, and a permanent seat at the UN Security Council. They both want to continue to be able to deploy force internationally and are both engaged in military operations across the globe at almost all times. Both states are often leading ones in African operations and they are the central actors in NATO.

These states have the ambition to continue to be global actors and great powers. In order to manage to do this, they need military power that is commensurate with this role. This is increasingly expensive and both countries try to find ways to keep up their military capacities, *inter alia* through cooperation with each other. The so-called Lancaster House agreement of 2010 is intended to enable savings through cooperation as well as promote political cooperation on security and defence policy.

As I wrote in 2013, Britain has not lost a major war since 1776, when it lost its American colonies in the American War of Independence, and is concerned with force posture and position in the state system as well as with fighting abroad. Politically, Britain has traditionally faced threats from strong European powers, from Napoleonic France to modern Germany, and sought to balance powers on the Continent. There is still an

---

I draw on my chapter on Britain in my book *European Union Security Dynamics: In the New National Interest,* Palgrave Macmillan, UK, in the introduction to this chapter.

© The Author(s) 2018

J. H. Matlary, *Hard Power in Hard Times,*

https://doi.org/10.1007/978-3-319-76514-3_7

interest in such balancing, some argue, and Britain continues to see its interests as global before European.

As mentioned at the beginning of Chap. 6, the British parliament does not have any formal powers in the area of security and defence policy. The foreign policy prerogative obtains, and Parliament does not approve sending troops abroad and all details pertaining to deployment; however, as we have seen, Parliament's role is increasing in this field. Johnson notes that the public has been critical of recent military interventions, in particular in Iraq, but also in Afghanistan and Libya, and that public opinion grew more negative after the Chilcot inquiry, which investigated the government and Prime Minister Blair's role in supporting the US in Iraq.[1] The result, he argues, has been that although British forces are able to intervene and fight across globe, the 'willingness to do so had largely evaporated' in the wake of these wars. This is an important change away from the traditional support that British public opinion has generally entertained towards their military, which is captured in the social contract between people and the armed forces.

A 'covenant' exists between the people, the state, and the army which warrants quotation as it defines the role between the military and the people in a state with a strategic culture:

> Soldiers will be called upon to make personal sacrifices – including the ultimate sacrifice – in the service of the nation. In putting the needs of the nation and the army before their own, they forgo some of the rights enjoyed by those outside the armed forces. In return, British soldiers must always be able to expect fair treatment, to be valued and respected as individuals, and that they (and their families) will be sustained and rewarded by commensurate terms and conditions of service. This mutual obligation forms the military covenant between the nation, the army and each individual solider; an unbreakable common bond of identity, loyalty and responsibility that has sustained the army and its soldiers throughout history.

In Britain, there is still such a military culture that respects and supports the work of the soldier, although the government's choices in security and defence policy are increasingly distrusted by many in the public. Most deployments are uncontroversial, and Parliament takes little interest in and has few powers regarding security and defence policy. Nonetheless, British soldiers complain that there is less and less spontaneous support for what soldiers do, that there was a lack of gear and equipment in Afghanistan, and that the government fails to take proper care of war veterans. Gordon Brown, when prime minister, had to reiterate that it was in the 'British national interest' to be in Afghanistan.[2] Thus, an important issue is the growing concern that British strategic culture is changing. The public is thought to be war-weary after 13 years of participation in Afghanistan, Libya, and other international operations.

Goodman argues that there are significant changes to the role of the FPP in British decision-making on the use of force.[3] There is, however, not much evidence that the British public wants to scale down the role of their country in the world. Yet in contrast to France—which will be discussed in the next chapter—Britain is undergoing some change in its strategic culture at present. Johnson notes that there is more discussion about and discontent with the actual use of force in operations than before, and that the strategic ability of decision-makers is sometimes very poor. Even Conservative governments put the economy above defence, he argues, and the Chilcot inquiry on Iraq revealed a 'poor grasp of the design and execution of strategy'.[4] In addition, the current Labour party leader, Jeremy Corbyn, would like to dismantle large parts of the military, including the nuclear deterrent, were he to be elected, something which may happen given the weak May government and the divisive issue of Brexit. Another tendency is the pressure to make 'politically correct statements over hard choices', says Johnson.[5] Thus, the 'insulation' of unitary, quick, and, therefore, strategically relevant decision-making that we find in France is not quite replicated in Britain where one experiences some of the problems that characterize other more postmodern states, including rapidly changing public opinion, 'having to justify military decisions in civilian terms', increasing parliamentary power in the sector despite the existence of FPP, and so on, he argues. Britain is still a strategic power, but many examples from recent years underline that both Parliament and public will make new demands on decisions being made and operations under way. This may impinge on the government's ability to make the right decisions at the right time, he maintains.

Since 2010 Britain has had a National Security Council which meets frequently, advising the prime minister. In this connection, it is important to note the system of checks and balances enshrined in the British constitution allows for robustness in decision-making, as it ensures that discussions are held and that no one actor decides alone. The problem emerges when these actors are not informed by strategic needs, but rather by civilian issues and concerns.

In recent years, Britain experienced both a major reduction of its defence budget, as laid out in the 2010 Strategic Defence and Security Review (SDSR), and an increase in the same budget in 2015. The debate about the review in 2008 largely concerned two issues: the diminishing purchasing power of the defence budget and its implications for the two ongoing wars (Iraq and Afghanistan),[6] as well as the relationship between the army and the public.[7] Soldiers returning from deployment were experiencing negative reactions and were therefore encouraged to parade, to wear their uniform in public,[8] and to generally be visible in society. The conclusion of the British parliament's report on the 2010 SDSR was alarming: 'We have found little evidence of sustained strategic thinking or a clear mechanism for analysis and assessment. This leads to a culture of *fire-fighting* rather than long-term planning'[9] [my emphasis].

Operations are carried out as a reactive response to events, the report continues, without strategic plans. In fact, using force for 'direct political ends' outside of war and strategy may be useful, but the results are usually short-lived. Can one use war in anything but limited and decisive ways to achieve political goals? ask the parliamentarians rhetorically. A couple of indicators from the Transatlantic Trends study cited at the beginning of Chap. 6 are informative: In Britain, there is disagreement whether civilian capacities are better than military ones for preserving peace, while in France 70–80 per cent agree that military force is necessary. Being asked whether one should use military force only when the risk is small, 60 per cent of Britons disagree with this line of reasoning, whereas only 30 per cent of Germans disagree.

Regarding confidence in their armed forces, 81 per cent of Britons are 'a lot confident', while only 25 per cent of Germans and 63 per cent of French are the same. When asked about how international politics should be conducted, there was a very strong preference for civilian means in Germany, but not in Britain or France. The acceptance of risk was also markedly different between Britain and France, on the one hand, and Germany, on the other: Fear of casualties among their own forces, and conviction of the need to avoid these casualties, is three times higher in Germany than in the other two states. Finally, high-risk military ventures are accepted in Britain and France, but not in Germany.[10]

These figures suggest that the public supports the soldiers but remains cynical about the missions.[11] This lack of public support constitutes a major and growing problem because the public must understand why force is used, and basically approve of its use. The problem is thus not in the strategic military culture in Britain or in the public's lack of support for soldiers and the military profession, but in the political leadership and its lack of strategic insight and culture.

Another key problem in sustaining a strategic culture is economic, as mentioned above, and by the beginning of 2018 a furious debate on Britain's defence spending erupted where the head of the Army, General Sir Nick Carter, warned of Russia and said that Britain is increasingly unable to deter and defend itself.[12] But before the current review of spending cuts, which is ongoing, there were other rounds of cuts:

In recent years, the defence budget in Britain has seen several major cuts. The greatest drawdown in 50 years was announced in the SDSR of 2010, which reduced the budget by 8 per cent, 'leading to a 20–30 per cent reduction in the UK forces' operational ambition and deployable capability'.[13] Increases in the plan were confined to cyber and special forces. However, the 2015 SDSR brought changes. President Obama is said to have warned the British premier that Britain had to meet the 2 per cent NATO target, lest Britain 'set a bad example'.[14] Intense criticism of the planned British cuts was voiced in the US, and the status of Britain as that country's key ally was in jeopardy, it was said. The defence cuts amounted to a 'slow motion crash', says the director of Royal United Services Institute (RUSI), Professor Michael Clarke. The 2 per cent is highly symbolic, he pointed out, and the US spends 4.4 per cent of its GDP. That Britain now may dip below 2 per cent is therefore both a military and a political problem.[15] The need to cooperate with other states is therefore an imperative, not an elective. The 2010 Lancaster House agreement with France concerns both cost-cutting and strategy in terms of operational impact, as does the Joint Expeditionary Force (JEF) with North European states. But there are more national cuts discussed nonetheless, as buying power in the defence sector will diminish as a rule, given the cost of new technology. Even increases in nominal terms will therefore lead to less buying power. In late 2017 there was another budget problem that came to the fore: The MOD asked for an additional four billion pounds over a four year period in order to offset new cuts, as the budget assumes major saving through efficiency cuts which may not materialize, while the cost of replacing nuclear missiles is rising, in part due to the depreciation of the pound following the Brexit vote, something which has added another 178 billion pounds to the cost over a ten-year period.[16] There is a need to save two billion pounds per year, something which means cuts. The suggested cuts are two amphibious ships, 15 per cent of Royal Marines, and cuts to the army:

'The government had promised not to go lower than 82,000 soldiers, but the current figure is around 77,400, and the fears is that it could go as low as 60,000.'[17]

This situation is familiar in all European states: defence has few lobby groups and inevitably seems to suffer when budgets are decided on—schools, health, and infrastructure matter more than defence in peacetime. In addition, buying power is diminishing much faster in the defence sector than in the civilian sector because there is no real competition in the former. Also, as much procurement involves American-made equipment, so the price of the dollar has an immediate impact. All this means that the strategic ability of Britain suffers, as it cannot sustain its political ambitions on its own. As stated at the outset of this chapter, both France and Britain retain their global ambitions and want to have a global military reach, but both are under economic pressure. This can be 'solved' through military cooperation, or even integration, as exists in the Lancaster House agreement between the two states. Yet the more national ambition and national defence capability are out of step, the more national strategic ability will suffer. This is a general point that does not affect Britain critically for the moment, but which will become more important in the future. It is also of vital importance in Britain's so-called special relationship with the US, which is a demanding partner. When Britain almost 'dipped' below the 2 per cent goal in 2017, the US applied major pressure to hinder this.

British strategic culture at the *military* level does however not show any indication of changing. However, the political level shows little appetite for strategy. When Tony Blair was prime minister, the refrain was that British military power was a 'force for good' and humanitarian intervention. This position could easily be justified politically, carried little risk, and demanded little, if any, strategic thinking. Using force like a 'fire brigade' when violence was intolerable required only one political decision, whereas deterrence, coercion, and containment require clever strategy and risk willingness on the part of the government. The lack of these features has been amply criticized by British top brass. The publication *British Generals in Blair's Wars*[18] contains ample empirical illustrations of the points made above concerning the campaigns in Iraq and Afghanistan. The underlying theme and major conclusion of all the contributions in this volume is that the political leadership did not understand strategic thinking when deciding to use force. After hearing Prime Minister Blair talking about Iraq, an officer drily remarked: 'His statement is the strongest case I have heard for politicians to study military history'.[19]

Finally but importantly, Brexit will render Britain less able to influence continental developments in the EU, which is developing its defence role at present.[20] Although France clearly wants to retain its closeness to Britain as far as operations and strategic action are concerned, it will become the only European power which is at once a nuclear one, a member of the UNSC, and member of the EU—a point that has been underlined by President Macron.

The exit clause was activated by Prime Minister May in March 2017, and in the formal letter about this there was mention that security and defence might suffer as a result. A debate ensued in Britain: was this a veiled threat? After some time, the British position seemed to have been reversed regarding this position. May's Lancaster House speech on 17 January 2017 had emphasized the need for future cooperation, including in the area of security and defence, and in September the same year the emphasis in her much-quoted Florence speech was on cooperation and finding 'win-win' solutions with the EU. She offered a sum of 20 billion pounds as a 'down payment' before negotiations started and full cooperation on security and defence. A government White Paper entitled *Foreign Policy, defence and development: A future partnership paper* was issued.[21] The document sets out to discuss the contents of a British-EU partnership in detail. First, it is underlined that the EU and Britain share the same values, in addition to facing the same risks and threat. It is then pointed out that Britain currently has a leading role in European defence and security policy and that this will continue through, *inter alia*, 'strengthened bilateral relationships'.[22] Emphasis is also placed on the leading role of NATO in European security and defence. Nonetheless, Britain wants a 'deep and special partnership with the EU that goes beyond existing third country arrangements' (ibid.). The scope of this partnership is 'foreign policy, defence and development' or, in other words, all external relations.

The White Paper lists the British contributions to the EU's Common Foreign and Security Policy, and they are major ones: a commanding role in Operation *Atalanta*; a leading contributor to Operation *Sophia* and the training of the Libyan coast guard; key leadership roles in the EU Operation *Althea* and missions in Ukraine, Georgia, Kosovo, and Somalia; provision of operational HQs for EU battlegroups and the HQ at Northwood for an EU military exercise in 2017; provision of strategic airlift, including to the French-led Operation Barkhane in Mali, and so on.

The paper further discusses Britain's leading role in the defence industry and notes that the EU has launched a European Defence Action Plan (2016) which has led to the creation of a European Defence Fund (EDF) that will co-finance common defence projects. It goes on to list British assets in foreign and development policy, as well as to describe what this new and special partnership should look like:

This should be 'deeper' than any such relationship in existence. It is also meant to be 'unprecedented in its breadth, taking in cooperation on foreign policy, defence and security, and development, and in the degree of engagement [envisaged]'.[23] In particular, the EU and Britain should consult closely on foreign and security policy issues with the option to agree to joint positions on foreign policy issues.[24]

It is suggested that Britain work with the EU 'during mandate development and detailed operational planning'.[25] Further, Britain offers to work on the EU-NATO relationship where a clear division of work is of paramount importance, as 'NATO will continue to be the cornerstone of our security'.[26]

When it comes to defence industrial development, the paper suggests that Britain participate in the EDA and their projects, the Commission's EDF, the European Defence Research Programme, and the European Defence Industrial Programme. In short, the bid is for British participation to the fullest in all EU foreign, security, and defence policy. Here one may assume that France will be the key actor, and that it would want Britain to be a partner in this work inside the EU, but clearly Britain cannot act as if it were a member after Brexit.

At present, France is in many ways in a better position regarding strategic action than is Britain. In addition to the issues mentioned above—namely the increasing role of public opinion and Parliament in strategic decision-making and pressure on and cuts to the defence—there are the uncertainties posed by Brexit. Negotiations are set to begin in early 2018 after a protracted and fruitless period of nearly nine months in 2017 which brought no clarity on the modalities of these negotiations, a period during which Britain was clearly the weaker party. Nevertheless, in the area of security and defence, Britain remains a strong actor, whose cooperation the EU will need; but that fact did not seem to matter at all in the deliberations in Brussels in 2017. The truth is that both the EU and Britain need a 'win-win' result, but instead Britain has so far been forced to agree to EU demands, given May's weak mandate and the divided government and nation. My point is that if the EU had considered Britain's importance as the only other strategic actor in Europe beyond France, it would perhaps have seen the importance of reaching a 'win-win' solution. But that did not happen, and the conclusion can thus be made that strategic issues play only a small role in the EU, and that the Brexit negotiations may become very turbulent going forwards, which is likely to weaken British strategic autonomy.

In sum, Britain has retained its strategic and military culture, but this culture is under pressure from three sources: politicians who do not know much about strategy or care about its importance—thus letting parliament decide on the use of force; governments that refuse to fund defence properly; and public opinion that regards the recent operations as only somewhat successful, or even as fiascos. Britain's participation in Iraq became very problematic and is largely seen as a major mistake now; the deployments to Afghanistan led to many fallen and much questioning about effect; and finally, Libya was a military success but not a political one. The British public has become more engaged in questions about the use of force than before, and Parliament seems to have acquired a new role in decision-making in this policy at the expense of the FPP. In addition, the cost of defence is increasing but budgets are not. The 2 per cent GDP goal has been reached, but is under pressure.

THE BRITISH REACTION TO RUSSIAN REVISIONISM

Britain was notably absent from the political work on dealing with Russia after the annexation of Crimea. There was the run-up to the general election in 2015 which seemed to preoccupy all political energy at home. After the surprising victory, Prime Minister Cameron called for a referendum on EU membership in 2016, and again the country was fully occupied with a domestic political issue and voting process.

Criticism of Prime Minister Cameron mounted throughout 2014 and 2015. 'Where is Britain?' asked recently retired General and Deputy SACEUR Richard Shirreff as the events in Ukraine unfolded and President Hollande and Chancellor Merkel headed to Moscow to negotiate with President Putin on 6 February 2015. Their move came in response to American pressure to arm Ukraine in order to improve the country's bargaining position with Russia. This trip was undertaken by the two European leaders on their own initiative and the meeting with Putin lasted for five hours; however, nothing came of it. The main actor was Merkel, Hollande-in-tow, but the remarkable issue was the absence of Britain which traditionally plays a key role in all European security and defence matters. Its diplomacy is known as realist and very capable, and is sought after for this very reason.

Chancellor Merkel arrived at the Munich Security Conference the same weekend, straight from the talks with Putin, and intervened to say that more arms would only lead to more bloodshed and that negotiations must continue. Several key US Republican politicians like John McCain and Lindsay Graham characterized this stance as appeasement. 'Foolishness', said McCain, a term that recalled Chamberlain and the Munich Agreement with Hitler in 1938. But Britain's prime minister was absent here also, another remarkable fact.

It was surprising that the British prime minister did not join the duo that went to Moscow. In fact, Hollande was less likely a choice than Cameron as a partner to Merkel in this situation, although France's historical rapport with Russia perhaps meant that Hollande was in a better position to mediate with Putin. Yet this argument does not preclude Cameron's presence as well; one could even argue that a trio consisting of the leaders of all three major European powers would have made eminent sense and indeed strengthened the cause by showing Putin that there was full solidarity in the European camp. Even if Britain had been close to the position that was emerging in the US in favour of arming Ukraine, it would only have added weight to the negotiations. Indeed, the absence of Cameron in the delegation is strange and unusual for Britain, which prides itself in being in the lead in all matters of hard power, sometimes alongside France in their now longstanding bilateral cooperation.

This criticism was echoed by many in the military profession and in the press. 'Absent without leave' was how an editorial headline in *The Guardian* characterized Britain's status with regard to current events.[27] The complaint was that the prime minister was absent, not only in the Ukraine case, but also in the fight against Daesh. A parliamentary committee found that British contributions to the latter were 'strikingly modest'. Cameron was as stated absent from the Munich Security Conference in February 2015, where all the main politicians of the West were present, along with figures like Foreign Minister Lavrov from Russia. The 2015 edition of the conference was of particular importance given the Ukraine war, but Cameron 'avoided the challenge of Munich in favour of a Midlands marginal'.[28] The British leader's absence from the Ukraine talks and from the Munich conference is an indicator of Britain's reluctance to play its usual great power role at this time. The most likely explanation was

BRITAIN   185

that, Britain was facing a general election, and domestic politics trumps security policy, yet one should expect Britain to retain its strategic leadership role also at such a time.

It must be added that the then British Defence Secretary Michael Fallon 'compensated' for Cameron's absence at the rhetorical level in Munich, calling Putin a nineteenth-century tyrant who was acting in violation of all international rules. In an interview some days later, he also predicted that the Baltics would be Putin's next target, citing Putin's testing of NATO by flying bombers over the English Channel. The two sides were 'warming up' and NATO had to be ready to respond.[29] The tone of the interview—much more forward leaning than is usual for European leaders talking about this subject—might also have been calculated to meet the domestic criticism of inaction.

British criticism of government inaction grew in 2015. The *Economist*, whose analysis had been consistent throughout the Ukraine crisis, intensified its message in February 2015 with a cover announcing 'Putin's War with the West'. The accompanying editorial underscored that the Europeans had been naïve in their handling of the crisis. The lead article, entitled 'From cold war to hot war', diagnosed 'Russia's aim as a broad and dangerous confrontation with the West'.[30] The authors pointed to the high defence spending in Russia, quoting a security analysis firm's assertion that '[s]pending on defence and security is expected to climb by 30% this year and swallow more than a third of the federal budget'.[31]

The belated criticism of British passivity fanned out from military officers—mostly retired—to the wider public debate. The cuts in the defence budget in Britain, combined with its smallish contributions both to the Daesh operation and to the RAP, have led many to ask whether Britain should stop claiming a global role and stick to defending its own shores.[32] There is a debate simmering 'beneath the surface of British politics, but [it] has yet to graduate into a full-on national debate. It brings together [the country's] diplomatic stance, [its] future military capability and how [it sees itself] in the world. All those elements are currently in flux, in a way that could change the UK and its self-image forever.'[33] Col Robert Stewart, a former commander who is now a Conservative MP, even called on top officers to resign in protest over military spending cuts.[34]

The Times and other sources further reported that Downing Street had prevented the then Chief of Defence Staff (CHOD), General Sir Nicholas Houghton, from giving a talk in February 2015 for fear that he would criticize defence cuts. Such a move represents a very unusual and strong intervention by politicians.[35]

The Economist wrote that 'Britain's strategic ambition has diminished even more than its defence budget'.[36] Citing a recent poll on attitudes about defence, *The Telegraph* said that Britain has been 'little more than a backseat driver' in the Ukraine crisis despite the fact that two-thirds of the public want the country to remain a great power.[37] The general public retains its high trust in the armed forces and supports military action, albeit with some reservations. The newspaper also points to some positive factors: the British are in charge of the NATO reaction force, which will be deployable by 2017, and the joint projects in the bilateral French-British cooperation. Yet the major problem remains money—the procurement plans require growth of 1–2 per cent, not cuts.[38]

One commentator notes that 'despite the resurgent Russian threat … cutting the defence budget is considered a far greater priority than having adequate measures in place to guarantee our security'.[39] However, some signs of thinking anew about deterrence are evident in the army's top echelon: For example, by organizing a new 'Chindit' brigade that combines all the tools of hybrid warfare, General Sir Nick Carter, the head of the British army is promoting an emphasis on 'political warfare'. This new approach emphasizes 'psychological operations, deception, and media operations', and the new brigade is 'designed to help the army win non-kinetic battles in an age of internet warfare and cyber attacks'.[40]

Overall, however, the British reaction to Putin's moves in 2014 and 2015 was surprisingly passive. The British pride themselves in being a great power in world politics and they have a global military posture and a strong military and strategic culture. Yet in this case, the British political class seemed to be preoccupied with national elections to an almost alarming extent at the risk of neglecting international security concerns. Not only was the prime minister absent from the Munich Conference—in itself remarkable, as most other political leaders from Europe and the US were present—but he was also absent from the usual foreign policy troika in Europe in meetings and negotiations with Putin. It is strange indeed that Cameron 'let' the German-French duo deal with the Ukraine crisis together with President Obama.

The special relationship between Washington and London has always been most eagerly pursued by the British, and in this case the Americans played the role of 'bad cop' to the two European leaders' 'good cop'. Prior to the Minsk negotiations in the beginning of February, President Obama called Putin and was heavy-handed, which suggests there was a transatlantic strategy behind these negotiations. In light of this, it is all the more remarkable that Britain did not take part in the discussions in Minsk, if not only to give weight to the negotiations, but to bolster its own standing in international politics. The prestige factor is well-known in diplomacy; if two out of three great powers partake, the third ought to do so as well.[41]

If British political rhetoric has sometimes been tough on this issue in this period, and this it can be interpreted as compensatory and intended for domestic audiences, amounting to little more than a kind of 'symbolic politics'. When the foreign secretary slammed Putin at the Munich Conference and called him a nineteenth-century tyrant, it seemed like a rhetorical ploy to garner headlines. Similarly, his prediction that Putin would attack the Baltic states next rang a bit hollow—did he know something others didn't? It was almost a populist move, indicating frustration rather than strategic planning.

The public debate in Britain on Russia-Ukraine relations seems both late and sometimes uninformed. There are many examples of crying wolf, but the level of generality is a problem. There was a lack of informed discussion about issues like deterrence, and the complaints about Britain's absence at the decision-making table have been strong in terms of indignation but often weak in terms of analysis. Along with this, the debate about the defence budget lives a life of its own, seemingly unrelated to the return of inter-state rivalry in Europe.[42] Britain's lack of surveillance ability at sea after scrapping maritime patrol aircraft led to a need for allied help to hunt for a foreign submarine off Scotland. This in turn led to some consternation, but it is an isolated case.[43] Britain's initial reluctance to promote sanctions, the West's weapon of choice so far, was very possibly related to the major financial investments and actors from Russia in Britain. When the US decided on sanctions, Britain followed suit.

Paraphrasing Gibbon, an editorial in *The Times* entitled 'Decline and Fall'[44] argued that Britain's main ally, the US, needs to lead more: 'Greater resolution in foreign policy requires a lead from Britain's most important ally, the United States. Under President Obama, that is not forthcoming.'[45] Yet this argument ducks the issue of European leadership; now is supposedly the time for Europe to lead itself in its own region of the world. Yet as we have seen throughout this book, Europe has continually relied on the United States: US military assistance was sorely needed in the short and limited war in Libya; and when deterrence was on the table in Europe again, it was President Obama who had to go to the Baltic states to provide its political underpinnings.

The editorial has another point, unrelated to the quest for American leadership: 'Britain's role in the world has less to it than meets the eye'.[46] Downing Street defended itself against the criticism over its absence in the diplomacy related to Ukraine saying that it had been agreed long ago that Britain would not be present at these talks.[47] A House of Lords report on the handling of the crisis points out that Britain has a special responsibility to assist Ukraine since it is in fact a guarantor of the inviolability of its borders as one of the signatories to the 1994 Budapest Memorandum. However, '[t]he government has not been as active or as visible as it could have been', their conclusion reads.[48]

Late in February 2015, probably in response to his critics, Cameron announced that he would dispatch 75 military trainers to Ukraine. This was a most unstrategic move. First, it was militarily nonsensical: Ukraine needs weapons to fight separatists if any at all, not a handful of trainers who will be located far away from the battlefield, in the west of the country. Second, sending troops to Ukraine, albeit only 75 trainers, plays into the hands of Britain's strategic opponent. With the presence of British military personnel, Putin will have 'evidence' that NATO is an actor in Ukraine. While 75 trainers hardy comprises the 'NATO legion' of which Putin has spoken, the political spin possible regarding their presence is limitless. Cameron's decision was justly met with another barrage of criticism and discounted as a rather desperate move to make up for his lack of serious engagement in security policy. 'The problem of western engagement in Ukraine has been the problem of indifference, leaving it in limbo and allowing Putin to feel he can intervene to construct a sphere of influence', said David Clark, an expert on Russia.[49] The British move was echoed by the American decision to train four companies of the Ukrainian National Guard near the Polish border.

The problem with this type of military assistance is that it furnishes Russia with political ammunition while having no military impact on the civil war in Ukraine. It is a 'lose-lose' game for the West. Yet these kinds of interventions can placate a critical public that does not grasp the strategic game by showing that something is being done, even if that something is useless and even counter-productive. In the UK, the real issues were whether to stick to the 2 per cent of GDP target for the defence budget,[50] the national election, and the lack of a British role in Ukrainian high politics. In light of the actual issues, the deployment of 75 trainers looked like a pathetic attempt to distract attention from the main questions.

In conclusion, Britain has so far not been a leader in devising strategy for containing and deterring Russia, although it tried to 're-insert' itself after the general elections in May 2015. Leading up to the elections, however, the government chose a passive diplomatic role, to the point of not participating with Germany and France in the great power troika of Europe. One can speculate about why a national election should mean that international strategic leadership is a problem; it ought to be the opposite, that statesmen of international stature are celebrated and re-elected, but in Europe today this does not seem realistic. This insight, if it is true, is yet another indicator of the lack of a strategic culture in Europe as a general phenomenon.

Britain regained its 'normal' position in the latter part of 2015, and when it published its new Strategic Defence Review in December of that year, it was clear that it would meet the 2 per cent of GDP target for defence. Britain also opted to join France in the aerial bombing of Daesh after the terrorist attacks in November, thus underlining both the military importance of fighting that organization as well as continuing its own cooperation with France.

Further, after the referendum on Brexit Britain has played its customary key role in NATO, being a major actor on devising deterrence and leading the work on the Joint Expeditionary Force (JEF) that is to be ready for deployment in 2018. Britain also initiated the Northern Group with all countries of the north and has taken the lead role in dealing with Russia as of 2016 onwards. Also the 2015 Security and Defence Review brought back British defence spending to the 2 per cent level and agreed major procurement: 'The UK's latest security and defence review is more coherent and ambitious than the previous version.'[51] Keohane's conclusion is clear: 'the main political message of the new defence review is that Britain is back as a serious military power'.[52] This undoubtedly has a lot to do with a growing awareness of Russian military assertiveness. Yet as we have seen, defence cuts are again on the agenda.

In sum, by 2018 Britain plays the key role in Europe as the leading state in deterring Russia through NATO arrangements that involve coalitions of the willing, such as the JEF. Britain also has a battalion in the Enhanced Forward Presence (EFP) in the Baltics, comprising some 600 soldiers. There is also much more political attention to the problem of Russian revisionism now than in the election years 2015 and 2016, so this 'absence without leave' must be considered an *exception* to the usual leading role that Britain plays in Northern Europe.

BRITAIN ON MIGRATION AND TERRORISM

With regard to these two issues, the British have continued their usual policies. On terrorism, Britain has a longstanding leading role in fighting the IRA. The 30-year period when this was a national terror problem taught the British resilience and toughness as a general attitude that minimized the impact of terrorism. Islamist terrorism has been met with the same attitude, and by an excellent intelligence service that is a key actor close to the Americans and the French. On migration, Britain has its own policy, not being part of Schengen and EU policy. It can also police its own borders more easily than continental powers. Migration played a role in the Brexit debate, being conflated with the EU's internal market. In fighting Daesh in Iraq and Syria, Britain was after a while also a key actor along with France.

In sum, Britain is a leading actor in the fights against terrorism, both at home and abroad.

NOTES

1. Johnson, R. (2018, forthcoming), 'Britain's defence role after Brexit', Johnson. R. and Matlary, J.H. (eds) (2018) *Britain's Defence Role after Brexit: Coalitions and Partnerships*, forthcoming.
2. *The Guardian*, 16.06.2009, '230 more British Troops to be sent to Afghanistan'.
3. Goodman, op.cit.
4. Johnson, op.cit. p. 6.
5. Ibid., p. 6.
6. The top military leaders were openly critical of the government.
7. *Economist, The* (2007a). *Britain's neglected wars*, 18 August.
   Economist, The (2007b). *Military spending: Tarnished glories*, 8 December, p. 44.
8. This was not common practice in Britain for many years because of the IRA problem. Wearing uniform was too dangerous in light of the 'target value' of British military personnel.
9. Report, op.cit., p. 242.
10. Transatlantic Trends, op.cit., p. 158, table 38.
11. Strachan, Hew, vol. 51, no. 4, pp. 49–70, 'The Strategic Gap in British Defence Policy'.
12. 'They say that generals are always fighting the last war. This time blame lies with the politicians', Con Coughlin, *The Telegraph*, 23 January 2018.
13. See note 11.

14. 'Obama to Cameron: maintain UK defence spending or weaken NATO', *The Telegraph*, 12 February 2015, online.
15. 'The grim truth about our defence budget', *The Telegraph*, online, 11 February 2015.
16. 'Shoulder pips squeaking', *The Economist*, 9 December 2017, p. 35.
17. Ibid., p. 35.
18. *British Generals in Blair's Wars*, eds Jonathan Bailey, Richard Iron, and Hew Strachan, 2913, Ashgate Publishers, UK.
19. Ibid., Chapter 1 "Why we went to war and the mismatch between ways, ends, and means", by Jonathan Bailey, p. 26.
20. See Matlary, J. H. (2018) 'When Soft Power is not Enough: The EU's Military Ambition and Brexit', in Johnson, R. and Matlary, J.H. (eds) (2018) *Britain's Defence Role after Brexit: Coalitions and Partnerships*, forthcoming.
21. September 2017.
22. Ibid., p. 2.
23. Ibid., p. 18.
24. Ibid.
25. Ibid., p. 19.
26. Ibid.
27. *The Guardian*, online, 11 February 2015.
28. Ibid.
29. *The Telegraph*, online, 19 February 2015, 'Putin will target Baltic Next, Defence Secretary warns'.
30. The *Economist*, 14 February 2015.
31. Ibid., p. 12.
32. Dejevsky, M. 'Ukraine Crisis: Can the UK any longer aspire to a global role?' *The Independent*, 20 February 2015.
33. Ibid.
34. 'Col Bob Stewart: Defence chiefs should "resign over Army cuts"', *The Telegraph*, 4 March 2015, online.
35. *The Times*, Melanie Philips, 'A Feeble West emboldens the forces of chaos', 23 February 2015, online.
36. *The Economist*, 14 February 2015, 'Muscle Memory', p. 23.
37. 'Report on British Attitudes to Defence, Security, and the armed Forces', You Gov, 2015. See also 'Poll: The British People Still Back Combat Operations Abroad', *The Telegraph*, online, 8 December 2014.
38. 'Military spending cuts will leave UK vulnerable, says US commander', *The Telegraph*, 30 December 2014, online.
39. 'Was this the British army's last Hurrah?' Con Couglin, *The Telegraph*, 27 October 2014, online.
40. 'British army faces radical shakeup', *The Guardian*, 2 February 2015, online.

41. The importance of prestige is empirically evidenced in Davidson's study of why states contribute to international operations, see op.cit.
42. An exception is the article 'Armed forces cuts now look like a big mistake', editorial, *The Telegraph*, online, 23 February 2015. See also 'The British Army: cash-strapped, homeward bound, and looking for new roles', *The Guardian*, 25 June 2015, online, which conveys the needs to scale down on army size and capacities.
43. 'Britain forces to ask NATO to track "Russian submarine" in Scottish waters', Ben Farmer, defense correspondent, *The Telegraph*, 9 December 2014, online.
44. *The Times*, same title, 9 February 2015, online, see also R. Braithwaite's article in *The Independent*, 8 February 2015, online: 'Ukraine Crisis: If negotiations fail, there are few good choices', where he notes that 'Britain seems unengaged'.
45. Ibid.
46. Ibid.
47. *The Guardian*, 11 February 2015, online, 'David Cameron can influence events in Ukraine without racking up air miles'.
48. Ibid., p. 29, point 82.
49. 'UK Military training in Ukraine: symbolic move that risks Russian ire', *The Guardian*, 24 February 2015, online.
50. *The Times*, 'Osborne warns Cameron over blank cheque for the military', 25 February 2015.
51. 'Is Britain Back? The 2015 UK defense review', CSS, ETH Zürich, February 2015, by Daniel Keohane.
52. Ibid., p. 2.

REFERENCES

Johnson, R., & Matlary, J. H (Eds.). (2018). *Britain's Defence Role After Brexit: Coalitions and Partnerships*. UK: Palgrave Macmillan.

Matlary, J. H. (2018). When Soft Power Is Not Enough: The EU's Military Ambition and Brexit. In R. Johnson & J. H. Matlary (Eds.), *Britain's Defence Role After Brexit: Coalitions and Partnerships*, forthcoming.

Meyer, S. (2014a). *NATO's Post-Cold War Politics: The Changing Provision of Security*. Basingstoke/New York: Palgrave Macmillan.

Strachan, Hew. The Strategic Gap in British Defence Policy. *Survival, 51* (4), 49–70.

CHAPTER 8

France

Of all the states discussed here, France is the one where executive power is the strongest. As explained in the introduction to Chap. 6, unlike in Germany, in France there is no need for parliamentary approval of any aspect of sending troops abroad—including mandate, budget prior to deployment, ROE, or duration of the mission.

France, like Britain, is a great power with a global reach, but it faces difficulty in matching its ambition and its resources, just like British that again faced cuts to defence spending after the respite that the 2015 defence review gave.[1] France spends about 2 per cent of its GDP on defence, but still needs to cooperate with others, again like Britain. The two powers have a partnership dating from 2010, often referred to as the Lancaster House agreement.

France's actor capability is however formidable—the best of the three states in this study—because the president alone takes decisions on the use of force. He is assisted by a Security Council (*le conseil de défense restreint*) which nowadays meets several times a month and consists of the president, the prime minister, the defence and foreign ministers, and the minister of home affairs. The proceedings are secret and decisions are taken there. The duty of informing parliament of such decisions within three days was introduced by President Sarkozy, and parliament also has to sanction deployments if they last more than four months. But the real decision-making on hard power issues remains with the president and his very close and small circle of advisors.

© The Author(s) 2018
J. H. Matlary, *Hard Power in Hard Times*,
https://doi.org/10.1007/978-3-319-76514-3_8

The French decision-making system allows for strategic action. Hellmann writes that 'the French decision-making system with regard to defence and security issues is closed. On the one hand it is a system in which the military and the political spheres are kept distinct and where the military is forbidden to express political views ..., but on the other hand it is a system where the president consults with his military security advisors on a daily basis.'[2]

In my previous study of French strategic culture I wrote:

> The French constitution of 1958 places all power for foreign and security policy in the hands of the president. The French parliament is not involved in the ratification of defence treaties, military cooperation agreements, or any other treaty related to security matters. This is a very comfortable position for the president. He can simply make the decision himself, aided by his own advisers. The role of public opinion is equally unproblematic: it is mostly not able to play any role in presidential decisions.[3]

These conclusions hold today as well: Public opinion plays no role in decision-making, but may play a role once an operation is ongoing; yet in most cases it is very favourable public opinion. Thus, in the French case, the domestic political situation is entirely different from that of most other states, especially that of Germany; but as we have seen in the previous chapter, also in Britain public opinion matters in defence matters.

In 2013 a White Paper[4] on defence was published, serving as the basis for a new French defence plan (*Loi de la programmation militaire*). The publication of new White Papers generally occurs at long intervals in France, with previous ones being published in 1972, 1994, and 2008. The chairman of the commission for the 2013 White Paper on Defence and National Security Jean-Claude Mallet remarked that the key issue was to develop and solidify the European Security and Defence Policy (ESDP): 'France must take the lead in in the EU in defence matters.'[5] There is a continuous EU interest on the part of French security and defence actors, as we also shall see below. A speech by then Defence Minister Le Drian at the *Institut des hautes études de défense nationale* on 5 October 2012 outlined the French strategic vision of an EU that 'must become a producer of defence' and its own strategic mission based on the region around Europe, with particular attention to the Sahel.

The White Paper presented French strategic analysis and responses: among the threats we find instability in the MENA region and sub-Saharan

FRANCE   195

Africa and general instability in the world. The French response is listed in terms of strategic priorities: first, secure territory and nation, including overseas territories; second, guarantee European security; and third, stabilize the regions around Europe, especially the MENA region.[6]

There is major emphasis on the need for 'strategic autonomy', something which is assured through the French nuclear deterrent which remains a cornerstone of sovereignty in the French analysis. This *'force de frappe'* is regarded as a defensive and general deterrent, for which the French term is *dissuasion*, meaning to persuade someone not to do something. In addition to this deterrent, French analysis has it that a strong conventional military force is a condition for real independence and sovereignty. This is very different from the EU's traditional emphasis on 'soft power' and from Germany's view of sovereignty as something that is enhanced and even constituted by multilateral cooperation, and especially European integration. In sum, the 2013 White Paper contains a clear presentation of French strategy and its priorities, which are basically in the South, namely in the Maghreb, and relate to terrorism. The paper makes clear that France will not allow havens for terrorists in these areas. When France intervened in Mali in 2013, this was exactly how the strategy envisioned French forces would be used.

The election of Francois Hollande brought no visible change in strategic culture, but austerity affected defence. 'For much of the past three decades there has been a virtual consensus on defence issues across the French political divide.'[7] Economic austerity and not ideology will determine how France develops, he argues.

The French also cut their defence budget, but not as radically as Britain. The cut in 2013 was only 1 per cent, but in 2014 it was 7 per cent. The deployment of soldiers overseas, in particular in Africa, was reduced to only about 10,000. A flat nominal budget of €33 billion was established for the following next six years starting in 2014, implying a cut of 34,000 military jobs, of which 14,000 are in the expeditionary sector, although the nuclear deterrent and aircraft carriers were retained.

The Sahel was by that point seen as a 'strategic risk of prime importance' and Hollande said that 'France's destiny is to be a global nation' whose duty it is to 'guarantee not only [its] own security but that of [its] allies and partners'. France invested in aerial refuelling (12 new Airbus planes) and medium-altitude long-endurance drones.[8] The British ambassador to Paris Sir Peter Ricketts was on the defence commission of France that developed the White Paper, a sign of the close bilateral cooperation between the two countries.

In November 2017, another major strategic document was published: *Revue stratégique de défense et de sécurité nationale.*[9] The text is a detailed analysis of the threat and risk environment for France and a recommendation for a strategic response. As in the White Paper, there is an emphasis on the importance of the strategic deterrent—namely France's nuclear weapons which are sea-based and airborne.

In the preface, President Macron writes,

> *j'ai décidé le maintien de notre stratégie de dissuasion nucléaire et le renouvellement de ses deux composants: elles sont la garantie ultime de nos intérêts vitaux, de notre indépendance, et plus largement, de notre liberté de décision*[10] (I have decided on the continuation of our nuclear deterrent and to renew its two components, they are the ultimate guarantee of our vital interests, our independence, and in a wider perspective, of our freedom of decision-making—my translation).

This is very interesting from a strategic viewpoint: French doctrine is that strategic action requires the ability to act alone without depending on others. Unlike Britain, which depends on the US in terms of nuclear technology and always praises that so-called special relationship, the French have chosen a different security strategy since the time of President de Gaulle. One might say that they are independent in a way that neither Britain nor Germany can be.

While the 2017 strategic document continues the emphasis found in the earlier White Paper on the unruly neighbourhood, it places much more emphasis on terrorism as a major threat from the South, as well as on migration shocks. France's main strategic priority is to defend state and nation, and then to be able to respond to a crisis in the neighbourhood. Today such a crisis could affect France directly, and the MENA region is therefore more important than ever. France must be able to intervene militarily, alone if necessary. The type of crisis where this may happen is thus not only related to terrorism but can also be *'un conflit a forte dimension humanitaire et migratoire'* (a crisis with a heavy humanitarian and migratory component—my translation).[11] This is listed as the second priority in French strategy. Clearly mass migration, instability, and terrorism are seen as complex security problems that may call for military intervention.

FRANCE   197

Third, the review emphasizes the French spheres of influence, *zones d'intérêts*, where France has special responsibilities. These are the states and former colonies in the MENA region, such as Morocco, Lebanon, Tunisia, Jordan, Algeria, and Egypt, as well as defence partnerships in sub-Saharan Africa. In addition, there are partnerships with the UAE, Kuwait, and Qatar. '*Le golfe Arabo-Persique est ... un éspace stratégique éssentiel pour la France*'[12] (the Gulf is of special strategic interest to France—my translation).

This French strategic review is very logical and well-structured. Its point of departure is the need for so-called strategic autonomy, provided by the nuclear deterrent and a strong army in addition to a cohesive and patriotic *nation*. The review stresses the importance of national resilience and community, and tasks the armed forces with socializing citizens into such patriotism: '*La cohésion nationale et la résilience des fonctions éssentielles à la continuité de l'Etat comme à la vie de la Nation constituent le fondement indispensable de notre liberté d'action .... Dans ce domaine, les armées jouent un rôle de socialization*'[13] (National cohesion and resilience essential to the functioning of the state as well as the life of the nation make up the indispensable basis for our freedom of action ... in this area, the armed forces play a role of socialization—my translation).

France has a global reach and global interests, and will intervene on its own if need be when these interests are at stake. As we have seen, threats from the South—namely the MENA region—constitute the *second* priority in terms of such interests, after attacks on France itself. These threats include terrorism, migration, and insurgencies that can spill over to or threaten France. The *third* priority, as mentioned above, is the French areas of interest and protection in Africa and the Middle East. Thus, as the review clearly shows, the risks and threats from the South are the key ones for France, a position which is consistent with the 2013 White Paper and previous strategic documents. Northern Europe and Russia are much less discussed and only concern France to a small extent. The main strategic orientation is, not surprisingly, to the South.

The threats from this region have intensified over the last few years: Terrorism, with Daesh as the key actor; unruly states like Libya; and mass migration via Libya and other states in the Maghreb. France is and will want to remain the key military and political actor in this region. The review points to the importance of *geography*, which is another way of saying that geopolitics determines a country's strategic interests: '*la géographie continuera ainsi d'être un paramètre important dans la définition de*

*nos priorités ... Une partie des flux physiques (trafics, migrations illégales ...)
qui affectent notre sécurité sont eux aussi fonction de la géographie*[14]
(Geography continues to be an important parameter in defining our priorities ... physical flows—trafficking, migration, illegals—which affect our security are themselves also a function of geography—my translation). For geographic reasons, Russia is the key dimensioning factor in Northern Europe's strategic thinking. For the same reasons, the dangers from the South determine French strategic interests.

The review contains a significant analysis of the importance of the EU and European autonomy in defence. France wants to intensify the EU's work in this field, and describes the need for 'pragmatic' progress on this issue.[15] France is undoubtedly the leading actor in developing the EU's role in the security and defence field, as it always has been. President de Gaulle wanted European autonomy in hard security, and present-day French strategy uses the same language, referring to *'une autonomie stratégique européenne'*[16] (a strategic European autonomy—my translation). Being autonomous does not mean rivalling NATO, which is described as the key element of European security.[17] Yet France places serious weight on the defence clause of the Lisbon Treaty, Article 42.6, which it invoked after the terrorist attacks on Paris on 13 November, 2015. This little-known article is, in its wording, more stringent in terms of alliance obligations than NATO's Article 5 which plays the pre-eminent role in Western deterrence. It is unclear whether France wants the EU to develop a real defence union with a mutual defence guarantee, but it is remarkable that France invoked the former article and not the latter after it was attacked. The case is similar to the 9/11 attack on Manhattan which elicited NATO's activation of Article 5 the next day; however, the French opted to invoke the EU article instead.

France's plans for the EU, as articulated in the review, are however basically 'bottom-up' and voluntary. These include the new defence fund, Permanent Structured Cooperation (PESCO), and other initiatives, which will be discussed in Chap. 9 on the EU. But there is a keen insistence that the EU should develop an autonomous *strategic culture* and the EU's document on strategy, adopted in 2016, is recognized.[18] In the French strategic review there is however no suggestion of an integrated defence union, a 'top-down' type of creation, but rather a pragmatic approach that allows for individual participation in projects.

France does not want supranationality in EU defence, but rather, as we have seen, to preserve national strategic autonomy. At the same time, however, it wants much more streamlining of member states' defence policies in order to create a common actor capability in the EU. It is clear that France is pursuing the old vision of an EU that can act alone and take its own initiatives. In this vision, EU common action is important; but in this review France outlines and describes various partnerships that it pursues and does not challenge the primacy of NATO. Moreover, it underlines that the special partnership with Britain is vitally important, as Britain is the only other European state with a nuclear deterrent, a permanent seat on the UNSC, a global scope, and global interests. Further, the US remains a vital link, and there are other partners as well.

The key issue in this description is the criterion of military cooperation that France cites: '*Dans la nouvelle Europe qui se dessine, la France doit proposer des partenariats de défense ambitieux à ses partenaires, selon une logique différenciée, et en priorité aux pays européens* **volontaires** *et* **capables**' (In the new Europe that is being drawn up, France can propose ambitious partnerships with its partners according to a logic of differentiation, prioritizing European states that are **willing** and **able**—my translation and emphasis).[19] It is clear that France prefers to cooperate with states that bring strategic and military ability to the table along with interesting military capacities.

In terms of military procurement, the EU programmes provide a useful format, and France has developed detailed policy regarding what can be integrated and shared and what must be kept under national control. This is impressive, as few other states, if any, have such a clear view of what sovereignty requires in this age of economic pressure for military integration. A chart depicting French ambitions for technological and industrial cooperation shows four different categories—areas that require sovereign control; areas that involve cooperation with other states; areas in which there is 'mutual dependence'; and finally, areas that can be market-based—and classifies capabilities in all five domains of defence (land, air, sea, cyber, and space) into this matrix.[20]

From this analysis, it is very clear that the French place great value *on autonomous strategic ability*, both in terms of decision-making independence (from public opinion, parliament, and dependence on other states) and in terms of owning and controlling vital military capabilities. Moreover, France believes that their partners should match this strategic autonomy— be able to decide on the use of force quickly and for strategic reasons and have useful capabilities to bring to an operation. The review also presents a clear strategy for when France will intervene militarily, emphasizing the need to be able to act alone, as well as a section on the need to be first, or *'entrer en premier'*, including utilizing the momentum of surprise, attacking the centre of gravity of the enemy, achieving air dominance in the first phase of combat, and so forth.[21] These are classical operational considerations that play a part in any military strategy but which are not often discussed in Western strategic documents.

Yves Boyer writes that 'strategy is deeply embedded in the power of the French state'[22] He continues: 'In the military domains the French defence organization … has been purposely organized to be efficient and to maintain the coherence of the French defence posture.' The president decides to send troops, and 'in "small" operations in Africa, Parliament is seldom consulted'. He adds that 'nuclear deterrence has become the central and structuring element of French defence policy … Paris is determined to retain a robust nuclear posture, still benefitting internally from a large political consensus'.[23] The aims of deterrence are to deter any attack on French national interest and to have complete autonomy strategically, 'to guarantee the ability of a limited nuclear warning shot against any adversary who may misread the delineation of French vital interest'. And thus[24] France retains the right to strike against an existential threat as well as to deter with its nuclear weapons.

In other words, there is a clear military and firm strategic culture in France.

The French Reaction to Russian Revisionism

We might expect France to play a leading strategic role with regard to Russian revisionism, but this has not been the case. When President Hollande used force in Mali in 2013, his low ratings at home changed for the better. The same happened to former President Sarkozy when he started the Libya campaign in 2011. France is a country where people are proud of their great power status and take for granted that military power must support such a role in world affairs. Retaining France's *grandeur* was already a key concern for de Gaulle, as it has been for every French president since.

Thus, it would be logical to predict that France would take the lead in dealing with Russia. Yet in the strategic review just discussed, there is hardly any mention of Russian revisionism. There is only the admonition that a strategic response to Russia based on both deterrence and dialogue is needed, and that NATO, including the French participation in the EFP in the Baltic region, is the key actor in this respect. The lack of discussion of Russia as a specific security and defence risk in Europe is noteworthy.

France has a strong and longstanding close relationship with Russia; the two states share(d)[25] not only the ideas of the French Enlightenment, which were imported to Russia in the eighteenth century, but also an interest in a multipolar world order. Despite this history, France, along with the rest of the West, did not develop strategic relations with Russia after the Cold War, something which was a major mistake according to Heisbourg.[26]

Writing on France's Russia policy in 2007, Thomas Gomert states that 'Russia is a strategic partner that is vital to [then President Jacques Chirac's] vision of ... a multipolar world where power is shared' and Russia is 'an unpredictable but unavoidable partner'.[27] Yet the more democracy's values are undermined in Russia, the harder it is for France to maintain this relationship. Writing this time in 2014, Gomert argues that '*Poutine est davantage dans une logique d'esacalade que de provocation ... son durcissement de ton s'accompagne, sur le terrain, d'un deploiement des forces militaires russes*'[28] (Putin behaves provocatively and escalates ... his tough tone is accompanied by the use of force—my translation).[29] Thus, Russia increasingly behaves in way that makes it very difficult for France to act together with Russia as a partner.

France only entered into NATO's military structure in 2009, but its presence since has been very much appreciated, and French generals lead and have led the Allied Command Transformation (ACT), the second highest post after Supreme Allied Commander in Europe (SACEUR). French military contributions are key in all UN and NATO operations, and France has cut its defence budget less than Britain. Yet because of France's traditional close relationship and strong economic ties with Russia, this new role in NATO has created tensions in both Franco-Russian and Franco-European relations. During the Cold War, France tried to play the role of the third way, or *la troisième voie*—a partner in the middle between the two superpowers.[30] When German reunification became possible after the Cold War, President Mitterrand even tried to stop it, as it would undermine the balance of power in Europe, a belief shared by Prime Minister Thatcher. At the time, it was unclear how the security architecture of Europe would develop, and Mitterrand proposed a great power organization that would include Russia, like in the 1915 Congress of Vienna and later Yalta. The point I make is that Russia's inclusion in the European architecture as a great power is not without historical precedent.

This is the Russian policy plan as well, as discussed in Chap. 2. France was also sceptical of EU enlargement to the East, and the eastern states were adamant that Russia must not be included in the security arrangements in Europe. As events unfolded, the French view lost to Eastern enlargement of both the EU and NATO. As we recall, France was not central to NATO's decision-making at this time, being outside the integrated military structure.

As we will remember from Chap. 2, the French played a key mediating role in the Russo-Georgian war in 2008. At that time, both NATO and the US retreated from playing any role when Russia used hard power, instead asking Nicolas Sarkozy, who was at that time serving as EU president, to find a solution. On the whole, this represented a defeat for both NATO and, especially, for the US, which had pioneered the idea that Ukraine and Georgia should join NATO without the obvious strategic consideration that such an act would entail Article 5 obligations. The French mediation resulted in the successful Russian retreat of forces and cessation of hostilities, but also in permission for the Russians to 'transform their military gains into political ones, as the final agreement did not insist on the territorial integrity of Georgia'.[31]

France's 2011 decision to sell warships (helicopter carriers) to Russia was heavily criticized in NATO. Nevertheless, France decided to go ahead with the €1.4 billion contract, which secured more than 1000 shipyard jobs in Saint-Nazaire—an important move in a country with very high unemployment and major economic problems. Once the Ukraine crisis erupted, however, the contract came under renewed and much heavier criticism. The US and other allies asked France to postpone or cancel delivery of the first warship, the *Vladivostok*, but France resisted. Only later in 2014, when it became clear that the fighting in Ukraine would continue, did France yield: 'After resisting months of pressure from the US and European allies to suspend an arms deal to sell sophisticated warships to Russia, France has finally taken a step in the right direction', reads one editorial.[32] This did not happen without much infighting, however. Four hundred Russian officers and sailors were already in Saint-Nazaire for training when the decision was made in November 2014 to postpone the handover.

When French Defence Minister Le Drian announced at press conference some weeks later that the Mistral class warships might never be delivered, Russian Foreign Minister Lavrov replied angrily that France had to fulfil its obligations.[33] Eventually France paid reparations to Russia and the two ships were sold to Egypt.

Overall, the French were very reluctant to back out of their deal with Russia and originally only postponed delivery of the first ship. However, they faced heavy and sustained criticism from the US and Germany—criticism that no doubt carries more weight now that France's position in NATO has become an important issue in French security and defence policy. As Putin's policies on Ukraine got ever more aggressive and as the EU, including France, levied sanctions, it simply became impossible to go forward with the delivery of warships to Russia. The decision not to sell the ships to Russia was not the result of French strategy, but rather of French capitulation to pressure from its Western allies.

A similar case is that of the petroleum industry, where Russia is of key importance for French oil companies. When the sanctions were launched, the Head of Total Christophe de Margerie flew to Moscow to personally assure President Putin that he and his company were against the sanctions. As he was leaving, his private plane was mowed down by a snow-plough machine at the airport, tragically killing him along with the crew. Some weeks later, his replacement as CEO repeated the same message during a visit to Norway, underlining that the French president fully supported the continuation of normal trade and business with Russia in the petroleum sector. Here we see how important business interests are, and not only to France: they also played a countervailing role to security concerns in Britain and Germany. In France, however, they seemed to dictate the policy response. In addition it should be recalled that Ukraine and Russia are not among France's key strategic priorities. Its priorities lie to the South and relate to failed states, terrorism, and broader policies in the Middle East and Africa encompassing Mali, Chad, Burkina Faso, CAR, Daesh, Iran, and Libya. Only after these areas have been addressed is France concerned with Ukraine.[34]

The French reaction to the Ukraine crisis should thus be understood as a consequence of both France's longstanding strategic relationship with Russia and the fact that its strategic priorities lay elsewhere. To these factors must be added very substantial trade interests, including in the arms sector. The fact that France contracted with Russia in 2011, before the current crisis, to build the warships discussed above shows that it considered its relationship with Russia at the time to be that of a normal partner, not of a potential adversary. When this position became untenable, and indeed incompatible, with both full NATO membership and EU membership, France had to postpone delivery of the ships. The contrast between selling arms to Russia and boycotting Russia was too glaring at that point.

It was only in the late days of the crisis that President Hollande became an actor on the international stage along with Chancellor Merkel. No French politician held keynote addresses about how to handle the strategic challenge posed by Russia, either at Munich or elsewhere. Hollande seemed to play a minor role in support of Chancellor Merkel. France, with its impressive military and strategic culture, opted for silent cooperation with Russian business interests for as long as possible and was reluctant to accept that Russia had become an adversary. The French led in Libya and Mali, but their strategic interest in Russian partnership remained constant throughout much of 2014 and 2015. President Hollande is even said to have stated that Ukraine should never join NATO. This is probably not an expression of appeasement but of French strategic thinking about Russia which is based on *Realpolitik* and a model of multipolarity which has been favoured by France since WWII.

France could have played the key role with regard to Russia in the Ukraine case. It had a unique historical relationship with Russia in the area of security policy, which Germany lacked. Germany was and is the key trade partner with Russia, but its *Ostpolitik* is economic and diplomatic. France, however, could have developed a strategic plan for the European-Russian relationship. Yet France opted not to play such a role. This is not because France is unused to strategic thinking or planning; it is a choice based on French strategic interests. France wanted to trade in weapons with Russia, only reluctantly giving up the delivery of the Mistral ships, and continued to work with Russia in the fight against Daesh, as seen below. Rieker writes that while France needed Russia's cooperation in the Middle East, and thus wanted to balance between Russia and NATO for as long as possible, it gradually became necessary for France to criticize Russia on alleged violations of the Geneva conventions regarding the siege of Aleppo.[35] She notes that the relationship between Russia and France deteriorated significantly beginning in 2014, even though the National Assembly adopted a resolution to drop the EU sanctions on Russia in 2016. The president decided to ignore this recommendation and also to cancel the Mistral ships. One must assume that it was impossible to maintain a type of third way after Russia annexed Crimea and instigated fighting in Ukraine because France is fully a member of NATO.

Russia and France were both attacked by terrorists belonging to Daesh or similar groups: In 2016 a Russian plane with tourists from Sharm-el-Sheikh exploded in mid-air killing everyone onboard, while France was attacked several times at home. France thus had common cause with Russia in fighting Daesh, but Russia's intervention on the side of Assad in Syria constituted a major problem. France was in line with the rest of the West in wanting Assad to leave and siding with the opposition; Russia, on the contrary, supported Assad and helped him prevail militarily. In doing so, Russia also received a lot of criticism from the West, including from President Hollande, over alleged violations of humanitarian law in the bombing of Aleppo. During the autumn of 2016, for example, when President Putin was invited to open a Russian cultural centre in Paris, Putin cancelled the visit on short notice in response to criticism of Russian bombing in Syria. When President Macron was installed in 2017, he invited Putin to Paris, but was very firm with him on the alleged Russian interference in the election campaign that had just ended. Hacked material from the campaign of Macron's party, *En marche!* had been published, and Russia was ostensibly behind this.

To some extent there are differences in interest between France and the rest of NATO with regard to Russia, but Russia's revisionism and its decision to side with Assad in Syria have made it impossible for France to continue its 'third way' and try to include Russia as a key partner in a European security architecture arrangement. France's commitment to NATO and Western values has become very clear in the last few years. Its key role in the EU also implies that it promotes liberal democracy and is open to enlargement to the East.

France on Migration and Terrorism

When Paris was attacked by Daesh terrorists on Friday, 13 November 2015, the reaction was a response to a declarant of war (*'une acte de guerre'*), to quote President Hollande. The subsequent air attacks on Syria brought France closer to Russia, which had also been the object of a major attack when a civilian airliner full of Russian tourists was blown up leaving Egypt. Russia and France coordinated their aerial bombardments and appeared to be leading partners in the fight against the terrorist organization.

France notably did not turn to NATO and invoke Article 5 as it could have done in such a serious situation; instead, it preferred to turn to a rather dormant and certainly unused paragraph in the EU's Lisbon Treaty,

Article 42,6, which calls for solidarity. With this choice, France retained its freedom to shape a coalition of the willing, which it could lead itself, while pointing out that the EU ought to act as a security organization (which it did not). In any case, France opted out of participating in a common NATO response to the Daesh attacks, thereby allowing for closer coordination with Russia. This is consistent with French strategy.

France's reaction with an 'act of war' is similar to the American reaction after 9/11: both states saw the attacks as attacks on the state and the nation and responded with hard power. Treating terrorism on this scale as war, as France did, was something many European states had criticized the Americans for doing—wasn't this a police matter? The French answer to this question was as 'tough' as the American one had been: this was war. And in the case of France, it also meant the introduction of a state of emergency which lasted until the end of 2017, when a new anti-terrorism law allowing extraordinary measures for police and military was created, thus changing the role of the hard power institutions in French politics permanently. The French response to terrorism has thus been very resolute and very much based on making hard power effective. Not only *gendarmes*, but also soldiers were deployed all over France in order to stop terrorists.

The French response to terrorism also extended beyond its borders, involving military action against Daesh and other groups in the Maghreb. At the NATO Cardiff summit, the US assembled a coalition for fighting Daesh, which both France and Britain joined. They contributed more than 1000 troops each, deploying combat aircraft, and providing materiel, as well as intelligence and mentoring.[36] Saxi notes that 'British and French pilots have flown 3–4,000 sorties and carried out hundreds of airstrikes against IS targets. In 2015 and 2016, France also temporarily reinforced the coalition with its carrier strike group, led by the aircraft carrier *Charles de Gaulle* embarking 24 *Rafael M* combat aircraft. British and French ground troops have trained Iraqi and Syrian forces.'[37] This response goes to show that France is fully committed to fighting Daesh militarily.

France also led in the use of military power against terrorists in other theatres in MENA. As foreign-trained terrorists entered France and attacked there, France went after them at home, as it were. The 'intervention in Mali must be recognized as an important part of France's new counterterrorism approach abroad', Rieker notes.[38] She adds that invoking the term 'war' in relation to terrorist attacks has legitimized not only a state of emergency lasting almost two years at home and new counterterrorism legislation, but also new military interventions against terrorists abroad.[39]

But also in other theatres in the MENA France did lead in the use of military power against terrorists. As foreign-trained terrorists entered France and attacked there, France went after them at home, as it were. The 'intervention in Mali must be recognized as an important part of France's new counterterrorism approach abroad', Rieker notes.[40]

France has a long history of being a target of terrorism. The Islamists of Algeria, named GIA (*groupes islamistes armes*) that emerged during the civil war there in 1992 declared jihad on France and abducted and killed French diplomats and politicians, hitting in France as well as in Algeria. Rieker recounts that France was attacked by 13 terror plots between 1994 and 1996.[41] Prior to this other Islamic terrorism had hit the country, and France was early among Western states in forging a strategy for domestic security with a 'whole-of-government' approach and also made deals with regimes in North Africa and the Middle East.

In the present period France has been able to detect several planned attacks and has developed counterterrorism strategies that allow for swift action and extensive powers for magistrates and police. There is also a French insistence that border control and EU anti-terrorism measures need to improve very much: France gives 'primacy to hard security practices', Rieker writes.[42] The EU is seen as unable to deal with hard security issues and 'priority has generally been given to national measures and intergovernmental cooperation and less to a transfer of sovereignty to the EU in this area. These measures have also been predominantly in the area of hard security, such as strengthening the capacities of the police and intelligence services.'[43]

The French are the leading actors in military interventions in both the Maghreb and sub-Saharan Africa. There were more than 19 interventions from 1960 to 1995, and in 2015 there were more than 7000 soldiers stationed in Africa. 3500 were in the Sahel, 900 in CAR (Central African Republic) and the rest in various other operations.[44] In 2012 the Islamists took charge of Northern Mali and then President Hollande launched an operation, *Serval,* to take back the North. This was a counterterrorism operation as France had been hit by Islamist terrorism and regarded this as the key strategic challenge. While seeking UN approval and acting on the invitation of the government of Mali, France was the undoubted leader. The EU has become involved as a result of the French asking with a small training force (EUTM Mali), the UN operation MINUSMA is of greater importance.

This operation is a major one in several respects: The US is greatly appreciative of it, it has UN backing and an accompanying UN force, and it is well received in Africa as being very helpful in fighting Islamists. As mentioned, operation *Serval* ended in 2015, to be replaced by Operation *Barkhane* with all of the Sahel as the area of action. This operation consists of a 3000-soldier strong HQ in Chad and a regional base in Mali. There are five former colonies involved, all in the Sahel: Burkina Faso, Chad, Mali, Mauretania, and Niger. In addition, Gabon in affected as a key former colony with a large expatriate French population. Rieker concludes that 'The French strategy in Mali worked well, by denying the Jihadists a safe haven from which to organize ... but it was not successful in preventing further attacks in France ... recent attacks have all shown that France is particularly vulnerable to foreign fighter. That also explains the French willingness to engage beyond Africa and the Sahel region.'[45]

The fight against Daesh has been a key one for France. It was an early actor in Syria, recognizing the opposition as the formal government in 2012, and it was the only country ready to strike at Assad after the regime used chemical weapons in 2013—but as we recall, neither President Obama or Prime Minister Cameron decided on such use. France was also a leading force in organizing the fight against Daesh in Iraq, organizing a conference to this end in Paris in 2014, and participating in the US-led coalition in Northern Iraq, Operation *Chammal*. The French also fought inside Syria and have operating bases in Jordan and the Emirates. The French announced a lead role in the coalition and explored possibilities of cooperating more with Russia in this, but as we noted above, Russian support for Assad implied a distancing of the French-Russian relationship, as did Russian bombing practices in Aleppo.

'French leaders today seem to have become far more militaristic in their approach to counter-terrorism', notes Rieker,[46] pointing out that they used to criticize the Americans for calling this a 'war on terror'. Now the French are like the Americans, she argues—declaring that they are at war with Islamic terrorism, making laws that provide far-reaching mandates to hard security actors, deploying the military inside the country to fight terrorists, and being the leading military actor in the near abroad in this fight. Interestingly this change of policy has also meant closer cooperation with the US, and 'practical cooperation at the level of the military and intelligence has been strengthened since 2001'.[47]

In sum, France remains a clear strategic actor, but its strategic interests are not the same as those of Britain. France is the leading actor in international operations in Africa, both in the Maghreb and in the Sahel, and has a military culture of risk-taking and audacity.

NOTES

1. 'We can't afford to rule the waves anymore', 12 January 2018, *The Times*.
2. Hellmann, M. (2016) 'Assuming great power responsibility: French strategic culture and international military operations', in Britz et al., op.cit., p. 27.
3. Excerpt from the chapter on France in my book *European Union Security Dynamics: In the NEW National Interest*, Palgrave, 2013, UK.
4. *Livre blanc défense et sécurité nationale 2013*, Direction de l'information légale et administrative, Paris, 2013.
5. '...*la France devait mener de front la relance de l'Union européenne en matière de la défense*.'
6. Livre blanc, Chapters 3 and 4.
7. Boyer, p. 96.
8. French strategic defence review published on 29 April 2013; article in *The Economist*, 4 May, p. 33.
9. This document, which was ordered by the new President Macron is shorter than the White Paper, but it presents an updated view of threats and risk.
10. Preface, p. 6: 'I have decided to continue and to renew both parts of our nuclear deterrent; it is the ultimate guarantee of our vital interests, our independence, and more broadly, our freedom to make decisions.'
11. Ibid., p. 53, number 152, 'a strong conflict regarding humanitarian and migratory issues'.
12. Ibid., p. 64, number 210, 'the Gulf is an essential strategic area for France'.
13. Ibid., numbers 173 and 175, pp. 56–57 ('national cohesion and resilience in the fundamental functions of the state and nation constitute the indispensable basis for our freedom of action ... the armed forces play a socializing role here').
14. Ibid., p. 55, number 167 (Geography continues to be an important parameter in determining our priorities.)
15. Ibid., p. 59–60, numbers 185–189.
16. Ibid., see heading on p. 58: '*La construction d'une autonomie stratégique européenne*.'
17. Ibid., p. 60.
18. 'Shared Vision, Common Action: A Stronger Europe: Global action for the EU's Common Foreign and Security Policy', EU Commission, adopted by the member states in June 2016.

19. Ibid., p. 63: 'In the new security architecture that is developing France will propose various formats for integration to various states according to the criterion of the "willing and able."'
20. Ibid., p. 69.
21. Ibid., p. 82, 'Entrer en premier'.
22. Boyer, 2013, "France: The State with Strategic Vision", p. 143.
23. Ibid., p. 149.
24. Ibid., p. 149.
25. These ideas were firmly suppressed by the Russian Revolution and have not been resurrected thereafter.
26. François Heisbourg, 'Preserving post-Cold War Europe', *Survival*, vol. 57, no. 1, pp. 31–48.
27. Gomart, op.cit., p. 147.
28. Les Echos, online, 'La violence des propos de Poutine soude les Européens', 17 November 2014.
29. Ibid., 'Putin is more in a logic of escalation than of provocation … the hardening of his tone is accompanied on the ground by the deployment of Russian military forces.'
30. Rieker, P. (2017) *French Foreign Policy in a Changing World: practising grandeur*, Palgrave Macmillan, UK, p. 61.
31. Rieker, op.cit., p. 71.
32. *NYT*, 6–7 November 2014, 'A Wise Delay on Warships'.
33. *NYT*, 'France says Russia may never receive two warships', p. 3, 6–7.12.2014.
34. French strategic defence review published on 29 April 2013, conversations with experts on French strategy, 2–3.2.2015.
35. Rieker, p. 75.
36. The International Institute for Strategic Studies, *The Military Balance 2017* (London: Routledge for The International Institute for Strategic Studies, 2015). 304–306.
37. Saxi, Håkon L, op.cit., p. 13.
38. Rieker, op.cit, p. 145.
39. Op.cit., p. 146.
40. Rieker, op.cit, p. 145.
41. Op.cit., p. 137.
42. Op.cit., p. 142.
43. Op.cit., p. 145.
44. Op.cit., p. 52.
45. Ibid., p. 149.
46. Ibid., p. 151.
47. Ibid., p. 152.

REFERENCES

Boyer, Y., "France: The State with Strategic Vision", pp. 141–160,in Matlary, J. H. and Petersson, M., 2013, *Nato's European Allies: Miltiary capability and Political Will*, Palgrave Macmillan.

Direction de l'information légale et administrative. (2013). *Livre blanc défense et sécurité nationale*. Paris: Direction de l'information légale et administrative.

EU Commission. (2016). *Shared Vision, Common Action: A Stronger Europe: Global Action for the EU's Common Foreign and Security Policy*. EU Commission, Adopted by the Member States in June 2016.

Faure, S. (2018, forthcoming). La Cooperation franco-britainnique malgre le Brexit. les deux roles du Royaume-Uni. ler premier role militaire et 'en meme temps' un second role industriel. In J. H. Matlary & R. Johnson (Eds.), *Britain's Defence Role in the Age of Brexit: Coalitions and Partnerships*. Basingstoke: Palgrave Macmillan.

French strategic review, 23rd November 2013.

Hellmann, M. (2016). Assuming Great Power Responsibility: French Strategic Culture and International Military Operations. In Britz et al., op.cit.

Rieker, P. (2017). *French Foreign Policy in a Changing World: Practising Grandeur*. Cham: Palgrave Macmillan.

CHAPTER 9

The EU: 'Soft Power Is Not Enough'

At the outset, it is useful to make clear that the EU and NATO—which will be discussed in the next chapter—are, for the most part, not actors in their own right in all but a few policy areas. The EU has supranational powers in monetary policy and it can be argued that the EU Commission and the European Court of Justice (ECJ) are supranational actors regarding market policy and justice and home affairs because decisions are made by majority voting in these policy areas. But neither organization has supranational powers in the field of security and defence, apart from the event that NATO's council would declare an Article 5 situation, something which would require unanimity. But even then, member states have considerable freedom in deciding whether they can meaningfully contribute to an Article 5 operation.

The EU is largely intergovernmental in this area, as I have shown in my book on French-British leadership in the establishment of the battlegroups and the EDA.[1] This means that the EU by and large has an arena function and not an actor function in security and defence policy. This is also the case when it comes to economic sanctions: all 28 states must agree to them. But the EU institutional assets play a role nonetheless—agenda-setting or framing of a policy proposal, timing of decisions, and so on. Decision-*shaping* is not decision-*making*, but that does not rob it of

---

Commission President Juncker said this in a speech in 2016 in connection with the launching of an EU strategic document.

© The Author(s) 2018
J. H. Matlary, *Hard Power in Hard Times,*
https://doi.org/10.1007/978-3-319-76514-3_9

213

political importance. Moreover, even great powers do not act alone in a case like Russia-Ukraine; they act in concert and/or through IOs. It is therefore necessary to study both the IO and the states that make use of it in order to understand the political dynamics of the European response to external shocks.

With regard to NATO, there is no formal supranationality, but the integrated command structure matters very much for actual military operability. Moreover, the role of the US is of paramount importance. NATO is dependent on unanimity for it decisions, but some actors are much more important than others. In a recent study of NATO's bureaucracy, Mayer concludes that 'treaty-based IOs do remain vital sources of legitimacy and valuable tools for coordinating multilateral operations. [This is] in agreement with Matlary who contends that post–Cold War NATO has been transformed into a rather loose, yet useful and legitimacy-providing arena for risk-willing members and partners.'[2] We can therefore speak of NATO as a platform for coalitions of the willing and able, with the US as the pivotal actor. The US covers more than 70 per cent of the total defence cost in NATO.

Member states in both organizations own the military assets and therefore wield major influence over their deployment and terms of use. Operations typically revolve around one major leading actor, such as the US, Britain, or France, supported by smaller states; and apart from International Assistance and Stabiliation Force Afghanistan (ISAF) in Afghanistan, no NATO operation has contributions from all member states. It thus makes sense to study how major state actors design policy and *use* these two IOs as arenas, with the caveat that they both possess key institutional assets. The main actors are, however, the major states.

Let us now look at the EU and the question of whether or not it has a strategic culture.

The EU: Crisis Management and 'Force for Good'

Former British Prime Minister Tony Blair often said that the military tool should be a 'force for good', but his Iraq experience ended in electoral loss and a major government inquiry into the problems this invasion presented for British politics. Blair's expression 'a force for good' is also found in the EU's 2003 Security Strategy, the only one that the organization had issued until 2016, when it published its latest strategy, which is analysed below.[3]

Since 1990, the military has not been deployed in defence of existential survival in Europe, but ostensibly in defence of values such as democracy, rule of law, and human rights. This is what allowed the EU, as a 'post-national' organization, to develop a security role—as it did between 1998 and roughly 2006. The idea that emerged in the 1990s that humanitarian intervention is a right and duty put the emphasis on human security rather than state security. The EU as a law—and the norms-based international actor—seems well positioned to achieve legitimacy in this policy field. By definition an IO cannot pursue 'national interests' and defend its territory—these are the key duties and privileges of states.

The key to understanding the EU's role as a strategic actor lies in this use of military force and in its justification, aptly captured in Blair's remark. The question with regard to the EU is whether the 'soft model of hard power' is possible at all. The EU has been somewhat successful in structuring the new democracies of the East through political conditionality, with either membership or close trade and cooperation agreements as the incentive. But this is different from threatening the use of force as a deterrent strategy or applying coercion, let alone deploying forces to fight in sharp operations.

In terms of actually deploying force, the EU has shown that it is able to do so, but the only sharp operation so far has been *Artemis* in the Democratic Republic of Congo (DRC) in June 2003—15 years ago— which was initiated and led by France, which also bore the brunt of the military risk. Other deployments involved police tasks and post-conflict stability. EUFOR Althea in Bosnia and earlier missions with more limited mandates were all 'very post-conflict', taken over from NATO after the heat of battle.

In 2003 in a bilateral Anglo-French cooperation scheme, the EU decided to create 13 battlegroups, each with about 1500 troops and a deployment time of six days. They are multinational, can operate on a rotational basis, and can be combined with NATO forces if need be. However, when we look at the deployment of these battlegroups, it comes to a standstill in 2006, and after this time neither France nor Britain seems willing to 'use' the EU as an arena for operations any longer.

As we have seen, these are the two European states that stand out in military terms. Both have long traditions of high-intensity warfare as well as of 'imperial policing', which relies on local and political knowledge. Both nations are capable of fielding HQs and assuming 'lead nation' roles for multinational operations, and both committed ground troops in Bosnia and Kosovo. The view of risk in these key European states is thus very different from the maximum force protection that US forces demand.

It is useful to distinguish between strategy, defined as the ability to deter, coerce, and deploy in an interaction with an adversary, and security and defence policy, which is really only policy, often called 'industrial policy', integration, or capability development. This distinction is all the more important today because the resurgence of state security concerns in Europe requires strategic action as opposed to mere policy. As mentioned in Chap. 2, the requirements of strategic action are twofold: *unitary actor capability* and *risk-willingness and relevant military ability*. We often call these two elements a strategic or military culture, as elaborated on in the discussions of Germany, France, and Britain in previous chapters. Before any strategic action can be taken, there must naturally be an ability to analyse strategic problems and interaction, or in other words, to devise a strategy as well as the ability to decide on one.

IOs will, for obvious reasons, rarely be able to act strategically. In NATO however, there will always be leading actors—in most cases, the US, but also the European leading powers, France and Britain. In the EU, we see the very same logic unfolding: in 2003, for example, when the EDA and the EU battlegroups were developed, France and Britain were the key actors. At the same time, a coalition-type mechanism for decision-making called Permanent Structured Cooperation (PESCO) was introduced. This framework—which was first introduced as an appendix to the Lisbon treaty and later incorporated into the treaty—allows two or more states to go ahead with concrete operations and deployments, provided that none of the other states object.

As stated, the battlegroups did not result in major EU military activity as they were only deployed twice; once immediately following their creation in 2003 when the French arranged for an African deployment primarily by French forces as an EU mission named *Artemis*; and again in 2006 when the German battle group on rotation was stopped by German politicians and the French again had to be the leading actor, doing the risky job on the ground in the DRC while Germany was the *pro forma* commander of the operation out of their Potsdam HQ. Already at this point it was clear that *only the states with a military and strategic culture* were going to deploy in risky operations.[4] The battlegroups have since stayed put, so to speak, as very expensive rotational forces for the member states, and when Gordon Brown became British prime minister in 2006 he decided against their use. He did not share his predecessor's enthusiasm for EU security and defence policy. From the experience of battle group deployments—or rather, the lack of it—over the last 15 years, we can safely assume that the EU will not be in a position to deploy in sharp operations unless the actors that actually undertake this job are France and Britain, either alone or together. They will be seconded by other states, but the leading role will be undertaken by one or both of them. This is a very important element of assessing strategic ability for the EU: the former directly depends on one or both of the strategic powers above. One analyst concludes that 'the EU's battlegroups are destined never to see active service', arguing that 'making the battlegroups viable would open up a can of sovereignty norms'.[5]

The EU is not a strategic actor in terms of military force; it was not one back in 2003, and 15 years later, nothing has changed in this regard. Nevertheless, its role in developing cooperation in capability building may increase. While the EDA was not much of a success initially, new initiatives from 2017 show more promise.

Military modernization and integration in Europe take place under the aegis of either NATO, which is the most important actor, or the EU. The process of military modernization in NATO is not directed in any firm 'top-down' manner, informed by political strategy; rather, it is the result of advice and consultation in NATO's transformation command ACT (Allied Command Transformation). But advice to member states remains just advice. Thus far, in the EU, there is no 'grand design' in this area, although the new initiatives may come to play such a role. But for the time being, the processes that integrate and cooperate in military transformation are voluntary and 'bottom-up', which constitutes a considerable problem from the point of view of cost-effectiveness rationality, not to mention politically.[6]

For as long as out-of-area engagement remained the key of European military operation—roughly from 1990 to 2010—military integration and the development of a strategic culture were not pressing concerns. However, when the tables turned during 2014 and state security presented itself as the key defence issue again, there was little or no preparation for this in Europe. Because expeditionary warfare had been the primary operational need for so long, base structures, weaponry, and exercises had emphasized this. Not much thought had been given to deterrence in the event of a direct threat to national or European borders. While the Cold War had not returned, certain aspects of it had.

Given the predominantly intergovernmental nature of the security policy of the EU, there was little risk and much potential gain for major states—they could act alone or together, but did not have to become embedded in supranational structures of the EU. Britain changed its traditional reluctance to EU security and defence policy during Tony Blair's premiership, knowing that it was fully possible to retain national control over defence policy in so doing. Britain invoked several reasons for their change of heart regarding European security policy at the St. Malo summit in 1998, including the need for European states to modernize militarily and be able to act as one; the fact that Britain was not in the other important 'core' group of the EU, namely the Economic and Monetary Union (EMU); and the compatibility between an intergovernmental model of the security and defence cooperation of the EU ESDP and NATO/US interests. The British influence over the first EU's strategy document, the European Security Strategy (ESS),[7] was extensive.

The unanimity requirement for major decisions in both the EU and in NATO become very important, however, when we deal with treaty changes or solemn policy commitment. For this reason, we cannot expect any major common policy developments that imply a transfer of sovereignty in this field. But the 'core logic' described above will most likely function in questions of concrete operations. The political decision to deploy is intergovernmental, but the core logic works strongly. In the case of Operation *Artemis*, it was the UN Secretary General who asked for an EU contribution and France took the lead in suggesting the intervention force, also assuming the major military responsibility. The many EU states that did not participate were only asked not to oppose the intervention, which was easy for them to do as the mission involved stopping genocide and had a UN mandate. However, as the Iraq case evidenced, there was major disagreement among EU states. We can assume that operations that are without a UN mandate and which involve a 'competition' with NATO—in other words, in cases where NATO has not declined to send a mission—will involve the same major disagreements in the EU. Thus, the scope for EU missions is rather limited.

When it comes to coercive diplomacy, the EU has much experience in using political conditionality through the policy tools of enlargement as well as economic and political agreements with third countries. The criteria for EU membership are very clear, and major structural changes in candidate states have been effected through the threat of non-membership and the occasional suspension of negotiations. The EU Commission has recently started a process of depriving Poland of its voting rights in the European Council as punishment for not observing the principle of balance of power in Polish politics, the EU's claim being that the judiciary is being placed under government control.[8] However, there is a principled difference between such conditionality and the threat of use of military force.

The EU defines itself as an international actor according to the Copenhagen Criteria: it is based on democracy, rule of law, human rights, and market economy principles. Both membership and cooperation with third countries are premised on this. Whereas a traditional state is based on the concept of a specific nation with a common history and with '*national* interests'—notably not '*state* interests'—the EU is defined in terms of its underlying values, cast as the Copenhagen Criteria. While the human rights basis of politics is gaining ground today, traditional nation-states are still a 'halfway house' between an ideology based on human rights and one based on national traditions and values. This is an important point with regard to security policy: if the 'new' security policy is based on these values rather than on territorial interests and state-to-state conflicts, then the EU is logically at the forefront of this development.

THE 2016 STRATEGY DOCUMENT AND THE 2017 PESCO

In June 2016, the EU published its *Global Strategy for the EU's Foreign and Security Policy,* its first strategic document since the 2003 ESS. The fact that 13 years had passed before the EU strategy document was updated says a lot about the unimportance of strategic concepts in the EU. NATO's strategic concepts are updated much more frequently and are much more detailed and specific than the two EU strategies.

Why an EU strategy? The answer is plain: there are new risks and threats in and around Europe: 'The purpose, even the existence, of our Union is being questioned. ... Our wider union has become more unstable and more insecure. ... This is no time for uncertainty: our Union needs a strategy.'[9] In terms of its style, the document is very general and very rhetorical, using phrases like 'this is no time for global policemen or lone warriors'. It reads more like a pep talk promoting the virtues of the EU than a precise analysis of the reasons why the EU should become a strategic actor. It is not an analytically serious document, but a call to general action in the direction of strategy.

'Strategy' in this document refers to policy, not strategic interaction with enemies or adversaries; and the term is not primarily concerned with the use of force. High Representative Mogherini makes the claim that the EU needs 'strategic autonomy', but what this means is never defined or explained. Although security and defence issues are central concerns in the document, they are not described in any detail. On the contrary, the strategic scope is as wide as foreign policy itself: the EU will promote a secure

Europe, foster societal resilience (which is never defined) in states in the East and South, promote conflict resolution within all dimensions, develop a cooperative regional order around Europe, and do the same for international governance. These five policy themes are called the EU's 'vision', and the document goes on to say that unless it can deliver on them, it must 'invest in a credible, responsive, and joined-up Union'.

Exactly how these lofty goals are to be realized is never presented in any credible way. Taking security and defence as an example, it is asserted that 'the EU will ... guarantee the security of its citizens and territory' and 'enhance its defence, cyber, counterterrorism, energy, and strategic communications'. Although the term 'strategic autonomy' is used several times in the document, it is not explained. In addition to 'joining up' with other IOs, the EU is also going to develop military capacity of its own: 'NATO remains the primary framework for most member states [yet] European security and defence efforts should enable the EU to act autonomously while also contributing to and undertaking actions in cooperation with NATO.' Here one recognizes that the battlegroups, the only existing autonomous EU capacity, face both 'procedural, financial, and political obstacles' to being deployed. The fact is that these groups have not been deployed since 2006, 12 years ago; something which testifies to the reticence of member states to use force under EU auspices.

In sum, this strategy document does not amount to a strategy,[10] as there is no clear analysis of risks and threats to the EU, no clear set of priorities, and, most importantly, no explanation of how the EU will build military capacity. The document provides a general outlook on the world surrounding Europe and puts forth five tasks for the EU, but does not go into any detail about how to reach policy goals in these areas. Moreover, it is very superficial and simple in style, clearly aimed at enthusing an audience, and contains more slogans than precise analysis.

Compared to NATO's strategic concepts, or its conclusions after the 2016 Warsaw summit, there is a world of difference in terms of precision and clarity, although all these documents are the result of diplomatic bargaining processes. Moreover, if we look at the timeline of so-called strategy development in the EU, we see that there are only two documents that can be called strategies, 13 years apart. Further, neither of them offers a concise analysis of threat, risk, and action, but rather a general outlook on the region and the world. They do not contain criteria for the use of force, unlike, for example, the French strategic document analysed in Chap. 8. Nor do they specify which military capabilities the EU needs or

THE EU: 'SOFT POWER IS NOT ENOUGH' 221

the decision-making procedure for deploying military force. There is no mention of deterrence or military coercion.

Measured by any criterion of what constitutes serious strategic analysis, these documents are not strategies and the EU is not a strategic actor nor likely to become one.

However, the other initiatives that we can term 'security and defence procurement policy' are more promising and offer something new compared to the EDA from 2003.

In the beginning of November 2017, an agreement on Permanent Structured Cooperation, or PESCO, was signed by 23 EU member states. On 12 December 2017, the Council of Ministers formally adopted the PESCO treaty. Faure makes the point that France, the leading actor behind EU military policy in general, may have wanted fewer states in this coalition because decisions can be made more quickly and with a more far-reaching effect in a smaller group, therefore allowing for the emergence of a strategic culture in the EU.[11] In Chap. 8 we saw the strategic character of French thinking about the EU's role: France believes the EU should become an actor able to decide and deploy quickly, an actor in a strategic sense, not simply a 'bottom-up' policy sense. With 25 signatories when adopted by the European Council in December the same year, and perhaps more to come, PESCO will not acquire actor-like qualities.

PESCO is the term used for the decision-making procedure on security and defence issues in the Lisbon treaty. As stated, it was invented by the French and the British in 2003 when these two states launched the 'autonomous military capacity of the EU which consisted primarily of the battlegroups, but also included the EDA which was intended to streamline EU states' defence spending. The current PESCO is wider and more ambitious. It is a binding commitment to spend more wisely on defence by integrating military capacities and undertaking missions together.

PESCO is defined as being about increased cooperation and investment in defence. As Mogherini said at a summit in Latvia on 7 September 2017:

> What we are offering is a platform for joining investments, joining projects and in this manner, overcoming the fragmentation that is characterising currently especially the environment of defence industry in Europe. In this way, the European industrial framework in the sector of defence will be enormously enabled to play a major role globally, and the European Union would then be, I think, really a credible security provider globally.

Thus, PESCO is not about operational military deployments but basically about investigating whether European states can cooperate in procurement, maintenance, and industrial policy. It defines itself thus:

- *PESCO is both a permanent framework for closer cooperation and a structured process to gradually deepen defence cooperation within the Union framework. It will be a driver for integration in the field of defence.*
- *Each participating Member State provides a plan for the national contributions and efforts they have agreed to make. These national implementation plans are subject to regular assessment. This is different from the voluntary approach that is currently the rule within the EU's Common Security and Defence Policy.*
- *PESCO is designed to make European defence more efficient and to deliver more output by providing enhanced coordination and collaboration in the areas of investment, capability development, and operational readiness. Enhanced cooperation in this domain will allow decreasing the number of different weapons' systems [sic] in Europe, and therefore strengthen operational cooperation among Member States, increase interoperability and industrial competitiveness.*
- *PESCO will help reinforce the EU's strategic autonomy to act alone when necessary and with partners whenever possible. Whilst PESCO is underpinned by the idea that sovereignty can be better exercised when working together, **national sovereignty remains effectively untouched.***
- *It is about providing an umbrella for such examples of regional defence integration as the Belgian-Dutch Navy or the European Air Transport Command.*
- ***Military capacities developed within PESCO remain in the hands of Member States** that can also make them available in other contexts such as NATO or the UN.* (my emphasis)

It is thus clear that although PESCO is to be a binding treaty, it is not supranational. As underlined in the text, military capacities remain national and subject to national sovereignty. Thus, PESCO is like a stronger version of the EDA with more commitment. However, it also resembles various force registers, in that states put their national capacities on lists that are made available to NATO, the UN, and perhaps the EU.

Prior to this 'relaunching' of PESCO, the foreign ministers of the EU agreed to reform and expand the Common Foreign and Security Policy

THE EU: 'SOFT POWER IS NOT ENOUGH' 223

(CFSP) at their meeting in November 2016 and they also adopted a fund for EU defence cooperation, the European Defence Fund (EDF).

The attempt to rationalize spending on defence in Europe is old, stemming from the EDA, which was drawn up by France and Britain in 2003, but never amounted to very much, given its voluntary character. At the time, the two states clearly differed in terms of policy: France favoured a centralized mechanism, while Britain favoured a market facilitator. What will become of the current policy of a common defence fund is an open question that cannot be analysed at this point in time. The same is true for the 'defence union' and the 'common EU army'—what exactly, if anything, do the officials in Brussels have in mind?

The problem of multiple military capacities (planes, ships, guns, etc.) in Europe is very real, and it would be very useful if the Europeans could agree to produce and buy fewer systems. Likewise, there is a great need for military integration across state borders as few states can afford the three services army, air, and marine with perhaps around 30 military capacities. If they refuse to spend more on defence, the only option is to share capacities with other states. The new mechanism, PESCO, may be able to succeed in this, but so far both NATO's Allied Command Transformation and the Nordic Defence Cooperation (NORDEFCO) have tried and not succeeded spectacularly. Thus, we should not expect that a newcomer will suddenly find an answer to these very difficult questions that affect national sovereignty at its core. All European states are labouring under chronic defence austerity; even France and Britain have to find solutions to share costs with others. Given this state of affairs, the EU's new initiatives may become very important—but only to the extent that states will it so. France is the key actor in this respect, remaining the driving force of EU developments in this field.

PESCO is accompanied by three other new EU mechanisms, the Co-ordinated Annual Review of Defence (CARD), which builds on former initiatives in this field, the Capability Development Mechanism of 1999, and the 2001 European Capability Action Programme (ECAP). As one commentator puts it, 'those two initiatives (the former two) fell by the wayside, largely because member states balked at the prospect of revealing gaps in their national defence capacities'. This is an indication of the importance of sovereignty in this field. There will also be a small EU HQ erected, able to direct operations in Africa. It will comprise only 25 persons, but is something Britain always has opposed but is no longer in a position to stop.[12]

The CARD will use the EDA as the hub for annual reporting on defence gaps if states decide to open up about this. In addition, there will be an economic incentive in the new defence fund, the EDF, which will co-finance new products and projects if three or more states agree to work together on common capacities. Funding for such projects is secured until 2020 at present, but this fund is not part of the normal EU budget and will have to be included as a permanent item from this time onwards. Whether this will happen remains to be seen.

The current EU process recalls similar processes around the turn of the twenty-first century. At that time, the main actors were France and Britain. Now Germany and France are the main actors, with Britain knocking on the door. At that time, the two protagonists wanted military action capability and designed the EU battlegroups as well as the EDA. Neither was a success. The EDA also failed in its attempt to optimize EU military procurement simply because member states were not willing to integrate if that meant giving up sovereignty. Here the British model was one of coordination as in a marketplace, whereas the French model was one of top-down management. Perhaps the current initiatives will fare better, but the difficulties NATO states have had in procuring wisely in terms of both choice and coming up with funding do not bode well. In NATO, there have been ongoing attempts to find solutions to the 'critical mass' problem for smaller states for many years, but even in NATO this has to be a bottom-up process, not a top-down one. Yet NATO does not offer co-financing like the new EU fund.

EU DEFENCE UNION?

The history of the EU is replete with calls for common defence and security policy. This has always been a French priority. Indeed, it was the main strategy of General de Gaulle, whereby Europe would become a serious international actor on the global scene and a great power, not dependent on the US. Thus, French policy priorities are and have always been clear and consistent in this field, but few other EU states besides France have invested much in this field. Finland and Sweden were interested in transcending neutrality through the creation of the CFSP and partook more than willingly in the peacekeeping operations that came along. Germany had a similar interest in legitimizing its contributions to international operations, but only so long as these were labelled 'crisis management'. This is very different from the idea of developing common military capacity, something far more controversial and opposed by NATO and the US alike. The prospect of a common defence clause was relegated to a future point in time in the Maastricht treaty; such a clause exists in the Lisbon treaty, but is not really heeded by anyone.

Nonetheless, a defence union is again on the agenda of the EU: The Lisbon treaty opened up the possibility for such a union, and over the last two years EU leaders have developed policy proposals for one. The European Parliament has voted to install a defence union and Commission President Juncker has proposed three scenarios for a defence policy, one of them a union, after having stated that 'soft power is not enough' at a meeting in Prague in the summer of 2016.

The backdrop to this rather dramatic about face is both the current crisis in the EU, due among other things to *Brexit* and the clear need for the EU to be able to deal with hard power policy issues. In his so-called State of the Union address in 2016 Juncker stated that 'Europe can no longer afford to piggy-back on the military might of others. (...) For European defence to be strong, the European defence industry needs to innovate.'[13] The Commission's rapporteur adds that 'with a worsening security situation in Europe's neighbourhood and a strong economic case for greater cooperation on defence spending among EU countries, the Commission believes now is the time to make strides towards a Security and Defence Union'.[14]

The EU High Representative for Foreign Policy, Federica Mogherini, stated that

> security and defence are priorities for the European Union because they are priorities for all our citizens. Since last year, we are stepping up our European defence to be more and more effective as a security provider within and beyond our borders, investing more resources, building cooperation among member states and taking forward a closer cooperation with NATO. The world is changing rapidly around us and we have to tackle new challenges every day: as the European Union, we have taken the responsibility to address these challenges.[15]

There is a principled and major difference between 'human security' and crisis operations, and defence, deterrence, coercion, and military confrontation, which is the essence of traditional state security. State security is back with Russian geopolitics and the rise of China, and the EU now speaks about forming a defence union against such threats.

However, one way of assessing the likelihood of whether such lofty proposals may actually materialize is to look at the requirements for substance that they entail. As mentioned, hard power policy must be concrete in terms of power resources; for instance, one cannot control a border without sensors, police, intelligence, and sufficient manpower on site. Likewise, one cannot halt migration in Libya without physical power on the ground. Hard power policy will not work unless it is part of a real plan, and such plans often have to deal with strategic interaction with adversaries. As the EU now moves from soft to hard power—by its own account—it is possible to glean much from recent hard power policy attempts by the EU: were they successful?

If judged by the criteria of strategy outlined in this book, EU strategy is pretty much non-existent: unitary action capacity in a strategic game and military capacities to act with hard power. PESCO and related initiatives may prove to be important, but they fall in the category of industrial policy or general security and defence policy, building capacity in a voluntary, 'bottom-up' perspective.

It would be useful if PESCO and related initiatives were to become a supplement to NATO, concentrating on bringing more economic rationality into defence procurement. Indeed, NATO Secretary Jens Stoltenberg welcomed PESCO as just such an 'added value' when it was adopted on 16 December 2017. Yet other forces in the EU see the new emphasis on defence there as a reaction to the US and President Donald Trump. Indeed, the two main EU leaders voiced sharp criticism of the new American president upon his assuming office. In an early reaction to Donald Trump's election, EU President Donald Tusk referred to Trump as an 'external threat' in a letter sent to all EU member states ahead of the summit in Malta in late January 2016.[16] The German chancellor voiced similar concerns after having made an official visit to the US and having a long telephone conversation with Trump in January 2017 during which she lectured Trump on immigration. This open criticism is dangerous, one commentator pointed out, as the US security guarantee in NATO is not automatic.[17] He noted that Merkel's congratulations to Trump on the election had been a veritable *Morallektion*—a morality lesson. She was prepared to cooperate with him on the basis of human rights, rule of law, and democratic norms. This kind of talk is very unusual, and even undiplomatic, among allies that are liberal democracies, and must have been received as something of an insult. Tusk's letter, too, was a clear insult, a kind of diplomatic declaration of war.

The transatlantic relationship was in the balance, and the talk in the EU turned to a defence union and the ability to defend itself. One journalist even argued that the EU had set out to develop a 'European union to supersede NATO'.[18] The announced 'defence union' was also made possible by the Brexit vote, and enthusiasts for the old project of autonomous EU military capacity praised the prospect of such a development. Mogherini stated that Europe could no longer take American security guarantees for granted, and the US criticism of the European lack of willingness to spend on defence paradoxically seemed like proof of this. But was it likely that European states would spend more on defence in an EU context than in NATO?

At the same time, there was also talk about the possible need for a nuclear deterrent in Germany, a most unlikely topic in that country. The idea was that French nuclear weapons would be the core of a so-called Euro-deterrent, but as Brexit had been decided already, Germany would have to develop its own weapons. This debate has not matured, and is not very prominent, but the fact that a German nuclear deterrent was even discussed shows something of the extraordinary character of politics in Europe after the election of Trump.[19]

In sum, the most important tangible new EU development is the EDF, the fund that provides fresh funding for procurement in a co-funding scheme. By 2020, EUR 500 million per year will be made available.[20] In addition, PESCO will demand more commitment on all aspects of procurement from member states. Yet all this remains in the realm of bottom-up defence policy, mainly in the defence-industrial area, and the steps taken are likely to be small.[21] The EU's leadership is simultaneously conducting another type of political rhetoric—that of a defence union which can act autonomously to defend the EU. And as we have seen, the Lisbon treaty contains a mutual defence clause, Article 42(7), which was invoked by France after the terrorist attacks on 13 November 2013. Commission President Juncker has even stated that 'soft power is not enough', a major deviation from the EU ideology that maintains that soft power is, in fact, enough—that rule of law and democratic incentives make for a different foreign policy actor.

How serious is this talk? Is there a possibility that common procurement will lead to integration into a defence union like NATO? As we saw in Chap. 5, the requirements for strategic action are political ability, including unitary and swift action, and military capacity. The EU clearly lacks a strategic culture—its recent strategy is nothing more than a list of foreign policy goals and betrays a thorough lack of understanding what strategy is. Even with PESCO as the decision-making procedure—with decisions being taken by only a few states (not all 25 signatory states)—having a '*directoire*'—a leading group of a few states—would contradict EU policy of including all states in important decisions. Strategic action—for instance deterring Russia—belongs to this category of vital decisions, and one would be hard pressed to think that Germany and France, for example, could decide alone on behalf of the EU in a given situation. Therefore, EU strategic action capacity seems an impossibility. Each time major EU powers have hinted at the idea of having a *directoire,* the other member states have baulked. PESCO is therefore unlikely in areas other than procurement and perhaps mission deployments with battlegroups in the familiar format of crisis management.

The joker in the deck with regard to a future strategic role for the EU is France. Germany is unable and unwilling to act as strategic leader, but France is the key strategic actor in Europe. Most likely, France will try to develop the EU in the direction of unitary actor capability to the extent that this is possible, and to this end it will need Britain. And as we have seen, Britain is more than eager to join all EU defence initiatives. Germany nevertheless remains the actor with means, and it suits Germany very well to be the 'framework nation', a state that undertakes defence coordination and planning in a regular policy process. It does not, however, suit Germany to act strategically—deterring Russia, for instance, or launching surprise attacks in the Middle East or Africa, to mention but two examples.

The EU's bottom-up defence-industrial policy can therefore be led by France and Germany, but not a strategic actor role for the EU. Yet France clearly desires that the EU develop such a role, albeit not in competition with NATO. How this relationship will look is unclear. The French would like the EU to have hard power, and to be able to play a global role alone if need be, but also to preserve the close relationship with the US and, therefore, to retain NATO. Yet for the French there is no contradiction between autonomous EU military capacity and NATO/US continuation. Sometimes Europe alone will act, sometimes Europe and the EU is a logical line of reasoning.

France does not depend on the US, and neither should the EU. Yet this vision requires not only a European nuclear deterrent but also major arming of Europe—not a likely or palatable choice for EU states that already refuse the 2 per cent of GDP goal for defence in NATO.[22] Moreover, talk of an autonomous EU defence union serves to further alienate the

US—hardly what anyone, including France, really wants. Thus, we can also assume that the French ambition for the EU remains in line with the 'complementarity model' between NATO and the EU, as was the case when the battlegroups and EDA were established in 2003. The Trump administration is serious about wanting Europe to do more in NATO, and if that does not happen, could be equally serious about weakening its commitment to Europe. France is not likely to gamble with the relationship with the US, given the weakness of most European states both in terms of spending and strategic culture. One could add that the talk about creating a European defence union is counter-productive given the realities of spending and the lack of willingness in the EU to be a strategic actor with the risks entailed in this role. Why alienate the US more than necessary when there clearly is no alternative to the American security guarantee? As discussed in Chap. 1, many European politicians accept neither the necessity of having to deal with *Realpolitik* and hard power issues nor the implications of being an actor that is capable of doing so. European leaders like Merkel and the EU leadership continue to talk about integration in defence policy as if it were just another policy area of low politics. They do not seem to understand what a defence union is and what it requires. Perhaps they simply think that cooperation on procurement will result in a defence union of sorts. While this may be, it is not helpful to float the idea of such a union, especially after having criticized President Trump in such an undiplomatic manner, unless Europe is really prepared to defend itself with the full spectrum of capabilities, including a nuclear deterrent. Yet it should also be mentioned that for Germany it is vital to be able to point to a robust EU role in defence as it legitimizes a key role for Germany itself as it had become the most populist and richest country in Europe, seeking to gradually normalize its defence role accordingly. For this reason the Germans strongly favour a European army and similar set-ups.[23]

The EU's easy talk about forming a defence union betrays its naïveté about strategic requirements, as does the EU strategy published in 2016. This is regrettable from a logical and rational point of view, but it also is disquieting in terms of substance. If the EU's leadership can talk so easily about the most serious policy field—launching a defence union which lacks both substance and strategy—this seems to indicate that it is not politically competent. This lack of competence and, more broadly, of substance in European policy is also evident in another key political issue, migration, which I will discuss below.

We now turn to the evaluation of whether the EU acted strategically in the cases examined in this book.

THE EU REACTION TO RUSSIA: SANCTIONS

As a response to the annexation of Crimea, the EU and the US decided on sanctions against Russia, which were implemented in various stages: first, immediately following the annexation when Russia was excluded from a G8 meeting, and then on 23 June 2014. The US initially launched sanctions and put pressure on the EU to do the same. Thus, the sanctions were an American initiative, not a European one.

The sanctions regime implemented by the EU and the US was designed to be imposed gradually, and can therefore be intensified. This in itself is an intelligent design. Since 2014, the sanctions have been upgraded to a more serious level and were renewed in June 2017, despite disagreement among member states of the EU.

The US sanctions decided on by President Obama were complemented by a new set of stricter sanctions by the US Congress in 2017 as a reaction to Russian interference in the US presidential election. President Trump, himself under investigation for collusion with Russia during the campaign in the independent inquiry led by Robert Mueller, could not refuse to sign the latest sanctions for this very reason. Europe, represented by the EU, did not follow suit on these sanctions, which remain purely American and an act of punishment for alleged election interference. In rejecting these sanctions, the EU argued that not only would the sanctions hit European energy interests, but they may even be intended to do so, targeting the Nord Stream 2 pipeline between Russia and Germany: 'For the bill's European enemies, among them the Netherlands and France … the sanctions are a thinly veiled excuse to promote American LNG exports and meddle in the European energy market.'[24]

Another proposal for sanctions against Russia was occasioned by the 'sickening atrocities' in Aleppo during the Russian and Syrian siege of the city in 2016. At that time, Britain, France, and Germany all agreed to the sanctions, but other states in the EU did not.[25] Italy, a long-time close ally of Russia, led the opposition, which consisted of Spain, Austria, Greece, Finland, and others in East-Central Europe.[26]

This shows *how divided Europe has become* over sanctions against Russia, even if the initial EU sanctions are still in place and have been renewed several times. However, as these initial sanctions were 'imposed' on the

EU by the US, we can assume that US pressure explains why they have not been lifted in spite of major opposition. There are major divisions among the EU states in terms of how Europe should respond: Greece, Finland, Bulgaria, and Italy has been sceptical of the sanctions to the point of trying to lift them; Hungary, which is dependent on Russia for gas imports and the renewal of its Paks nuclear power plant, wants a careful balancing, as do Slovakia, the Czech Republic, and Romania. German leadership in the sanctions policy towards Russia, which 'has been progressively down-graded to the traditional *Ostpolitik* slogan '*Wandel durch Handel*' (Change through Trade), is very shaky. France has a major economic interest in maintaining normal ties with Russia; its order for delivery of warships to Russia overshadowed security policy throughout 2014. The French leadership was increasingly opposed to continued sanctions throughout 2015 and 2016. We could add that the third great power in Europe, Britain, likewise preferred the *status quo* with its strong degree of Russian investment in London, both in real estate and in finance, at the beginning of the Ukraine conflict.[27] Yet Britain became much more critical of Russia in 2016 and 2017. Prime Minister May presented very blunt criticism of Russia in her talk to the City of London governors in November 2017,[28] and, as we have seen, promoted the idea of EU sanctions as a reaction to Russia's bombing in Aleppo. The latter response was also supported by Germany and even France, although it appears to have been a poorly developed idea since the impact of such sanctions would hardly be to stop Russian support for Assad in the decisive battle of Aleppo.

These three sanctions attempts—the initial EU sanctions caused by US pressure; the 'humanitarian' sanctions proposal over Aleppo; and the later US Congress sanctions adopted as punishment for alleged Russian interference in the American elections—give considerable insight into European thinking and policy. First, the EU sanctions were adopted and have held because of US insistence on having a unified Western response to Russia. The considerable opposition to these sanctions shows that they would not be continued otherwise. They are not the result of EU strategic action.

Second, the 'humanitarian sanctions' proposed by Britain and seconded by the other two great powers of Europe, France and Germany, were not adopted due to opposition led by Italy. These sanctions were not developed as a strategic tool at all, having no possibility of stopping Russian bombardment of Aleppo in the critical phase of war-fighting. Instead, they should be seen as a 'values-based' reaction that was partially a response to media and public outcry. As such, this reaction fits with Europe's 'valuesbased' foreign policy and shows how important these values are for European governments: France, Russia's traditional ally, and Britain, not unused to the logic of war and the terrible consequences for civilians of siege warfare, were both in the forefront of this sanctions proposal.

Finally, the sanctions of the US Congress, signed reluctantly by President Trump, were simply rejected by European states as contrary to their interests. These sanctions have not been implemented by the Trump administration at all, and thus no pressure from the other side of the Atlantic has been brought to bear as a result of this decision.

In these three instances, European states reacted to their own public and media outcry over humanitarian issues in war to such an extent that sanctions against Russia were, in fact, proposed by the two major military powers, France and Britain. Thus, we can conclude that following the Geneva conventions in war is really very important to both states. As we can see, the proposed sanctions did not have an intended strategic effect; they were simply expressions of the values these states stand for. Second, the Congressional sanctions were rejected in Europe; it was possible to do so because President Trump did not make them a matter of transatlantic policy and solidarity. As for the initial sanctions, they have been maintained despite European opposition, in all probability because the US put pressure on the EU. In sum, there is no evidence of EU strategic action against Russia in coercive diplomacy as such.

Let us now examine the existing EU sanctions in terms of the requirements of strategic action—coercive diplomacy—which, as mentioned in Chap. 6, include calibration for effect in terms of clear conditionality, timeline, and, if possible, incentives for compliance.

The EU sanctions, modelled on the US sanctions, started as *targeted* sanctions, meaning that they were aimed at specific persons. They have since been extended to economic sectors and comprise both private companies and individuals and their personal assets, which have been frozen. Moreover, they affect financial markets (e.g., the EU has banned long-term loans to five major state-owned banks in Russia), the energy sector (the EU has placed restrictions on Rosneft, Transneft, and Gazprom Neft activities), and the defence sector (the boycott of all 'dual-use' manufacturers). The EU also boycotts all contacts and trade with Crimea as a consequence of its non-recognition of the annexation. Thus, we speak of sanctions that are both political boycotts and affect trade and finance, as well as persons.

THE EU: 'SOFT POWER IS NOT ENOUGH'   233

Russia retaliated with countersanctions on 14 August 2014. All imports of agricultural produce and fish from the sanctioning states—including all of the EU, as well as Norway, Australia, and Canada—were banned. For the EU, this meant a loss of 10 per cent of its exports in these sectors.

In addition to the sanctions, the sharp drop in price of oil in 2014 caused the value of the rouble to plummet. The recession that followed clearly impacted ordinary Russians as well as the elites on the individual sanctions list. Thus, while the sanctions seem to have had an economic effect, it is unclear how much of this is actually due to the sanctions and how much to the fall in oil prices.[29] The sanctions have an economic impact, especially on trade, but not so much on the financial world. Jones and Whitworth have analysed the economic impact of the current sanctions and find that they will raise the cost of capital in the long run—'so long as Russian banks and firms face the need to refinance existing foreign-currency obligations, yet cannot gain access to alternative markets'[30]—because of the prohibition to buy bonds or equity with a maturity beyond 90 days on the part of financial institutions owned by Russian authorities. This part of the sanctions will work to exclude Russia more and more from European capital markets. The authors make the interesting point that this will force Russia to look to alternative capital markets, something which, in the end, may harm European markets even more than the sanctions themselves.

They also make the point that there was a slow build-up to the sanctions in Europe, which created legitimacy for the decision to institute them, which was triggered by the shooting down of a Malaysian Airline flight over Ukraine in July 2014.

The most important effect on Europe has been on German trade. On the Russian side, the unintended trade consequence will be that Russia will look for new markets, something which will hurt Europe in the long run. The sanctions may also encourage Russia to build its own markets, institutions beyond Western influence, and in doing so, consolidate the BRICS (Brazil, Russia, India, China, and South Africa) group and an alternative world order. Should Europe decide to exclude Russia from the SWIFT mechanism, as it did with Iran in 2012, this would have very great consequences—it is 'a nuclear option'; however, Russia is already thinking about building its own alternative. Jones and Whitworth's point is that such steps will lead to counter-measures that may in the end hurt the West more than the sanctions hurt Russia. If the aim is to retain the Western international system, impetus to design an alternative order should be minimized.

In 2014, the flight of Western capital from Russia amounted to US \$150 billion.[31] This is a considerable amount, and in addition, the rouble has plummeted due to the fall in the oil price. The Russian GDP fell by 4.5 per cent in 2015 and was expected to fall by an additional 2 per cent in 2016.[32] On the European side, German exporters lost 20 per cent of their trade with Russia in 2014, and some EU states, like Greece, suffered greatly from the cessation of fruit exports to Russia.

Despite these effects on the Russian economy, there are serious weaknesses in the EU sanctions regime. First of all, it was the US and not EU states themselves that proposed sanctions; indeed, following US sanctions, the EU was basically put under heavy American pressure to follow suit. Sanctions and countersanctions have much greater consequences for Europeans than for Americans. The US has a 4 per cent import share from Russia, while the EU share is 40 per cent. Russia is the third most important trade partner for the EU, and the EU is the first trading partner for Russia. Moreover, the EU is the most important investor in Russia.[33] Moreover, for some EU member states, the issue is of vital economic importance; Finland, for example, has not only experienced renewed Russian attempts at 'Finlandization', but also depends entirely on Russian gas and imports 70 per cent of their oil from Russia. Finnish exports to Russia are also important, as is cross-border tourism. Finnish security interests are in line with the West, but the country's economic dependence on Russia is very great. Finland was thus in a true dilemma when faced with the EU sanctions regime and was reluctant to comply.

Not only is the risk of military conflict with Russia unpalatable, the cost of any type of conflict is real. Norway is another country where the government has always preferred to avoid conflict with Russia, but within clear limits; although Norwegian fishery exports have suffered as a result of the sanctions, but Norway puts security above trade and has sided with the US and the EU on sanctions and other Russia policy.

Other non-EU NATO member states have aligned themselves with the sanctions policy, among them Iceland, Liechtenstein, FYROM (Former Yugoslav Republic of Macedonia), and Albania, as well as Ukraine and Georgia. Thus, a large coalition of states subscribes to the sanctions, making for an impressive political statement. The question is for how long this coalition can hold, especially if the sanctions are tightened. One possibility is to shut Russia out of the international banking system SWIFT, a move that would isolate the country and have major consequences.

Have the sanctions had the desired political impact? As of the writing of this book, the political impact has been the very opposite of what was intended. The Russian population, which is suffering economic hardship caused in part by the sanctions, fully supports President Putin. In fact, he has never been more popular. Levada polls from September 2013 showed a support rate for President Putin of 60 per cent, whereas support was 80–90 per cent in the subsequent two years.[34]

One might object that Russian media are censored and that opinion polls cannot be trusted, but even with these caveats it seems clear that Putin is a popular president, and his rhetoric depicting NATO and the US as the enemy is clearer than ever. Putin has used the sanctions as 'proof' that the West seeks to bring about regime change, and, in a sense, he is of course right: the long-term goal of this containment strategy is to wait him out. Similar to the strategy during the Cold War, as outlined at that time in George Kennan's 'long telegram', the West is trying to contain Russia, waiting for domestic changes that will lead to a regime that can be dealt with on normal diplomatic terms.

There were sanctions after Russia attacked Georgia in 2008, but they were removed because the US wanted a so-called reset in Russian-American relations. Russia did nothing to meet the sanction demands at that time, and looks unlikely to do so this time. After all, de-annexing Crimea is all but impossible now, and Russian has never admitted to supplying arms to Ukraine. Moreover, the sanctions are not designed according to the minimum standards stipulated by the literature on coercion: a credible threat, clear demands, a clear deadline, and incentives, as discussed in Chap. 2. Under the current sanctions regime, there is no threat of using military force, and the economic threat is not big enough to be persuasive, especially since reciprocity is so important to Europe in terms of gas dependency. Furthermore, it is not clear what exactly must Putin do to have the sanctions lifted, or by when. The only criterion that is met is that of incentives; it is likely that the West will be more than happy to reinstate normal trade and diplomacy with Russia if it 'behaves' in Ukraine. But the 'misbehaviour' in Crimea and Donbas cannot be undone, thus there will probably not be compliance, only a cessation of war-fighting. But Russia could effect that regional elections are held without risking losing influence in Eastern Ukraine, and perhaps this is the key to the lifting of sanctions—some sort of negotiated outcome based on the demands made in the Minsk process. However, reversal of Crimea's status is not likely. I discuss these factors in the concluding chapter.

In sum, the EU sanctions seem to rest on clay feet, both in terms of support and in terms of self-damage. They have had no discernible political effect on President Putin; indeed, quite the contrary. Their long-term economic effect is, however, real and objective. But it seems to reinforce the political message that the West's goal is regime change, thus fostering a siege effect and mentality, which is easy to exploit in a dictatorship.

The EU sanctions of 2014 were prolonged for another six months at the end of 2015 in spite of major opposition from Italy's Prime Minister Renzi who argued that Germany dominated decision-making in the EU and was calling for opposition to Russia while benefitting from Russian gas imports. Italy stalled the prolongation of the sanctions for a full two weeks demonstrating that, although the sanctions remained in place, the EU was far from a unitary actor. The US kept the pressure on Germany; Germany kept the pressure on the rest of the EU.

The EU and Migration

The EU's policy on migration and refugees is comprehensive. The so-called third pillar of the Maastricht treaty was named Justice and Home Affairs (JHA) and was largely intergovernmental, consisting of various regimes for tackling terrorism, crime, and transborder activity like migration.[35] Schengen, named after the small town in Luxembourg where the treaty was signed, is the name of one agreement on common EU external border control that is carried out by the various states themselves. Several non-EU members, including Norway, are parties to the Schengen treaty, while several EU member states, including Britain, are not. Likewise, the Dublin agreement on return of asylum seekers to the country of entry in Europe is intergovernmental and not limited to EU member states only. This treaty stipulates that asylum seekers must apply for asylum in the country in which they arrive and if they do not do so, they will be returned to that original country from any later destination. The intention is to avoid so-called asylum shopping where people try to reach specific destinations.

In the Lisbon treaty, the JHA policy area is included in the majority procedure of the internal market, which was decided on by majority voting. This passed without much notice when the treaty was signed, but has

THE EU: 'SOFT POWER IS NOT ENOUGH' 237

become intensely controversial ever since the EU decided to impose refugee quotas on all member states in the aftermath of the 2015 migration crisis. At that time, German Chancellor Merkel had declared that migrants and refugees could enter Germany, which is where they wanted to go, thereby setting aside the Dublin regulations which stipulate that they be returned to Greece or Italy or wherever they first entered European territory. The havoc wrought by this mass influx quickly rendered both Schengen and Dublin useless: the external border was not controlled at all, meaning that everyone could enter in a chaotic fashion. The Dublin rule was effectively suspended by Merkel, and when even Sweden and Germany were unable to take in more arrivals. Merkel called for the distribution of refugees to other EU member states. This was voted on by the majority; and thus legally adopted, but rejected by the Visegrad states. These states do not accept supranational refugee quotas, arguing that they have a vital national interest in deciding how their own nations are to develop. The case has gone to the ECJ where the plaintiffs, Hungary and Slovakia, predictably lost; however, these two states, and the other three states in this five-state group, say that they will not accept this verdict and will pay fines rather than meet imposed quotas.[36] The Hungarian Foreign Minister Péter Szijjártó used uncompromising language about the court ruling, calling it an attack on security in Europe and on Europe's values and rule of law: 'The real battle is only beginning', he said.[37]

The EU has been very unsuccessful in implementing this quota policy: almost two years after the decision was made, only 17 per cent of the 160,000 refugees slated for resettlement have been relocated to other EU states. States resent having such quotas imposed on them and many already take so-called quota refugees through the normal mechanism of the UN's High Commissioner for Refugees. Moreover, they resent that Germany, which allowed everyone to come and is predictably overwhelmed, now wants other states to 'show solidarity'. As Hungarian Prime Minister Orbán pointed out, it was Germany that created much of the 'pull factor' for migrants in 2015. Moreover, illegal migrants—many of which were Syrian war refugees—also represented a security concern related to terrorism. As Norwegian authorities, for example, have revealed, no one knows the identity of all the people who arrived in the mass influx in 2015 because it was not possible to check the ID of so many people at the same time. In more than 50 per cent of the cases of Syrians entering Europe, there was no real control of their ID.[38] There is a real fear that terrorists have entered under the guise of being war refugees, and this can be assumed to be the case in other European states as well. The security problem posed by terrorists returning from Syria and Iraq should have led European states to not allow anyone without legitimate ID to enter their countries, is the argument. Instead some states, like Germany and Sweden, did not control their own borders and let everyone enter.

At the EU summit in December 2017, the president of the European Council, Donald Tusk, stated that the EU's refugee redistribution policy was a failure and that it caused unnecessary friction and conflict. Tusk, himself Polish, spoke about the reality of the situation, but was immediately upbraided by members of the European Parliament. As the ECJ had just ruled, the policy had been adopted by majority rule and was therefore valid. But what Tusk said was that this policy was not going to be accepted because it interfered in the core of state sovereignty. He advised the EU Commission to recognize this and to adjust to member states' views. Although the matter remains unresolved, this was an admission of a major policy mistake by the EU. Only some refugees have been resettled. The European Parliament underscored the issue by adopting a policy of limitless resettlement of refugees on the eve of the summit, something which led the Hungarian parliament to refuse a permanent quota system run from Brussels. The EU is deeply divided by the issue of sovereignty, including the questions of who belongs to a nation and who is responsible for its security. Of the European leaders, only Merkel continued to refuse to define an upper limit to the number of migrants and refugees entering her country, and no state wanted to take the necessary steps towards border controls and asylum application *beyond* Europe. Even with border controls, those without papers (and therefore visas) could not be simply shut out at a European border. They could not be returned without papers or, if they had papers, without the agreement of their home states. They were allowed to apply for asylum, and the moment this happened, they were effectively in Europe for a long time, often for good.

This policy problem is one where the human rights and global outlook of European elites clashed with reality in the sharpest manner conceivable. On the one hand, there was the imperative to welcome and help strangers; on the other, there was the need to secure Europe both from chaotic conditions caused by mass migration and from terrorism made possible by uncontrolled entries. Only Prime Minister Orbán did not mind being seen as tough on this issue. He closed the Hungarian border before anyone else dared to and did not let asylum seekers into Hungary before they were granted asylum, which was only in rare cases. For security reasons, migrants were kept interned at the border in closed camps. Because of its location, Hungary had been a major recipient of migrants; several hundred thousand had come during 2015. But after a while, the EU had to find a way to combine two opposites: the closing of borders and stopping everyone from applying for asylum in Europe. Yet no EU leaders, especially not Germany, were willing to commit to such a policy. It was unpalatable, and a rejection of the asylum policy principle so guarded by human rights groups and lawyers. No West European politician wanted to be 'shamed' in public opinion as 'heartless' and 'inhuman'. The publication of pictures from hard borders with police pitted against migrants was a nightmarish prospect. What to do in this emergency?

The EU's common policies—Schengen and Dublin—thus proved dysfunctional early on with regard to mass migration. The demise of the Dublin Regulations is related to two things: first, Merkel's *Willkommenskultur*, which allowed for just what Dublin was designed to stop, namely 'asylum shopping'—migrants wanted to get to Germany, not to Greece, Italy, or Hungary; and second, the overwhelming numbers of arrivals, which would have swamped Italy and Greece had they all stayed there. These states were fairly overwhelmed with arrivals and had called for solidarity before, but in previous years neither Germany nor other states beyond the Mediterranean had responded. The 'solution' was to let migrants pass through Italy and Greece—not to offer assistance or take asylum application as they were obliged to under Dublin, but to quietly become mere transit zones. Thus, it was impossible to honour the Dublin agreement if there were more than a small number of arrivals. Moreover, the agreement was a dysfunctional deal to begin with, placing special burdens on the frontier states in southern Europe.

However, the most important EU policy is the Schengen Agreement, which is based on the assumption that the outer Schengen border is controlled so that internal EU borders can remain open. Indeed, this is the precondition for the internal market. The outer border is to be closed to entry for anyone without a visa, but the control itself is to be carried out by the member states, aided if necessary by the EU border agency Frontex. However, all states have allowed anyone arriving at their borders to apply for political asylum. As discussed in Chap. 3, this asylum practice, originally intended for intra-European refugees after WWII, has become a magnet for migrants from all over the world. If refugees can make it to a European border, they can apply for asylum and stay until their appeals are exhausted; and during that time they can disappear or become unreturnable, even if their application is eventually rejected. Very few are actually returned once in Europe. This undoubtedly creates a major pull factor.

Yet the EU, with its porous borders, insisted on maintaining this asylum policy, and the mass influx of 2015 continued without abatement. What was to be done? As we recall from Chap. 3, state after state in Europe closed their own borders. Hungary built a veritable fence on its Serbian border; Croatia closed its border; Spain quietly built 20-foot high fences with barbed wire on top in Ceuta and Melilla and paid the Moroccans to keep migrants out; France closed its border with Italy; and Austria sent soldiers to the Brenner Pass.[39] The states located farther north were luckier, as they were shielded when the states on the front line of migration physically closed their borders. Even so, the Nordic states, including Sweden, used an emergency rule of the internal market and introduced border controls between themselves and insisted on detailed visa controls by all airlines landing in these countries. This brought migration almost to a complete halt.

But the southern border along the Mediterranean and into Greece still received thousands of people every day. Even if they could no longer move onwards through Hungary, Croatia, Italy, or Spain, something had to be done to stop this influx. The EU, led by Germany, forged a deal with President Erdoğan of Turkey. The deal, the terms of which are detailed in Chap. 3, involves large sums paid to Turkey to stop migrants and refugees before they reach European soil in Greece, from which point they can move onwards. The point is to achieve two things at the same time: to stop migrants and refugees, and to have them apply for asylum somewhere outside Europe where being granted asylum does not lead to a right to come to Europe, but to stay in a refugee camp, awaiting return to the country of origin when the conflict there has ended.

In both the media and public opinion, the migrant and refugee crisis has been defined as a human rights issue, rather than a security issue. Accounts of what was happening in Europe were not framed by security concerns; rather they presented a humanitarian crisis, with people in need fleeing war and poverty. The fact that migrant smuggling networks were so pervasive and well organized played no role in this framing. As we have seen in Chap. 3, the media upheld this framing and made it impossible to protest against the influx. Arguments for accepting few or no migrants were seen as right-wing and unacceptable, as was the Central European concern about preserving the Christian character of nations there. In this climate of opinion, the EU devised a smart plan, developed by German

THE EU: 'SOFT POWER IS NOT ENOUGH'   241

diplomats: The outsourcing of both border control and asylum application. 'The EU-Turkey agreement achieved this [stopping the influx to Europe] without ... breaking EU and international refugee law, which prohibits refusing entry to people who request asylum and sending them back without due process.'[40]

The impact of the EU-Turkey deal—spearheaded by Germany's Merkel, who faced an immediate need to stop the influx but refused to do so at Europe or Germany' border—was significant. Illegal border crossings into Greece fell from 856,723 in 2016 to 173,447 in 2017.[41] Yet those who had reached Greece before the deal was closed had to be allowed to apply for asylum there, and were to be returned to Turkey, wherefrom they came, in the event that their applications were rejected. Turkey was declared a safe third country by the EU. Nevertheless, since this plan was implemented, the legal procedures in Greece have dragged on and on, and very few people have been returned. Moreover, and far more serious, the resettlement of returnees to Turkey with refugee status into Europe, is dismal. As of 17 January 2017, only about 3000 out of a Syrian refugee population of 2.8 million in Turkey have been resettled as part of the EU quota policy discussed above.[42] Thus, it is very clear that EU states do not want a common migrant and refugee policy beyond closed borders and border control at the outer Schengen border. And when that border is not controlled, keeping migrants out, states compete in a race to the bottom, each trying to be as unattractive as possible to migrants, and, increasingly, even close national borders. Thus, it would seem that the EU can only have a common policy in terms of closing and controlling borders, not in distributing refugees and migrants. This conclusion concurs with Sophie Matlary's 2015 study of the EU's logic of action: states are in a joint decision trap, meaning that they want a common policy in the EU but not one that requires them to share the burden of dealing with refugees.[43] They prefer others to carry the burden while they enjoy a free ride. For this reason, an EU distributive policy will not work. At the EU summit in December 2017, Council President Tusk declared that the supranational refugee quota policy of the EU was a fiasco and should be abandoned, but he was immediately met by sharp criticism from the Commission which called his statement 'anti-European'.[44] Thus, the Commission reserves itself the right to call criticism 'anti-European', something which betrays a certain desperation. Tusk dared to say what everyone saw, namely that when member states oppose supranationalization of a policy area which is key to sovereignty, the

Commission should rethink its stance. The Visegrad 5 are not the only states that oppose such a development, both Denmark and Austria agree with them. By 2017 there was a deep and serious split between these states and the EU Commission, Germany, and France,[45] when Commission President Juncker called the Poles and the other Visegrad states 'racist' for not accepting the EU-imposed refugee quotas.[46]

Despite its apparent advantages, the EU-Turkey deal entails major dependencies for the EU.[47] The deal was intended to give all Turks EU visa freedom, a promise that has not been kept and which it is politically impossible to keep. Further, the negotiations for Turkish membership in the EU would be accelerated, another impossible promise given the extremely hostile relationship between Europe and Turkey at the moment. Turkey will not become an EU member, and the dictatorial policies of its President Erdoğan make any trust impossible. What remains of the deal is only the financial motive and Turkish interest in exporting to Europe. In all other respects, the relationship is highly conflictual. European states have given political asylum to Turkish officers and diplomats, and even the US-Turkish relationship is at a historical low. The Turks have threatened to unleash millions of migrants on Europe on a regular basis, and the EU can only pay up, in hopes that Turkey will not make good on this threat. By depending on Turkey to close Europe's borders, the EU has made itself extremely vulnerable. This arrangement is very unwise because it makes it easy for Turkey to put pressure on the EU, and there is no clear end to the deal—for as long as migrants continue to travel to Europe, Turkey will play a key role. At an EU summit in December 2017, the EU agreed to pay even more to Turkey for its work with refugees, another 700 million euros.[48]

The EU apparently thinks that the problem of migration should be kept out of sight, and thus out of mind. Instead of changing its asylum policy to allow people to apply from outside of Europe and tightening border controls of the Schengen border—which would effectively remove the incentive to travel to Europe and leave control in the EU's own hands—the EU chose to outsource the problem to a dangerous 'ally'. This is not a sustainable policy, and it entails dependencies that Europe should not have.[49]

The other EU policy designed along the same lines is the deal with the government(s) of Libya, discussed in Chap. 3. This is an even more desperate move than the Turkey deal, involving shady actors, including smugglers and militias. As the main influx shifted from the Balkans route via Greece to the Mediterranean, the EU, and Italy and France in particular, had to deal with this problem under duress. Once again, they have chosen to outsource the problem, ideally stopping migrants before they reach Libya, but also stopping them at sea before they reach international waters. To this end, the so-called Libyan coast guard is trained by EU trainers and with EU funds. There are few refugees arriving in Libya; almost all are migrants, and they are therefore to be returned. But the conditions under which they are held in Libya are awful and in breach of human rights law, and the actors in the game are profiteers of the worst kind. There is therefore a glaring discrepancy between the values professed by the EU and the reality of this deal.

Like the Turkey deal, the Libya deal has led to a halt to migration into Italy. Italy itself has taken charge of the situation, as discussed in Chap. 3, and is also sending its own soldiers to Niger to stop migration going north. Four hundred and seventy soldiers will go into the Sahel to close the major migrant route to the Maghreb.[50] French troops in Africa are also active in this endeavour. This shows that the EU policy is inadequate since it only pays for others' soldiers, without sending its own; and it also underlines the importance of the state as such: neither Italy nor France trust the EU to effectively solve the problem.

In sum, the EU has failed to deal with the migration problem. It has been totally unable to forge a common policy to address the refugee crisis and quotas; but this was to be expected, as this policy area raises sovereignty and identity concerns of the first order. But the EU has also been unable to act strategically in securing the Schengen border. Instead of changing an asylum practice that was designed for small numbers of intra-European refugees and physically secure outer borders, the EU has outsourced management of the asylum process and border control to undependable and outright hostile 'allies'. In doing so, it has become dangerously dependent on both Turkey and African actors. The EU is uniquely suited to devise large development programmes based on conditional returns and attempts to curb migration at home. It is starting to do so, but any such policy must be accompanied by the closure of European borders.

Notes

1. *European Union Security Dynamics: In the New National Interest*, Matlary, Palgrave, 2013.
2. 'Conclusion: NATO's Transformed Vision of Security', Sebastian Mayer, p. 309–310, in Mayer (ed) (2014) *NATO's Post-Cold War Politics. The Changing Provision of Security*, Palgrave Macmillan.

3. In 2016 a second security strategy was published, but we note that it has been 13 years since the first strategy was issued. This implies that strategy work is not serious in the EU.
4. My book *European Union Security Dynamics: In the New National Interest*, op.cit., provides a detailed analysis of this period in EU security policy and of the leadership exercised by France and Britain at the time.
5. Braw, E. 'EU battle groups are destined never to see active service', The Times, 20 June 2017.
6. lt. General Camporini—remarks at NDC, 5 April 2005—elaborate.
7. Not only the inception but also the very development of the ESS was handled by UK diplomats, from Richard Cooper, currently working for Javier Solana, to detailed revisions. Chr. Hill's non-paper shows this direct influence, 'Britain and the ESS', unpublished, 2004.
8. The Hungarian Prime Minister Orbán pledges to oppose such a move in the EU, and here we again encounter the intergovernmental character of the organization since there is a need for unanimity for depriving a state of its voting rights.
9. Introduction to the 2016 strategy by f. Mogherini, the EU's High Representative for External Affairs.
10. 'EU-Kommission: Europa kann militarische macht warden', FAZ, 12 June 2017.
11. Faure, S. (2018) 'La cooperation franco-britannique lagre le Brexit? Les deux roles du Royaume-Uni: le premier role militaire et "en meme temps" un role industriel', in Johnson, R. and Matlary, J.H., op.cit.
12. 'EU richtet militarische Kommandozentrale ein', *Die Zeit* online, 12 June 2017.
13. The EU Commission's report on defence union, summer 2016.
14. Ibid.
15. Ibid.
16. Bruno Waterfield, 'Trump is a threat to Europe', *The Times*, 31 January 2017.
17. 'Angela Merkels Lektion für Trump birgt Risken', Clemens Wergin, *Die Welt*, 29 2017.
18. Bruno Waterfield, *The Times*, 8 June 2017.
19. 'Fearing US withdrawal, Europe considers its own nuclear deterrent', Max Fischer, NYT, 6 March 2017.
20. 'EU will Ausgaben für Rüstungsforschung bündeln', *Zeit* online, 7 June 2017.
21. 'EU wächst militarisch zusammen – zumindest ein bisschen', Markus Becker, 8 March 2017, *Der Spiegel*.
22. 'Mike Pence Widens US Rift with Europe over NATO defence spending', *The Guardian*, 18 February 2017; 'Tillerson gets tough with allies as he sets deadline for NATO spending', *The Times*, 1 April 2017.

THE EU: 'SOFT POWER IS NOT ENOUGH' 245

23. 'Wie von der Leyen an der Euro-Armee bastelt', Der Spiegel, 3 January 2018.
24. 'The Sanctions Blowback from the EU Begins', The American Interest, Seam Keeley, *The American Interest*, 8 October 2017.
25. 'EU throws out sanctions plan to punish Kremlin for atrocities', *The Times*, 21 October 2016.
26. 'Italy scuttles new Russia Sanctions Proposal', *The American Interest*, 21 October 2016.
27. See, for example, Andrew Wilson, *The Ukraine Crisis: What it means for the West*. Yale University Press, 2014.
28. Speech to the Lord Mayor's banquet in London, 12 November 2017.
29. Shetsova, L. 'The Sanctions on Russia: How hard do they bite?', *The American Interest*, 4 April 2016, and Milov, V. 'Why sanctions matter', *The American Interest*, 14 August 2017.
30. Jones and Whitworth (2014), 'The Unintended Consequences of European Sanctions on Russia', *Survival*, no 56, issue 6, September, pp. 21–30.
31. Newnham, R. E. 2015, 'The Ukrainian Crisis and Western Economic Sanctions against Russia: Do they work or should they be strengthened?', Cicero Foundation, US.
32. Ibid.
33. European Commission, 2016, 'Countries and Regions, Russia', 29.4.2016.
34. Levada centre, 'Sanctions and Counter-sanctions, 2015, and ibid., September 2015 ratings'.
35. See for example, the chapters on justice and home affairs in Gareis, S. et al. (eds) (2013), *The European Union – A Global Actors?* (Barbara Budrich Pubs, Opladen), especially the chapters on terrorism and migration.
36. *The Times*, 7 September 2017.
37. Ibid.
38. Minerva, 22 August 2017, 'Syria-alarm: Sviktende identitets- og sikkerhetskontroll'.
39. 'L'Austria sfida Roma. 70 soldati al Brennero contro i migranti', *La stampa*, 22 August 2017.
40. European Stability Initiative, 'On Solid Ground? 12 Facts about the EU-Turkey Agreement', 25 January 2017, p. 1.
41. Ibid., p. 3.
42. Ibid., p. 7.
43. Matlary, Sophie, *A Joint Decision trap?*, op.cit.
44. 'EU-Kommission nennt Tusks Schreiben "anti-europaeisch"', FAZ, 22 December 2017.
45. 'EU Migration showdown divide deepens', *Telegraph*, 14 June 2017.
46. 'Poland is racist for turning away refugee, says Juncker', *The Times*, 10 January 2018.

47. 'Das Ende des Selbsbetruges', FAZ, 7 June 2017.
48. 'EU zahlt Hunderte Millionen Euro an Flüchtligen in Türkei', FAZ, 22 December 2017.
49. 'Deutschland droht Türkey mit Bundeswehr-Abzug', FAZ, 16 May 2017; 'Das Ende eines Selbstbwetrugs', FAZ, 12 June, 2017, 'Germany to move troops fightring ISIL from Turkey air bases, as diplomatic row escalates', *The Telegraph*, 5 June 2017.
50. 'Griper inn i Niger', *Klassekampen*, 16.12.2017, p. 25.

REFERENCES

Faure, S. (2018). La cooperation franco-britannique malgre le Brexit? Les deux roles du Royaume-Uni: le premier role militaire et 'en meme temps' un second role industriel. In R. Johnson & J. H. Matlary, op.cit.

Gareis, S., et al. (Eds.). (2013). *The European Union—A Global Actors?* Opladen: Barbara Budrich Publishers.

Jones, N., & Whitworth, J. (2014). The Unintended Consequences of European Sanctions on Russia. *Survival, 56*(6), 21–30.

Matlary, S. (2015). *A Joint Decision Trap?* op.cit.

Meyer, S. (Ed.). (2014b). *NATO's Post-Cold War Politics. The Changing Provision of Security.* Basingstoke: Palgrave Macmillan.

Newnham, R. E. (2015). *The Ukrainian Crisis and Western Economic Sanctions Against Russia: Do They Work or Should They Be Strengthened?* Washington, DC: Cicero Foundation.

Shetsova, L. (2016, April 4). The Sanctions on Russia: How Hard Do They Bite?. *The American Interest.*

CHAPTER 10

NATO's Deterrence and Détente Efforts

NATO is a unique military alliance and one that has lasted longer than any other alliance in history. Most military alliances have been instrumentally conceived to address an immediate problem, but NATO seems to be enduring. Thies argues that the explanation for this is that the members are all—or nearly all, if we exclude Turkey—democratic and therefore share such important values that the alliance remains deep and endures.[1] Yet one could also explain NATO's longevity using realist logic: the alliance was formed in 1949 to deter the Soviet Union, and that was its main purpose for 40 years. When the Cold War ended, NATO was not certain about its role at all, and major debates raged about the purpose of the alliance. It could even be said that the wars in the Balkans this decade supplied NATO with a new rationale of muscular peacekeeping, often called peace enforcement. In the Kosovo War in 1999, when attempts at coercion failed, NATO attacked Serbia, a sovereign state, without a UN mandate.

Since Kosovo, NATO has been heavily engaged in war-fighting in Afghanistan, particularly between 2006 and 2013, and it led the attack on Libya in 2011. The reality of NATO action has thus been one of conventional war-fighting in areas beyond its own, and deterrence has largely been off the agenda since the end of the Cold War. The discussion within NATO then was about expeditionary forces that were professional and self-sustaining, rapid intervention forces in theatres beyond the transatlantic

© The Author(s) 2018
J. H. Matlary, *Hard Power in Hard Times,*
https://doi.org/10.1007/978-3-319-76514-3_10

area, a role for NATO greatly favoured by the US. One American politician quipped that NATO must go 'out of area or out of business'. It became very important to be able to fight professionally with expeditionary forces and deterrence was no longer relevant to the internal conflicts that erupted around the globe where non-state actors like insurgents were the enemy. As discussed in Chap. 2, state-to-state wars continued, but not in Europe and not bordering on NATO member states.

This period in NATO's history ended about 2010. Russia intervened in Georgia in 2008. At the same time some states such as Norway tried to get NATO back 'in area' and this effort coincided with Russia's attack on Georgia. The latter had come as a shock to NATO which had assumed that membership could continue eastwards. The debate that had been between those who wanted NATO to become a global actor and the states that wanted it remain 'in area' suddenly became outdated. Russia brought NATO back to its own euro-Atlantic area. Today we can safely conclude that the 'traditionalists' have won the argument, spurred on by Russia's annexation of Crimea. Deterrence is back on NATO's agenda as the major task of the alliance, just as in the Cold War. Yet the present situation is not like the Cold War, and deterrence models from that period can therefore not be replicated without careful analysis.

This chapter discusses NATO's response to Russian revisionism as the main theme, but also deals with the much smaller role that NATO plays in fighting terrorism and stopping illegal migration.

THE AMERICAN SECURITY GUARANTEE REMAINS VITAL TO NATO

Former US Defence Secretary Robert Gates gave a major speech in his last NATO ministerial meeting in June 2011, arguing that NATO had become a 'two-tiered' alliance 'between members who specialize in "soft" humanitarian, development, peacekeeping, and talking tasks and those conducting the "hard" combat missions, between those willing and able to pay the price and bear the burdens of alliance commitments, and those who enjoy the benefits of NATO membership – be they security guarantees or headquarters billets – but don't want to share the risks and the costs'.[2] Since Afghanistan, NATO's fundamental security contract, Article 5, naturally still remains the defining characteristic of the alliance as a military pact, but the political dynamics of the alliance are not centred on a common strategic assessment and there is no political agreement on the importance of deterrence in the Baltics or on the role that NATO should play in general.

The Cold War has not returned, despite Russian revisionism, and Russia is mostly regarded as a northern European issue in NATO, not seen to concern the South very much, as we saw in the previous chapter on France. The formation of the Northern Group and the JEF are northern responses to Russia, and the participating states are all from this region of Europe. Thus, NATO is divided by strategic interest and strategic outlook—more than ever before in its history. In the Cold War there was but one strategic scenario, that of invasion from the East. NATO's contingency plans and its deterrence were designed with this in mind. After the Cold War there was no strategic plan at all, only a number of security challenges such as internal armed conflicts, terrorism, failed states, and the like. The emphasis then was on expeditionary expertise and modernization of armies in this direction. Multinational operations 'out-of-area' was the key focus. There was no need for strategic planning, deterrence, and forward deployment.

Then comes the present, from about 2010 onwards: Russia becomes a revisionist power, but it does not seek inter-state war with NATO. Rather it maintains that it has special interests in the former CIS states, but it also tests NATO in various ways and uses tools that are both military and conventional as well as hybrid. NATO must therefore deter Russia, but not invasion from the East. This is a very important difference—in the present situation, NATO must be able to act on an Article 5 situation, requiring deterrence of such high-end risks, but these are not likely and cannot therefore determine and determine the deterrence model adopted. One does not take risk and spend enormous amounts on a plan for deterrence that is very unlikely to be needed. NATO will therefore not roll our large forces like in the Cold War along the Eastern 'flank'. There is no such flank today and modern weapon development means that a slow motion build-up to a war where tanks are rolling across the great plains of the Europe will not happen. The situation is different along all dimensions—missile technology makes geography and distance much less important today, cyber technology makes attacks extremely swift and even non-military, and above all: the political intention is not to occupy states and lock their borders imposing an ideology called Communism. Today the use of military force is much more Clausewitzian; it is about gaining political influence over states and in states. Sometimes only hybrid means will be useful, sometimes a mix of military means and non-military ones, and the operations will be limited, perhaps local, and very small. Deterrence must therefore be smart and adaptable. There has been an ongoing discussion about all this in NATO since the annexation of Crimea, but this is very much work-in-progress. No one really knows how to think about deterrence for the present challenges, especially those posed by Russia.

The division in NATO between the serious military actors and the rest, as spelt out by Gates, remains a constant: the willing and able are the two main strategic actors, France and Britain, the smaller Nordic members Norway and Denmark, the Dutch, and the Poles.[3] The realities of coalition warfare have become very clear in terms of the demands for risk-willing, relevant military capacities. Some European allies participated in the ISAF despite high costs, both financially and in terms of lives lost, but many more offer only token participation. Thus, NATO today is divided both by actors—the few 'willing and able' versus the many who are not in this category—and by strategic priority—the northern states that see Russian revisionism as the most important strategic challenge versus the southern states that look to the Maghreb and terrorism and mass migration as the key challenges.

As discussed in this book, international organizations (IO) usually do not collapse or dissolve—they become marginalized if not seen as useful by states. The OSCE is an example of an organization that plays a miniscule role in international security today, but which was much more important in the period after 1990 onwards and in its heyday in the 1970s when it functioned as a meeting-place and forum for East-West negotiations. Performance, often through being 'used' by states as platforms for action, is the decisive factor. The question is therefore whether the US finds NATO useful for its global security purposes. NATO is under American pressure to spend considerably more on defence, especially since President Trump took office in 2017, and also under pressure to participate in deterrence operations against Russia. In addition, the US expects allies to contribute in their latest 'surge' in Afghanistan and to be ready to deliver in the event of a war against North Korea.

NATO is increasingly a platform for coalitions of the willing, in the sense that states seek military cooperation like the JEF when they share strategic interests. As we have seen, both the French strategic review discussed in Chap. 8 and the German *Weissbuch* mention this explicitly—the French list a great number of types of partnerships and coalitions; the Germans allow for participation in coalitions of the willing for the first time, detached from an IO. Yet NATO also remains an organization in which the US plays an indispensable role because only the US can guarantee that Article 5 remains the deterrent that all members seek. While the strategic challenges for NATO today do not include nuclear and/or conventional war with Russia as the most likely scenario, this is nonetheless the major scenario that should be deterred, simply because it is so terrible and must be avoided at all costs. Therefore, the United States' role will remain a key one, even if we are not looking at a new Cold War. Yet in the most relevant and likely security scenario, it is below Article 5, so to speak—and this is where European states themselves have to be able to act, including deterring Russia.

The Americans rightly assume that the Europeans must be able to manage their own security agenda short of inter-state war. Thus, the challenge to European NATO members is that they can assume US participation and US deterrence in the most serious situations, but these situations will rationally speaking be avoided by an adversary. The 'gap' between national responsibility for own security and defence and Article 5 can be very wide, and modern cyber technology makes it wider. There are very many ways of creating uncertain and unstable situations for European states that do not 'touch' Article 5. As discussed in Chaps. 2 and 5, hybrid and indirect ways of fighting are plentiful and it is not always possible to attribute an attack to the state behind it. Europeans must be able to detect, confront, and win such battles. In addition, the US remains the only state in NATO that can meaningfully deter major war or confrontation.

The proximity of Britain and the Nordic states to Russia implies a permanent security problem which is less severe than in the Cold War, but where the basic geopolitical issue of great power–small state neighbour remains. Thus, states that border Russia are concerned about possible future conflicts of interest and therefore seek close relations with the US.

The main rationale for NATO membership has always been, and remains, existential security, the so-called Article 5 guarantee, even though, after 1990, the existential threat from the Soviet Union was gone. However, Russia has remained politically important as a source of lesser threats and plays a key role in the security thinking of states bordering it. In the work on a strategic concept for NATO in 2010 and 2011, Norway, the Baltics, and Central Europe formed a group that emphasized the importance of being 'in area'. In the concept itself, the importance of maintaining an 'in-area' presence was recognized for the first time since 1990, and work towards military exercises and contingency planning is mentioned.

NATO's Response to Russia: Belated Deterrence

Deterring Russia was NATO's key priority during the Cold War, and has all of a sudden become so again today. After a 25-year 'peace dividend' in Europe, state-to-state rivalry is back, and with it the (distant) risk of state-to-state war. After the annexation of Crimea in 2014 the term deterrence became yet again the main focus in NATO meetings.

On the military side, at the summit held in Cardiff in September 2014, NATO agreed on a Readiness Action Plan (RAP) to speed up response time to security threats; this included the creation of a Very High Readiness Joint Task Force (VJTF) which deployed a pilot force to Latvia consisting of British, Dutch, and Norwegian troops soon afterwards. The plan was for company-size deployments to rotate and exercise in the Baltic states, including larger exercises. In addition, command and control nodes were to be stationed in East-Central European states as well as in the Baltics.

The British are also to lead the UK JEF, a multination brigade-size expeditionary force on high readiness. The contributing states are Norway and the Netherlands along with the three Baltic states. The aim is to make the JEF fully operational before 2018, but it can also be deployed in smaller formations before that.[4] In the summer of 2017 Sweden and Finland also joined the JEF, a significant move for these non-aligned states which brings them very close to core NATO states. The JEF is to be deployed very rapidly to a 'hot spot', which now also includes these two key states in the Baltic sea region. They have also joined the NATO's "Host nation"-policy which allows NATO to use their land, sea, and air territory in exercises and real crises and war. This is 'win-win' for both sides—NATO gets access to the Baltic Sea region and the Baltic states not only via Poland, which sits near Kaliningrad, but also through Sweden and Finland. For these states, they are de facto on NATO's side if a conflict occurs, and will then fight with NATO and be protected by NATO.[5]

The deployment of NATO Force Integration Units (NFIUs) in all the Baltic states and in Poland, Bulgaria, and Romania was announced in 2015. These are small command and control units, not real HQs, yet they can coordinate the high readiness force and national forces.

But why were these deployments so small? This has to do with both political reluctance among NATO members and strategic considerations. With regard to political opposition there was a clear divide between the US and Britain, Norway and Denmark along with the East-Central Europeans and Balts on the one hand, and Germany on the other. This was evident at Cardiff. The Germans did not want to talk about deterrence, only the vague unstrategic term reassurance. They did not want to create any more tension with Russia and were not keen on deployments in the Baltic area.

Thus, not only were the deployments to the Baltics and East-Central Europe small, but they were also late in coming, and made possible only because the US rather belatedly chose to deploy. But European NATO states were even more reluctant to go to the Baltics than the Americans. The NATO summit in the summer of 2016 in Poland finally agreed on something, after the US had made their decision to send a brigade on a rotational basis. The European contribution was the so-called Enhanced Forward Presence (EFP), consisting of four battalions, one stationed in Poland—an American one; the other three placed one in each Baltic state. The British, Germans, French, Dutch, Danes, and Norwegians made up these three battalions, along with soldiers from all the Baltic states. They were fully deployed in the autumn of 2017.[6]

While the US was active in reassuring the Baltic states about their security in the early stages of the Ukraine crisis, there was as said, little willingness to deploy beyond the very small nodes mentioned above. The Baltic states were not pleased. They pleaded for more troops and forward positioning of materiel, pointing to Russian activity in fomenting unrest among Russian minorities.[7] They also prepared for hybrid war with Russia, conducting exercises along the lines of smaller incidents and infiltrations.[8] They demanded permanent NATO forces on the order of a battalion in each Baltic state, but accepted that these would be there on a rotational basis. The point, however, was to establish a permanent presence of troops.[9] The US finally got more involved in deterrence of Russia in the Baltics and Central Europe in the spring and summer of 2015. It announced the deployment of heavy weapons to Poland and other allied states in June, including heavy battle tanks on the order of about 250 and 1200 vehicles.[10] Poland was actively seeking a special relationship with the US, demanding as much deployment of American forces as possible[11] and even talking about the possible stationing of some of NATO's legacy nuclear weapons there.[12] Thus, it was the US, not any European state, that took the lead on deterrence.

The Obama administration had drawn down their forward deployments in Europe and opted for a 'pivot' to Asia where the key security challenges of North Korea and China are. It took more than a year after the fighting in Ukraine started before the US decided on forward deployments of heavy materiel, such as Abrams tanks, to the Baltics and some Central European countries.[13] The US deployed an armoured brigade that would rotate throughout the Central European states, but this was a small deployment compared to the Cold War stationing of troops. All in all the US may have around 60,000 personnel in Europe, including personnel on bases and in staff. Only some years ago the US had four brigades in Europe.[14]

In addition, exercises were held, such as 'Noble Jump' in Poland with 2000 troops from 9 NATO member states in June 2015. A very large exercise was Anakonda-16, with 31,000 troops, held in Poland in June 2016[15]—it was this exercise that Walter Steinmeier, then foreign minister of Germany, called 'sabre-rattling', as mentioned in Chap. 6. There was also 'political signalling' from the US in the deployment of three B-52 bombers, intended for exercises over the Baltic Sea and states, to RAF Fairford in June 2015.[16]

Militarily, deterrence is aided by having an 'ear to the ground' in these states—by having sensors and intelligence of all sorts, being situationally aware at all times, and being able to share intelligence with NATO HQs in Brunssum and in the US. Military technology makes intelligence gathering possible without much visible presence at the border, but the presence of ground troops of some kind plays a major political role in deterrence, as argued above. Yet for deterrence to be effective, there must be a certain depth to the military capacity in place, not only in terms of intelligence. Air policing is necessary, and several NATO states have deployed jets to that end. Contingency planning must be developed and updated, exercises must be held, and there must be credibility that these plans will work in a real situation. The bottom line is that deterrence is successful only if the military threat is credible. The *political* aspect of deterrence—instilling fear in an enemy—ultimately depends on *military* credibility.

THE BALTIC THEATRE

NATO might very well have decided to deploy larger forces to the states mentioned above. It was Germany that kept insisting at the Wales summit that NATO continue to respect the Russia-NATO agreement of 1997 despite Russia's failure to do so. In this political agreement, both sides had promised not to station permanent troops in East-Central Europe, a promise that Russia violated by the annexation of Crimea and the heavy forward stationing of weaponry in Kaliningrad. Germany's position on this matter was in line with German domestic policy, but it can clearly be interpreted as appeasement. Heisbourg argues along these lines: 'NATO has every reason to move to a permanent military presence in Poland and the Baltics [beyond the current deployment]. ... The annexation of the Crimea [sic] removed the basis for the West's political renunciation of such a permanent presence during the 1990s.'[17] This assessment is seconded by senior British officers who believe that 'this commitment [the 1997 treaty with Russia] should now be dropped to allow a "forward deployment" of NATO soldiers in the Baltic states'.[18] As we have seen, this became US policy in mid-2015 when it decided on further deployments to the Baltics and Central Europe. NATO, however, has not agreed to revoke the 1997 agreement. Thus, it is the US that leads and decides to act, not NATO.

The Russian response to increased deployment to the Baltic states was very tough, at least rhetorically.[19] In a message delivered to Russian generals, President Putin threatened to deploy (more) nuclear-armed missiles to Kaliningrad. Once again, according to the Russian narrative, it was the US and NATO that had provoked Russia and acted aggressively, and these actions had to be countered.[20]

Militarily, deterrence requires more than a token presence, especially given the very short lead times of military operations today. Even if air power can be deployed very fast and there is Baltic air policing, planes need plans for bases, shelters, and air defence. If the adversary establishes air dominance, there is no possibility for ground troops to fight effectively or even for them to deploy in theatre. If effective deterrence from a military point of view is to be established in the Baltic states, much more needs to be done. Yet here we see the twin problems of lack of military capability to station troops in these states and political caution, or rather fear of escalation. For Russia, the 'hybrid' choice is a reflection of strategy; in a way, it is the ideal mode of operating in order to avoid serious counter-measures, in this case from NATO.

The Institute for Strategic Studies warned in its annual, *Military Balance*, that Russia's method of operation may inspire others, as 'it is essentially an effort to wage limited war for limited purposes'.[21] A limited war of this kind can start with subversive efforts in states beyond Europe, and NATO is unprepared and not mandated to tackle this kind of operation.

Yet there is another new aspect of the deterrence of hybrid operations that must be mentioned here. It is the role that the national governments

256   J. H. MATLARY

of the Baltic states and Finland should play to avert hybrid situations. The OSCE and the EU, and perhaps the UN, also have key roles here. The point is to ensure that minority policies are up to international standards to prevent any cause for complaint and uprising. For example, the Russian minority in Latvia must be treated according to all international legal and political norms. One way of ensuring this could be to host a high-level conference under the auspices of OSCE, the main organization for the question of minorities, with its own High Commissioner for National Minorities, of which Russia is also a member. The goal of such a conference would be not only to bring national policies in line with standards that are generally accepted by the community of states, but also to deter attempts at hybrid operations that use minority politics as a pretext. In a more general sense the EU should engage more in the East-Central European states and Finland to show presence and create a kind of 'seamless' deterrence: If a state or organization interferes in internal affairs in Hungary, for example, it will answer to the EU. Even if this is not primarily a NATO task, but rather the purview of the OSCE, the EU, and national governments, I discuss it under the NATO heading because the lack of deterrence of hybrid wars will make it almost impossible for NATO to act in such operations once they are launched. In other words, deterring hybrid operations is extremely important because it is far from certain that NATO will be able to respond to them. Yet deterrence has received very little attention from political leaders beyond the mere recognition that it is a major issue. To date, none of the Baltic states have taken the initiative to look critically at their minority policy or to invite international actors to join them in this. This will make it much easier for Russian actors to foment discontent.

This is what is called 'multilateralization' by single states, a tactic employed by Norway in the Cold War whenever Russia attempted to create a condominium in the High North and thereby establish a bilateral relationship between the two countries. In sum, Western states bordering Russia can and should do much political work as a form of deterrence against being put under pressure. The political actors, not the military ones, are the most important actors in a hybrid case. Yet preventive diplomacy has barely been discussed; the EU and OSCE have been rather passive, as have the Baltic states. There has been no evidence of thinking along these lines.

Again, strategic logic is interactive and the actions of one party influence those of the other. Europe's political action can influence the calculus

NATO'S DETERRENCE AND DÉTENTE EFFORTS 257

in Moscow. If Europe is not proactive, however, its counterpart in the East is likely to be emboldened. A reactive mode is the worst choice, both militarily and politically.

Given enough military hardware and planning, NATO will probably be able to deter Russia in a conventional operation. This is the normal way we think about deterrence. Yet there is another way—we can see a gradual loss of confidence in NATO's deterrence, a kind of 'salami slicing',[22] whereby the leading guarantors of deterrence have lost credibility in terms of their political and military will to act. Given the drawdown of Europe's defence budgets, this may be a consequence, combined with a post-national political mind-set. That leaves the US as the only real deterrent in NATO, as in the Cold War. Yet conditions then and now are very different—the US is weaker now and engaged in conflicts elsewhere. The confrontation that is most likely between Russia and Europe is a hybrid one in which it would likely be far from clear whether the principle of collective defence as stated in Article 5 of the North Atlantic Treaty is in play; US involvement is therefore not guaranteed. This gap between Article 5 and likely hybrid scenarios means that Europe itself must do much more and take responsibility, both for deterrence and for any response to eventual aggression.

Although NATO agreed on deterrence measures for the Baltics and Central Europe during 2014 and 2015, these were deemed insufficient by these states, which called for more deployments. Germany, however, was opposed to increased deployment, and the US was not very active in Europe until mid-2015 when it decided to deploy more heavy equipment in these states. The 'return' of the US as leader was greeted with relief, and it was seen as a belated but correct policy change. Yet it remains a fact that Europe itself, and NATO, as such, did not lead. US leadership was called for, and it finally presented itself. The eastern Europeans were relieved, welcoming the deployments.[23] But do these rather modest deployments really deter?

Does NATO Deter in the Baltics?

Summing up, the term 'deterrence' was used in the conclusions from the NATO summit in Warsaw in June 2016, and the text of the final communiqué was very sharp in tone regarding Russia. At the prior NATO summit in Cardiff in 2014, the term that had been used was 'reassurance', which seemed to signal that the Baltic and East European states needed to be reassured instead of their neighbour Russia needing to be deterred.

Naturally no one is 'reassured' in this kind of situation unless deterrence is in place, so the talk about reassurance was more of a diplomatic move to avoid the 'tough' term deterrence than something substantially different from deterrence. Yet deterrence is what NATO's strategy vis-à-vis Russia is about, and there is an extensive political as well as scholarly debate on what this means in the present age of electronic and 'hybrid' warfare. While entirely new technologies, such as cybertechnology, enable actors in new ways, present-day deterrence must also encompass the 'old' issues of nuclear brinkmanship and conventional war.

Deterrence theory was developed during the Cold War, particularly by American political scientists working on strategic games and game theory. The essence of deterrence is very logical and quite simple: to prevent an opponent from starting an action he plans to undertake or may think of undertaking. It is an essentially strategic concept where success is a function of whether said opponent is dissuaded from trying such an action. Deterrence has been described alternatively as the ability 'to persuade an adversary that the costs to him of seeking a military solution ... will far outweigh the benefits',[24] and as 'the power to dissuade as opposed to the power to coerce or compel'.[25] Other scholars phrase it somewhat differently, but the essence of the strategic logic remains the same: to stop someone from undertaking an action because the risk of failure is too great.[26] Usually deterrence theory is limited to military means of action, but there is no reason why this should be so, as Rostoks points out: 'Military means are at the core of deterrence ... [deterrence] is, however, not based solely in military means, which is also recognised by the authors that wrote about deterrence in the Cold War period'.[27] Nuclear weapons play much less of a role today than they did during the Cold War, yet they continue to be the 'ultimate deterrent' for both NATO and Russia, as well as for other states, including France and Britain. Current efforts to deter Russia must therefore take into account what we can call 'traditional' deterrence, as well as the new technology of cyber warfare and significant improvements in missile technology. Regarding the latter, so-called anti-access/area denial weapons, abbreviated A2/AD, play a central role: Russian denial capabilities from its bases in Kaliningrad will make it extremely costly in terms of risk and losses if NATO were to have to reinforce its deployments in the Baltic states. Thus, designing a deterrence regime for the present challenge of Russian revisionism is a complex task, entailing the full spectrum of possible uses of both military and hybrid tools.

NATO'S DETERRENCE AND DÉTENTE EFFORTS 259

Deterrence is usually divided into two types or models: deterrence by denial and deterrence by punishment. Denial is the 'best' or preferred option, as it simply concerns having the 'upper hand' militarily in a given situation. Being able to escalate at will means controlling the situation. If an opponent faces military superiority, he will naturally not want to try an attack. Ideally, therefore, NATO should be in this position if it wants to create the intended deterrent effect.

DENIAL: A PREFERABLE STRATEGY?

A much discussed RAND study[28] purported to show that Russia could take Riga and Tallinn in 60 hours and that NATO would need to deploy at least seven brigades in the area to be able to fight this. As we have seen, the deployment is four battalions. In the study the conclusion was that NATO in the event of conventional conflict over territory, like a capital in a Baltic state, stood to lose massively.

In a detailed analysis of what this kind of deterrence entails in present-day Europe, Colby and Solomon argue that although it is not likely that Russia would risk an Article 5 reaction from NATO if it tried to 'carve out a small portion of a Baltic or Scandinavian state', 'NATO does not necessarily own the advantage in a contest of wills with Moscow in a limited war'.[29] The risks for Russia of attempting such a strategic attack would be formidable, but so would the gains if it showed that NATO's Article 5 guarantee did not function. If Russia could maintain deniability, the risk would be considerably lessened. 'To allow this to happen would be absolutely devastating to the credibility of the Western alliance',[30] they continue, and NATO therefore has two options: to accept the higher risk strategy that Russia would not dare make such a move; or to deter Russia from making such a move. The latter choice involves deterrence by denial.

The requirements of such are very great, especially for European states that are unwilling to spend much on defence and, in many cases, also risk-averse. The authors point out that there are almost no fighting forces in the Eastern parts of Europe, and that the rapid response forces agreed to at Wales, the VJTF, can only be deployed in one place at any one time. There is a need for permanent NATO forces in this region, but these should be as defensive as possible in order to avoid instigating a spiral of arming, which is the well-known strategic problem with placing more forces in a given theatre. However, deterrence with a denial force would require 'several mechanised infantry-brigade combat teams', as well as substantial reinforcement in terms of forwards bases, fighter aircraft, and missile shields able to suppress Russian A2/AD capabilities.[31] In addition, there is a need to re-establish deterrent naval forces in the North Atlantic to protect the Sea Lanes of Communication (SLOCs), as well as a number of other conventional military capacities that I do not detail here, but which are discussed in the article. The authors conclude however that 'revamping NATO's posture along these lines would be controversial, to say the least'.[32]

More controversial is Jakub Grygiel's proposal that *offensive*—and not defensive—capabilities be given to the countries of the east.[33] In order to take the A2/AD challenge seriously,[34] extended deterrence must be created for the states in the east since 'Russia's integrated air defense system … covers every Baltic state and one third of Poland, all NATO members', he argues.[35]

If all states in the region arm themselves with similarly offensive capabilities instead of just relying on the US to be able to penetrate these missile shields, and that at great cost, they will deter more effectively. The US may not have much incentive to engage in this manner in the first phase of a conflict—thus making the deterrent value *smaller*—whereas states bordering Russia have every incentive to engage immediately. If they have offensive weapons that counter Russia's, the deterrent value increases, leading Grygiel to conclude that 'frontline US allies should be armed with offensive arsenals capable of targeting the common rival's strategic and military assets'.[36] This makes strategic sense, as the states in the region have an existential interest in making deterrence work, and there is no danger of interest asymmetry if these states have a capacity to inflict punishment on an aggressor. They can be counted on to do so, something which will influence the calculus of the former. Yet arming states with such offensive weapons will incur reactions, thus perhaps leading to escalation and is therefore a risky strategy.

A similar argument is made by Matthew Kroenig in his article 'Facing Reality: Getting NATO ready for the new Cold War'.[37] NATO needs a new strategy of deterrence, he argues, one that is able to deter conventional war in in the form of 'an invasion by regular Russian forces'.[38] This requires not only a forward presence in East-Central Europe, but also a new policy for tactical nuclear weapons in Europe because 'NATO has few good options for responding to Russian tactical nuclear aggression'.[39] He argues for forward stationing of nuclear forces in East-Central Europe in order to make deterrence real. This is necessary because Russian nuclear doctrine differs from that of NATO: ' Russian military doctrine relies on the integration of the nuclear elements of military capability with the conventional and assumes escalation from conventional to nuclear capabilities in order to "de-escalate."[40] This implies a forceful deterrent on the part of Russia, which 'actively uses nuclear forces for messaging purposes as part of an integrated approach to crisis and conflict'.[41] NATO, on the other hand, retains nuclear weapons as the ultimate deterrent, but not as part of an escalation model, and has no modern doctrine about how these weapons fit into deterrence strategy. Moreover, there is major opposition to any discussion of such strategy among NATO countries.

Thus, in the view of these authors, there is little strategic development in NATO at present that takes into account the major military challenges that Russia poses, namely its rhetoric and doctrine on tactical nuclear weapons as well as conventional war. NATO has not even mustered deterrence by denial strategy.

The likelihood of creating a denial deterrence mechanism in East-Central Europe is politically very low, but doing so may also not be a good idea from a strategic point of view. Deterrence is political in the sense that its effect is political. From a military point of view, having a system of deterrence by denial in place is ideal, as this is the most certain mode of deterrence. The deterring actor has escalation dominance.[42] The aggressor can thus be certain that he will meet overwhelming resistance and likely lose the battle. He will therefore refrain from attacking if he is even remotely rational.

Deterrence by denial was possible in an existential scenario like the Cold War, where it simply had to exist because the risk was so high, and the conditions for creating such deterrence were in place because the scenario was conventional. Moreover, at that time one could mass militarily without being accused of aggression. Today this is no longer possible. Were NATO to deploy massive forces in the Baltic states, next to Kaliningrad, Russia would certainly label it aggression and would counter any such move. In addition, the political will to mimic Cold War deterrence posture is simply not there.

A Punishment Strategy: The Trip-Wire

Deterrence by denial, while ideally the best form of deterrence, is not a viable concept in the present construction of NATO's strategy to counter Russian revisionism. This statement is a strategic assessment, not based on what is politically possible or impossible, argues Zapfe. Deterrence by denial should *not* be the preferred option strategically, he argues, because the threat is not invasion but 'a political threat to allied cohesion'.[43]

The risk ranges from 'high-end' war (least likely) to 'hybrid' war (much more likely). High-end war could result from increased tension between the US and Russia with a choice of escalation on Russia's part. Putin's mention of Russia's nuclear weapons serves as a threat and reintroduces the Cold War nightmare of brinkmanship, and in a scenario of increased tension, conventional war cannot be ruled out. Thus, deterrence for NATO currently entails every type of military operation, from the quasi-military hybrid mode to full-scale war, where tactical nuclear weapons cannot be ignored. Yet the most likely scenario is not conventional war in a limited way, therefore deterrence by denial is at present not the best model for the Baltics, he argues.

In a hybrid scenario, the problem is not major troop movements and follow-on forces, but rather determining and detecting what is really going on, as well as attributing events. The cat-and-mouse game that has been played in Ukraine since 2014 shows that Russia is capable of being an actor while denying it, which led to the absurd situation in which the non-actor Russia was the major diplomatic actor at the 2015 Minsk negotiations while also meddling in Ukrainian politics, advising Ukraine what to do, 'accepting' national elections in Luhansk and Donetsk in 2014, and telling Ukrainian troops to surrender in Debaltseve in February 2015 after the Minsk negotiations. It will require more than military means to deter a hybrid war in a Baltic state.

If Russia employs hybrid methods against one of the Baltic states, there will probably be much confusion and dissension surrounding the facts of the events, not to mention a deliberate propaganda war on the part of Russia. Sources in NATO described such confusion at the first North Atlantic Council (NAC) meeting after the occupation of Crimea.[44] At that time, there was no common situational awareness among the NATO ambassadors and much confusion about what was really happening in Crimea. We can assume that this will also be the case should another hybrid situation arise. Deterring such a situation is thus all the more important.

Zapfe starts his analysis by discussing the threat and risk picture and argues that many miss the key element of this, which is 'above all, a political threat to allied cohesion'.[45] This can result in essentially two types of actions on Russia's part, he continues, subversion or a *fait accompli*. Subversion can hit the forces of the EFP in the form of staged demonstrations and fights with NATO soldiers by locals in the Baltic states; allegations of crimes committed by the same soldiers, such as rape, violent brawls, and the like; or situations of unrest among the local Russian population involving NATO soldiers: 'The possibility of NATO tanks facing civilian protesters is not far-fetched.'[46] Another possibility would be a supposed terrorist attack on NATO forces or disinformation campaigns about troop behaviour.

Zapfe points out that if such incidents were to take place in the Baltic states, it could easily lead to political division in NATO since the EFP is made up of several national contingents essentially controlled by their capitals, much like the ISAF, where national caveats and differences made it virtually impossible to act in a quick and unitary manner. Thus, by instigating situations like the above, Russia could attempt to divide NATO politically. As this would be a risk-free strategy, it is the more attractive.

A *fait accompli* would be a riskier prospect, Zapfe writes, as it could lead to an Article 5 response. The 'land grab' problem is the key preoccupation of the strategic thinking behind the EFP, which constitutes a so-called *trip-wire model* of deterrence. The military problems involved in assisting the small EFP have already been discussed—namely, the A2/AD issue, which is the reason why NATO cannot easily create a deterrence by denial situation in the Baltics, even if it were politically possible among NATO states. As said, such a move would have the strategic effect of making Russian escalation and other possible reactions likely, thus increasing the risk of conventional armed conflict. There are thus good *strategic* reasons behind the decision not to create a deterrence model based on denial in this specific case, although a generally improved military deterrence situation for NATO in all of Europe is necessary in the longer run if one is to achieve the desired deterrent effect. But to escalate in the Baltic region now seems a poor idea, also for strategic reasons as discussed above.

But how can the 'trip-wire' deter? Zapfe writes that 'the Russian leadership appears to perceive international politics as part of a continuum of warfare, making no clear distinction between war and peace'.[47] Thus, what to Western states is a clear distinction between military means and diplomatic tools does not hold in Russian external relations. 'Cross-domain' coercion is therefore the norm, not the exception, and this makes the Western categories of conventional and hybrid, military and diplomatic, void of meaning and, in fact, a weakness. Russia is a unitary actor in a much more consolidated way than the liberal democracies of the West, and does not operate with one set of rules for military means of influence and another set of rules for diplomacy. The West defines deterrence as a military activity of conventional military means, whereas Russia is able to combine subversion and kinetic warfare in one and the same move. Here, the importance of the political is key—the effect of whatever means is used to gain influence is *always political*. Clausewitz' main point is of tremendous importance in analysing the strategic game between Russia and the West in the Baltics and elsewhere.

Zapfe makes the salient point that a *fait accompli* there would most likely result in a monumental decision-making crisis in NATO, showing that there is no unity behind Article 5: 'in the absence of agreed-upon contingency plans, the necessity for unanimous decision-making could well block NATO forces from acting decisively'.[48] Now, such an outcome would represent a massive political effect! One would be able to show that NATO cannot act in such a critical situation, something which weakens the art 5 institution considerably.

NATO's rapid reaction force, the VJTF, which is under SACEUR command, is supposed to be sent in first, but any follow-on force would require unanimity. The result of an impasse like the one described above would most likely be that the US would step in with key allies like Britain and a few others among the 'willing and able', what Zapfe calls NATO's 'silent conventional deterrence'. But were this to happen, the lack of unitary action capacity behind Article 5 would be revealed, irreparably harming NATO's credibility. Furthermore, we must assume that the adversary in this strategic interaction would not be so stupid as to provoke an Article 5 response. There is ample opportunity for creating 'domestic' armed conflict where deniability is possible, as in Ukraine. And even if it did not want to worry about deniability, Russia could find areas in NATO where the US would not be likely to step in at first notice and withdraw quickly, before a reaction was in motion, having made its point that Article 5 is 'permeable'. Thus, without contingency planning for deterrence by denial, the EFP remains politically quite risky, as it ultimately relies on the assumption that a smaller incident in a Baltic state will result in major escalation undertaken by the US.

Zapfe concludes that the EFP does not deter in any military sense, and that it 'may well enhance the threat to NATO's cohesion',[49] because it makes NATO soldiers vulnerable to the various risks discussed above. While this may be an overstatement, his admonition that 'NATO must not believe its own hype'[50] about the EFP is a good piece of advice. The 'trip-wire' concept is basically political in the sense that there is no plan for military deterrence in a meaningful sense. The idea is that the US will get involved should American soldiers be killed in a situation in a Baltic state, and that the same goes for the other Western states which deploy there. But would Germany react with military means if German soldiers were killed in a skirmish of some sort in the Baltic states? Would it demand Article 5 action in NATO? The answer is far from clear and probably negative—the risk being too great. According to Zapfe, the cumbersome unanimous decision-making procedure in NATO is not likely to produce an Article 5 decision quickly, if at all. *Therefore the 'trip-wire' ultimately rests on American willingness to react massively—to escalate—in a given situation.* If that situation is skilfully designed to not provoke or target Americans, it may not result in escalation or a military response. The 'trip-wire' would fail in deterring.

The question is really whether the EFP is planned as a deterrent in the military sense or whether it is mainly a political statement about NATO's reaction if the sovereignty of a member state is violated. Deterrence and coercion require both the political will and the military capacity to win a war if need be. The 'trip-wire' deterrent represented by the EFP does not constitute deterrence by denial, which is always the best kind of deterrent, provided it can be established without prompting adverse and dangerous reactions from the adversary. In this case, we can assume that heavy military build-up in the Baltic states would provoke a Russian response. Yet this is not necessarily the most important factor for NATO to consider, as reactions must be expected. The key issue is whether deterrence by denial is necessary to deter Russia in this theatre.

As we have seen, Zapfe argues that deterrence by denial is not necessary because Russia is primarily interested in low-risk subversion. Because the EFP provides ample opportunity for Russia to engage in such subversive activities, it has itself created vulnerabilities, he maintains. Yet his arguments are weaker when it comes to *fait accompli*, the other and more serious option that Russia is assumed to have. Sometimes called 'limited war', a *fait accompli* is a smaller violation of sovereignty serious enough to elicit a reaction, but not war in a traditional sense. In terms of Russia-NATO interactions, such an act might be considered 'too small' for Article 5 and American involvement. This is where 'trip-wire' deterrence leaves very open questions, for how realistic is it to react heavily, incurring great risk and probably many losses, to a limited situation in, say, Riga? Armed conflict in a Baltic city between local Russians and Balts that ends in Russian take over of government buildings and national media would seem to be a 'big enough' incident for Article 5, but can we expect a clear-cut case where there is evidence of Russian forces acting inside a Baltic state? Hardly. In the event that national minorities begin fighting inside their own home state, there is little reason for NATO to react. In Ukraine, despite there being much evidence of Russian assistance, there is little hard evidence of direct Russian participation.

The 'trip-wire' deterrent may be excellent at detecting what goes on, but there is no automatic escalation built into the EFP, as there was in NATO's deterrence in the Cold War, where it was much clearer what constituted an attack and where the stakes also were considerably higher. The present-day 'trip-wire' is still modelled on a clear situation, where diplomatic and military means are separate and where deterrence concerns military means.

DÉTENTE AND DIPLOMACY

In addition to deterrence, which is a necessary strategic measure, NATO tries to reinstitute meaningful diplomacy with Russia. Within NATO and the EU there is disagreement on whether to put priority on this at present—'In West, a debate over talks with Russia', writes the *Wall Street Journal*—citing a diplomat who says that 'meetings with Russians at NATO are like talking to the radio'.[51] Some argue that even if this is so, diplomacy and dialogue is the more important. This is an old adage of professional diplomacy—that it is when relations are difficult that diplomacy is the more important. This is also what the secretary general of NATO argues for in wanting an 'intensified dialogue' in 2018.[52] However, this does not amount to a normalization. The US Secretary of State Tillerson points out that the latter presumes progress on Ukraine.

The fact is that diplomacy is always necessary, and that is especially true for détente—measures to de-conflict, prevent military misunderstandings, and disarm if possible. On this score much ought to be done and there has been little by way of meaningful contact after 2014. In the Cold War there was a concerted effort to create conditions for détente, and several disarmament initiatives. This is not the case today, and there is a clear need to combine deterrence and détente again. NATO tries to get this process going, and this work must be intensified.

In sum, this chapter has argued that NATO's efforts at deterrence are the most important part of strategy to meet the challenge of Russian revisionism, but that it is the US that is the main actor in this endeavour. Deterrence by 'trip-wire' is mainly a kind of political deterrence, depending primarily on the US. This model is riskier than deterrence by denial, but installing such a type of deterrence in the Baltics today is not the best strategic option because it is too risky and too costly. However, in the long run, Europe itself should deter by denial, as this is the only type of deterrence that ensures escalation if need be, thereby deterring at the most secure. In other words, if the adversary knows that there is a military response superior to himself, he will most assuredly be deterred from taking the risk of confrontation. This fact implies that European states be willing to spend much more on defence, at least getting up to the 2 per cent goal of GDP. At present there is no indication that this is happening anywhere, especially not in Germany, the richest state in Europe. Also, in Britain there is currently a new round of cuts discussed.

NOTES

1. Thies, W. (2009) *Why NATO Endures*, Cambridge University Press, UK.
2. Gates, op.cit.
3. See the discussion in my book NATO's *European Allies: Military Capability and Political Will, co-edited with M. Petersson*, 2014, Palgrave Macmillan, UK.
4. 'International partners sign JEF agreement', Gov.uk., 25.3.2015.
5. See chapter on Finland and Sweden by Petersson and Møller in Johnson and Matlary, op. cit.
6. 'Abschreckung mit Speerspitze im Baltikum', FAZ, 18 May 2015.
7. *NYT*, ?, 'Stirring separatist fervor in Latvian region'.
8. The Moscow Times, 'Fearing Repeat of Crimea, Baltic States Prepare for "Hybrid War" with Russia', 3 June 2015.
9. 'Baltische Staaten fordern dauerhafte Nato-Präsenz', *Spiegel Online*, 14 May 2015.
10. 'US and Poland in talks over weapons deployment in eastern Europe', *The Guardian*, 14 June 2015.
11. 'US and Poland in talks over weapons deployment in eastern Europe', *The Guardian*, 14 June 2015.
12. These are currently in Germany, Belgium, Italy, the Netherlands, and Turkey. 'Poland considering asking for access to nuclear weapons under NATO program', *The Guardian*, 6 December 2015.
13. 'A new US brigade won't change the status quo in Eastern Europe', Stratfor GeoPolitical Diary, 1 April 2016.
14. 'USA verlegen Kampbrigade nach Osteuropa', *Die Welt*, 31 March 2016, 'Für die NATO ist Osteuropa das neue West-Berlin', *Die Welt*, 31 March 2016, 'pentagon to restore Obama's troops cuts in Europe to address Russian aggression', *The Guardian*, 31 March 2016.

15. 'NATO countries begin largest war game in eastern Europe since cold war', *The Guardian*, 6 June 2016.
16. *The Times*, 'American Bombers fly in to send Putin a Message', 8 June 2015.
17. Heisbourg, op.cit., p. 41.
18. General Jonathan Shaw, British defence staff, quoted in *The Telegraph*, 'How do we protect the Baltic states?' David Blair, 23 February 2015, online.
19. 'Russia says US troops arriving in Poland pose threat to its security', *The Guardian*, 13 January 2017.
20. *The Times*, 'Putin threat of nuclear showdown', 2 April 2015.
21. Quoted in 'Report warns Russia's "hybrid warfare" in Ukraine could inspire others', 11 February Radio Free Europe, online.
22. 'The Revisionists: Salami slicing and deterrence', W. Mitchell and Grygiel, J., *The American Interest*, 23 February 2015.
23. 'Eastern Europe cautiously welcomes larger US military presence', *INYT*, 3 February 2016.
24. Howard, M. 1983, 'Reassurance and deterrence: Western defence in the 1980s', Foreign Affairs, 61:2, pp. 309–324, p. 317.
25. Snyder, G. (1961), *Deterrence and Defense: Toward a Theory of National Security*, Princeton, Princeton University Press, p. 9.
26. See also A. George and R Smoke (1974) *Deterrence in American Foreign Policy: Theory and Practise*, Columbia University Press; A. Long, (2008), *Deterrence: From Cold War to Long War*, RAND Corporation, and I. Arreguín-Toft (2009) 'Unconventional Deterrence: How the Weak deter the strong', in *Complex Deterrence: Strategy in the Global Age*, T.V. Paul et al. (eds.), Chicago, The University of Chicago Press.
27. T. Rostoks, 'Deterrence: The Evolution of a Concept from the Cold War to Hybrid War', in ibid. (ed), *Deterring Russia*, Routledge, 2018 (forthcoming).
28. RAND Corporation, (2017) 'Reinforcing deterrence on NATO's eastern Flank', by D Shlapak and M Johnson.
29. E. Colby and J. Solomon, (2015), 'Facing Russia: Conventional Defence and Deterrence in Europe', *Survival*, 57:6, pp. 21–50, p. 29.
30. Ibid., p. 28.
31. Ibid., p. 34.
32. Ibid., p. 42.
33. Grygiel, J. (2015) 'Arming Our Allies: The Case for Offensive Capabilities', *Parameters*, 45, 3, Autumn 2015, pp. 39–49.
34. This theme is analysed in detail by S. Frühling and G. Lasconjarias in their article 'NATO, A2/AD and the Kaliningrad Challenge', *Survival*, 58:2, pp. 95–116, 2016. There are three major Russian base complexes that are protected by 'missile shields'—Kola, Kaliningrad, and Crimea. The authors make the point that the Kaliningrad base is a threat to both the Baltics and

NATO'S DETERRENCE AND DÉTENTE EFFORTS   269

Nordics, yet at the same time a base surrounded by NATO members, meaning that it could become 'a hostage to NATO', p. 107.
35. Ibid., p. 47.
36. Ibid., p. 49.
37. *Survival*, 2015, 57:1, pp. 49–70.
38. Ibid., p. 61.
39. Ibid., p. 63.
40. Corbett, A. 'Deterring a Nuclear Russia in the 21st century: Theory and Practise', NDC Research Report, NATO Defense College, June 2016.
41. Ibid., p. 8.
42. 'Nuts and bolts solutions to deter a resurgent Russia', *War on the Rocks*, 18 May 2016.
43. Zapfe, M. (2017) 'Deterrence from the ground up: Understanding NATO's Enhanced Forward Presence', *Survival*, 59:3, pp. 147–160.
44. Conversations with NATO diplomats in London, 30 October 2014.
45. Op.cit., p. 148.
46. Ibid., p. 151.
47. Ibid., p. 149.
48. Ibid., p. 153.
49. Ibid., p. 157.
50. Ibid.
51. Article by same name, WSJ, 27 December 2017.
52. 'NATO will Dialog mit Russland intensivieren', *FAZ*, 3 January 2018.

References

Arreguin-Toft, I. (2009). Unconventional Deterrence: How the Weak Deter the Strong. In T. V. Paul et al. (Eds.), *Complex Deterrence: Strategy in the Global Age*. Chicago: The University of Chicago Press.

Colby, E., & Solomon, J. (2015). Facing Russia: Conventional Defence and Deterrence in Europe. *Survival, 57*(6), 21–50. p. 29.

Corbett, A. (2016, June). *Deterring a Nuclear Russia in the 21st Century: Theory and Practise*. NDC Research Report. Rome: NATO Defense College.

Frühling, S., & G. Lasconjarias in their article. (2016). NATO, A2/AD and the Kaliningrad Challenge. *Survival, 58*(2), 95–116.

George, A., & Smoke, R. (1974). *Deterrence in American Foreign Policy: Theory and Practise*. Columbia University Press; A. Long (2008). Deterrence: From Cold War to Long War, RAND Corporation.

Grygiel, J. (2015, Autumn). Arming Our Allies: The Case for Offensive Capabilities. *Parameters, 45*(3), pp. 39–49.

Howard, M. (1983). Reassurance and Deterrence: Western Defence in the 1980s. *Foreign Affairs, 61*(2), 309–324.

Rostoks, T. (2018). Deterrence: The Evolution of a Concept from the Cold War to Hybrid War. In T. Rostoks (Ed.), *Deterring Russia*. New York: Routledge.

Shlapak, D., & Johnson, M. (2017). *Reinforcing Deterrence on NATO's Eastern Flank*. Santa Monica: RAND Corporation.

Snyder, J. (1961). *Deterrence and Defense: Toward a Theory of National Security*. Princeton: Princeton University Press.

Thies, W. (2009). *Why NATO Endures*. New York: Cambridge University Press.

Zapfe, M. (2017). Deterrence from the Ground Up: Understanding NATO's Enhanced Forward Presence. *Survival, 59*(3), 147–160.

CHAPTER 11

Conclusions

In this book I have examined five actors, three of which are actors in the sense of possessing hard power resources (police, intelligence, military) and being nation-states, indeed great powers. These are the key states of Europe today: France, Germany, and Britain. In addition, we have analysed the roles that the two main IOs in Europe play, the EU and NATO. These are argued to be platforms for coalitions of states for the most part, as the security and defence field is one where states rarely give up sovereignty and where they remain in command of their hard power themselves. Yet NATO plays a key unitary actor role when it comes to operations and naturally in an Article 5 situation, and the EU can be a unitary actor when all agree, such as in the case of sanctions aimed at Russia.

In this concluding chapter I bring the analysis together and to a close, first by concluding about strategic action and strategic actors: Who were they and why do they fall in this category? Second, I look at the three cases and whether these strategic actors acted in these specific situations, what they did and why.

STRATEGIC ACTORS?

As discussed in Chap. 2, a strategic actor is able to act in a unitary manner, take action quickly and timely, and does not need to consult widely in order to do so. In the states that have the Foreign Policy Prerogative (FPP), these conditions are met. Such states are the US, France, and Britain (as well as

© The Author(s) 2018
J. H. Matlary, *Hard Power in Hard Times*,
https://doi.org/10.1007/978-3-319-76514-3_11

271

some smaller states like Norway and Denmark). These states typically have a strategic and military culture, as we saw in the country chapters. There we noted that France retains the strongest strategic action capacity in Europe today, given its clear demarcation between presidential powers and parliamentary ones. The fact that the president can act on his own, supported by his inner cabinet, the Security Council, without time-consuming and public deliberations with parliament, makes this strategic ability a real one. There are many examples of swift French military action; for example, the attack on Libya in 2011 which started when then President Sarkozy ordered it during a luncheon with allies at the Elysee. Also, the French underline their sovereignty in terms of being totally independent from all other states in their nuclear and other defences. They do not rely on the US like Britain does, although this may be a rather theoretical issue in this day and age when both states are fully integrated in NATO. Yet France pays attention to *national* independence.

The French have a clear national security strategy and put priority on threats and risks from the South. They demand of their partners that they are able and willing, not that they are members of NATO or the EU. Their strategic vision is an intergovernmental EU with an autonomous military capacity, but the first criterion of cooperation with other states is as said, that these are professional hard power actors. For this reason Britain is the preferred partner to France despite Brexit. President Macron came on an official visit in January 2018, which was held at Sandhurst Military Academy, a sign of this close military relationship. During this visit he made further agreements on such cooperation, especially in development of missiles and drones.[1]

Also Britain is a strategic actor with autonomy, yet it maintains the closest possible relationship with the Americans. Like France, it has an FPP as decision-making model, but as we have noted in the discussion of Britain, this is not as 'insulated' as it used to be. The role of Parliament in making decisions about the use of force seems to have increased, and public opinion is much concerned about 'failed' wars like Iraq and Afghanistan. There is much at stake in British strategic culture at present and the weakness of the current May government makes for instability in terms of grand strategy. Will Brexit weaken Britain's role? Not likely, we have argued, but a Labour government with Corbyn as prime minister would have major negative consequences for Britain's role as a strategic actor. Thus, although Britain is traditionally a strategic actor on a par with France, its current politicians do not seem to appreciate the importance of this. The political

CONCLUSIONS 273

class does not show much strategic ability and continues to pursue major defence cuts, despite strong evidence of a return of Realpolitik in Europe.

Germany is not a strategic actor, nor does it have a strategic culture. There are historical reasons for this and they are still important to the Germans. There are attempts at changing into a 'normal' great power role, entailing leadership, but this goes very slowly, and the major role that the Bundestag plays means that decision-making is slow, subject to ideological battle, transparent, and entailing micro-management of troops. All this runs contrary to swift, decisive, and tough action. For this reason Germany is unable to deter.

The EU cannot act strategically with hard power, but can do so with other policy tools where there is supranationality. The EU's rhetorical commitment to a defence union and its strategy document do not mean what one normally thinks these terms signify. The EU's own role in military affairs is miniscule and is not set to increase. PESCO is not strategic action, but a bottom-up industrial plan for smarter defence. Operations under EU auspices will come about only when states decide to undertake them. For these reasons the battlegroups remain unused.

NATO is a strategic actor only when the Americans take the lead. The key actor in the alliance, the US, is the leading force for decisions. But unanimity means that NATO can easily be paralysed in making decisions. Therefore real decisions will only be taken by states that cooperate in coalitions of the willing and able. The trend in NATO is towards such coalitions. We have noted that the US-led operation against Daesh is such a coalition, as was the fight against al-Qaida in Operation Enduring Freedom. Also the Libya campaign of 2011 started as a coalition, under French leadership. Moreover, even Germany's recent *Weissbuch* notes that coalitions of the willing and able is the new and increasingly preferred way of warfare by the West.

We have also pointed out that the unanimity procedure in NATO most likely will make it extremely difficult to reach a decision on declaring Article 5 in a given situation, and that deterrence therefore suffers as a result. The US as the real deterrent in NATO is therefore more important now than in the Cold War, something which underlines that states and not IOs, even NATO, are the real actors in security and defence policy. For those who deplore dependence on the US this is not the news they would like, but it is clear that multilateralism is less important now than in the period after 1990. The recent US security strategy's[2] main message is that we are in a period of great power competition, mentioning China and Russia, something which also implies that states take the centre stage of action.

For Europe this means that on the one hand, there is only one state actor that is a strategic actor in its own right—France—but on the other hand, there is but one actor that is extremely close to the US and therefore the stronger in concert with the US—Britain. As discussed in Chap. 7, Britain would opt for the 'special relationship' with the US as the very first priority in its security and defence policy if it had to choose. The two states are integrated in intelligence cooperation and in general defence cooperation, and this means that Britain is the most important actor in NATO among the Europeans since they can be counted on to be 'teamed up' with the Americans at all times.

We now turn to the findings of this study with regard to the cases studied.

RUSSIAN REVISIONISM: STRATEGY IN EUROPE?

Russian revisionism has been met with deterrence and with sanctions, as well as with some attempts at diplomacy and détente. We have argued that deterrence is the key strategy, and that the best form of deterrence is deterrence by denial. Yet in the short term, in the Baltics, such deterrence is neither possible nor desirable for two reasons: One, it would lead to escalation in the form of Russian reactions and could therefore function as a dangerous move, creating a spiral of action. Two, it would not be possible politically in European NATO; there is simply no agreement on a major military build-up in the Baltic Sea region. One could add that it is not possible economically as well; European states would not pay for such a strategy. Inserting much military capacity in a region where Russia has key military interests—the Kaliningrad base—is strategically unsound because it changes the *status quo* rapidly, creating a 'new normal' that cannot be considered a 'normal' because it is not credible as such.

Therefore, the preferred deterrence model in the Baltics at present is the 'trip-wire', a small deployment that is composed of troops from the major Western states with one American battalion in Poland; and German, French, British, and other forces in the Baltics. This 'trip-wire' is designed to create major American and European involvement should any of their troops be involved in war-fighting there. It is a Cold War concept which is logically that of deterrence by punishment, meaning that the reaction to the killing of allied soldiers is going to be escalation to major war-fighting on the part of the alliance. This assumes that there is political will on the part of the US, Britain, France, Germany, and so on to escalate in such a

CONCLUSIONS 275

situation, even if that implies penetrating the very well protected air and sea domains around Kaliningrad and in the Suwałki gap between Poland and the Baltic states. Militarily this will be extremely costly for NATO to do, as one has not prepared for doing so in any serious manner militarily. The latter would imply a deterrence by denial *modus operandi* for deterrence. There is therefore a real dilemma involved in the 'trip-wire' model—it is cheap, politically easy to agree to (at least compared to deterrence by denial), and it does not lead to strong Russian reactions. But it is a vulnerable model in its core logic, for how credible is this form of deterrence? Will the US react if there is an unclear situation in a Baltic state? The best one can say for this model is that it creates uncertainty also on the adversary's side; he cannot know what the reaction will be, so should he take the chance? In the deterrence by denial model, both sides can be pretty certain of the outcome of transgression—there is enough military force in place to escalate if an aggressor tries his hand. It therefore deters with much more certainty.

NATO's current 'trip-wire' in the Baltics is in place and nothing special has happened as of the end of 2017. Deployed troops train together with Baltic troops and this functions very well; a Norwegian officer says, 'Unless we can fight together, there is no point in any deployment. The Baltic colleagues are very professional and realistic in their approach', after being deployed to Lithuania.[3] All the three states in this study have important roles in this deployment, and we note that Germany, which was initially reluctant to deploy there, is now the battalion leader in Lithuania. Also Britain leads a battalion.

Yet we also note that it was the US that took the lead in deploying in East-Central Europe in the summer of 2015, spurring others to follow suit. The US leadership on creating a 'trip-wire' is clear; *US decisions came before NATO's decisions* at the Warsaw summit in the summer of 2016. Also at the Cardiff summit in 2014, recently after the annexation of Crimea, it was US leadership that drove the decisions. At this time Germany was still reluctant to even speak about deterrence, but Britain was clear in its support of the US despite being politically preoccupied with national elections. This says a lot about the nature of the 'special relationship'—when the US acts in NATO, Britain is always there as the most supportive state. Thus, Britain has come to play the key European role on deterrence of Russia through its leadership of the Joint Expeditionary Force (JEF), the build-up of the Very High Readiness Joint Task Force (VHRJTF), and the Northern Group after having been 'absent' during 2015 and 2016. Britain is by now the key military actor in Northern

Europe; one that also Sweden and Finland look to and seek closeness to. They have joined both JEF and the Northern Group.

Germany remains a follower in this policy area, preferring a role that amounts to support rather than leadership. Yet Germany has, as noted, taken on the battalion leadership role in Lithuania, something which is a major step for this country. For the first time since WWII it deploys heavy material like Leopard 2A tanks to Eastern Europe.

France is also present, albeit in a lesser role. This also speaks to the importance of NATO obligations. It would indeed look strange were France to be absent from the EFP, given its reluctance to give up the sale of warships to Russia in 2015.

Beyond deterrence, the détente aspect is largely untried. There have been calls for 'dialogue' as some call it, but the fact remains that there is (far too) little interaction with Russia, unlike in the Cold War. There are military 'hot lines', but the Russia-NATO Council has only met a few times since 2014, despite NATO wishes to the contrary. From the NATO side one has tried to agree on policy for snap exercises, something that Russia has not agreed to, and on better rules for information on air activity, flying with transponders on, and the like. It is fair to say that there has not been any major improvement on détente in this period.

As for diplomacy on Ukraine, President Obama and Chancellor Merkel cooperated on this along a 'good cop'/'bad cop' plan. Obama initiated the sanctions and thereby put pressure on Russia, whereas Merkel and Hollande were direct actors in the so-called Minsk process. These were conducted in Minsk with the Russian and Ukrainian presidents, but as noted in our analysis, they were conducted based on the facts on the ground. The military status in Eastern Ukraine was a 'moving target', so to speak, and this implies that these talks were not really negotiations with clear positions, but concerned a truce. To silence the weapons, to stop the fighting was the objective of Merkel and Hollande, but this is not normal diplomacy, but attempts at reaching a ceasefire. The curious fact that Russia was a party to these talks also testifies to this: why would a neighbouring country figure in talks in Ukraine under normal circumstances?

Western strategy on Ukraine has throughout this period 2014–present been absent. There is no policy, let alone strategy. Early discussions on arming Ukraine fell to the ground, and this was probably for the best. Ukraine is neither a NATO nor an EU state and does not have any Western security guarantee. The fact that there was no clear idea behind the Minsk talks on the part of the Western states explains their failure and why they were so muddled. Merkel—who was the key actor, with Hollande 'in-tow' as a passive party—did not know how to go about this: on the one hand, the West had condemned the annexation of Crimea in the strongest terms and called for its reversal and also for a full stop to fighting in Eastern Ukraine. On the other hand, the West did not want to use military means in this area of Europe, arming Ukraine. Therefore the West had no influence on the vital means of policy there at the time, namely physical force. The West could not even get access to the bodies on the ground after the shooting down of the Malaysian Air Lines plane until permission was given.

In a situation where the military tool is used by one party and the other party refrains from this, the advantage lies with the armed actor who can manipulate the facts on the ground to his advantage as he pleases. The unarmed party becomes dependent on what the armed party does. This was in essence the situation in Ukraine. The West pleaded for cessation of hostilities and Russia agreed on-and-off, creating conditions for this that had to do with regional elections and a federalized structure of the country that would ensure a veto on future EU and NATO membership for Ukraine. These talks, of the latest round is called Minsk II, has not resulted in anything substantial. The fighting in Eastern Ukraine flares up and dies down and no one is responsible for this; attribution cannot be made. There is an OSCE observation force in place, but there is no momentum in the talks as of early 2018. The status quo in Ukraine is that it is a state with border conflicts and internal armed conflicts, facts that make it impossible to approach the EU or for that matter NATO, as candidates for membership.

For Russia, this is a good state of affairs as 'going West' seems to be permanently off the agenda and that was the main policy interest on Russia's part. As for the West, if one entertained the thought of Ukraine as an EU or NATO member some years ago, this is very far from the agenda today. If we use the term interest asymmetrically, it is clear that Ukraine is not of interest to the West today. This has to do not only with Russian reactions, but very much with the corruption in the country and with the EU's own problems with Brexit, Visegrád, and so on. The EU is far from being able to think about enlargement, and NATO would naturally not touch this issue after the 'lesson' of Georgia in 2008.

Germany has played the key role in talks with Russia over Ukraine, but these talks have been processes rather than result-oriented. The sanctions, intended to put pressure on Russia to implement the Minsk demands, have not resulted in any political concessions in this regard. The sanctions were initiated by the US and they were imposed on the EU. The EU states would not have levelled sanctions themselves, we can safely assume, being unable to agree on such a controversial move. We have seen that EU states strongly disagree on the sanctions, but that they are renewed because of pressure to stay united with the US. *The US thus was the leader whereas European states were the followers, like in the case of deterrence.*

The sanctions show no evidence of having the intended political impact, although having an economic impact as well as predictably leading to a 'rallying around the flag' effect in Russia. It is on the whole unlikely that Russia will reverse its annexation of Crimea as this is a base of key strategic importance to Russia, and we can be fairly certain that sanctions and diplomacy will not lead to such a result. The problem for the West is therefore what to do next: should one simply act according to *Realpolitik* and admit that Russia defines a 'sphere of interest' in Crimea and in Ukraine? Or should one pretend not to accept this and continue to insist that the sanctions and diplomacy will work, knowing that they will not? By *not having a strategy* at the outset, the West has painted itself into a corner. It reacted with major condemnation at the rhetorical level, demanding the reversal of Crimea, but has not been willing to do much beyond this. The 'rational' explanation for this is interest asymmetry, but there should then have been a logical relationship between the massive rhetorical reaction and the concomitant lack of any other action. This betrays the lack of strategy on how to deal with Ukraine. These situations are not uncommon in international affairs, and time solves problems that states cannot. Ten years from now few will remember the annexation of Crimea and the sanctions will be long gone. Ukraine's domestic development will determine where it goes politically. Outsiders cannot 'manage' a country's development. This case is similar to the conflict between NATO and Russia over Georgia which took place exactly ten years ago, now largely forgotten in the West, the Russian position consolidated. Russia could 'solve' the problem by making some concessions on Ukraine, a la Minsk, that would satisfy the West, but not significantly alter the situation in Ukraine. In all events, Ukraine will not be able to 'go West' until it solves many of its own problems and the EU would not want such a problematic country as a member.

What remains essential to the West is the NATO border. It constitutes the 'red line'. Deterrence of a real kind, the denial model, must therefore obtain in NATO's own area. This is a long-term project that requires steady investment in defence in Europe, and here European states with their defence cuts undermine their own alliance through erosion. Deterrence by normal military means is the most important strategy for Europe, and one that is not 'aimed' at any one risk or threat, but which is a general position of sovereign states. Here the defence cuts and the reluctance to even spend 2 per cent tell a tale of being in *denial* of reality. Again Britain and France stand out as the exceptions, although Britain again discusses serious defence cuts as of early 2018.

In sum, the key actor on Russia has been the US; it is behind the sanctions as well as deterrence efforts. The strategy behind the sanctions—coercion—is very far from perfect, but it was the US that took the initiative, not the Europeans despite the fact that the problem is a European one. Moreover, despite these events European states continued to deplete their defence budgets, a telling indicator of how little emphasis they place on being able to deter in general and for *la longue duree*, which is what really matters.

Deterring Migration and Fighting Terrorism

The strategy that is necessary on mass migration into Europe, which will continue as a mega trend because European states are preferable to all others in terms of welfare policy, political democracy, and rule of law, is one of deterrence at Europe's borders as well as development in the MENA so that sustainable state structures with rule of law can become a reality. Only then can young talented people see a future in their home state and opt to remain there.

The situation for refugees is that most of them are so-called war refugees and that wars end, hence the return to home states should be planned so that these citizens can rebuild their own states. Political refugees are rarer, but also for these the main intention should be to be able to return once political conditions change. However, this may not happen in a lifetime and beyond, implying that also European states must continue to accept quotas of refugees under the UNHCR. Europe will also have to be active in war prevention and international peace enforcement. Thus, deterrence of migration and refugee 'external shocks' must go hand in hand with a strategy of changing the conditions in the regions that generate such exodus. Here conditionality must be streamlined into all developmental and political aid programmes—return of migrants-agreements, terms for rule-of-law and democratic developments, and so on.

In order for the attraction of Europe to be diminished it is also necessary to change the way asylum policy is being practised. Political asylum should not be possible to apply for inside a European country, but in centres at the Schengen border and preferably beyond, in designated sites operated by the UNHCR. In this way, the selection of those who will be included in quotas for European destinations will receive a fair treatment in a process of determining who will be allowed in, and it will be possible to establish ID for all who apply. Moreover, there will be a common standard for reviewing applications.

We can also assume that far fewer migrants will travel to Europe if it is impossible to apply for asylum there, as this process and appeal possibilities often imply that if one makes it to Europe, one stays. The vast majority of arrivals across the Mediterranean are African migrants, and they not only risk losing their lives on this journey but also become ruined economically because of the trafficking industry. The ethical issues involved here are complex, but it is clear that citizens of a state, even a poor and dysfunctional one, have a primary duty to remain and build their own state, and that only those states that want migrants will take them. Migration remains a state's sovereign policy area.

The conclusion is that the EU's ability to deal with the migration shock was non-existent. Germany's Merkel changed the rules of the Dublin system *de facto* by not insisting that all seek asylum at point of entry into Europe and allowed everyone to come to Germany, something which created a major pull factor. When Germany was also unable to cope with more arrivals, it insisted that an EU quota policy be adopted by majority rule, to the protestation of the *Visegrád* countries. Yet this policy was imposed on them and constitutes a major source of conflict in the EU today. These states will not accept a supranational policy on migration and refugee quotas; insisting that this is a vital area for a sovereign state. Prime Minister Orbán says that he will accept the quota policy of the UNHCR, but not of the EU.[4]

The EU should have controlled the Schengen border, and the fact that each state is responsible for the actual border control does not change the long-term policy of control of the outer border in order to open internal borders and thereby make the internal market a reality. When the external shock occurred in late 2015, nothing was done to stop it or to control it. The result was predictable: state after state started to control its own borders again. Also this situation quickly became untenable, as it led to congestion at borders and long delays in transport. The only solution was to

CONCLUSIONS   281

control the outer border, but the political will (and ability) to do so was absent, Germany's Merkel drew up a policy plan in the name of the EU to outsource border control as well as the asylum application process to Turkey. *Thus, both Germany and the EU realized that borders had to be controlled and closed in some instances, but opted to pay others for doing this.*

The deal with Turkey is not only expensive, but more importantly, implies strong dependence on the part of the EU on the dictatorial and unpredictable President Erdoğan. The EU is the dependent, and therefore the vulnerable, party. This is strategically speaking, extremely foolish and shortsighted. European states need to be able to control their own borders as a basic condition of being sovereign, and not depend on 'unlike-minded' and unfriendly states like Turkey to do it for them. The deal with Turkey halted the migration flow into Europe by almost 90 per cent right away, so it worked well in that respect. But it also compromised the values that the EU stands for since the partner Erdoğan cracked down on all elements of the rule of law, human rights, and democracy.

The second deal of this kind that the EU made is with Libya and its lame-duck government(s). As migration shifted to the Mediterranean route, the EU shifted its focus to Libya and made a desperate deal with various actors there. Called 'assistance' to the 'coast guard', the EU financed their operations to stop and return boats with migrants before they reach international waters, at which point they have to be taken to Europe. This is what the EU wants to avoid, therefore it is necessary to make the Libyans return them to Libya. Further, there they are deported by the International Organisation of Migration (IOM) back to Africa, a very sensible and necessary policy, but the conditions in the detention centres where they are held are absolutely appalling. They are subject to all sorts of abuse and extortion. Again the values of the EU clash with the policy of the EU, but the deal works: Migration from Libya has almost stopped completely.

Two other states have designed similar policies to stop migration from Libya: Italy and France. They pay militias in the south of the country to stop migrants. Stopping migration is also part of the security and defence policy of France, as we saw in Chap. 8, and France has thought seriously about how to do this in the Sahel as well as in the Maghreb.

In the British case, there is a policy of border control and as Britain is not in Schengen and it is not part of the EU's policy. It is thus able to control migration, both politically and at the border.

As for NATO, it has refused to get involved in border controls for the most part, pointing out that the migration issue belongs to the police.

On terrorism, closely related to the border issues and to mass migration, neither the EU nor NATO have major roles, although NATO still has an operation in the Mediterranean, 'Active Endeavour' which is actually an Article 5 operation because it resulted from NATO's declaration of Article 5 after the attack on Manhattan in 2001. It surveys the Mediterranean.

But the fight against *Daesh* was carried out by a coalition of states led by the US. These ten NATO member states met at the margins at the NATO summit in Cardiff in 2014, but have continued as a coalition of the willing and able. France has played a key role here, as discussed in Chap. 8, while the British role has been somewhat more modest. The US and the French must be termed the leading actors in fighting *Daesh*, although many other states contribute to training the Kurdish *Pesh merga* which bore the brunt of the heavy fighting on the ground. Also Russia has been an actor if not an ally; a valuable military contributor to the destruction of the territorial power of this terrorist organization, undoubtedly agreeing with defence secretary Mattis' statement that 'we have shifted from attrition tactics, where we shove them from one position to another in Syria and Iraq, to annihilation tactics where we surround them. Our intention is that the foreign fighters do not survive the fight to return home ... we are going to stop them there and take apart the caliphate.'[5] He added that civilian casualties are unavoidable in this kind of siege warfare, something that both President Obama, President Hollande, and Prime Minister May had criticized the Russians over regarding the siege of Aleppo.

The military and very conventional sieges of Mosul, Raqqa, and other *Daesch* strongholds yielded victory to the Western coalition and Kurdish *Pesh merga* forces during 2017. The terrorist organization was broken and although terrorists remain and will attack in the West—as they did on many occasions in recent years—the centre of gravity of the organization has been destroyed, much as Clausewitz would have prescribed. Thus, although terrorists cannot be deterred, they can be destroyed. Also al-Qaida was destroyed militarily through the same attrition and annihilation tactic. This military action carried out by the US, France, Britain and some others has weakened the terrorists in a major way, and its importance can hardly be overstated. Germany has not fought *Daesh* but armed a brigade of the *Pesh merga,* a major step for Germany.

CONCLUSIONS   283

France has been a leading strategic actor in the coalition fighting *Daesh* as well as in fighting terrorism in the Sahel and especially in Mali. It has also taken a very active approach to fighting terrorism at home, similar to the American approach after 9.11, declaring that France is at war with the terrorists.

In sum, we see that the two strategic actors in Europe, France and Britain, figure in all three cases as leading actors. Yet the main actor in two of the cases—Russian revisionism and fighting terrorism—remains the US. France is however an actor in its own right in the MENA, not depending on the US. Britain's strength is on the contrary its closeness to the Americans, almost always acting with them.

Moreover, this study has shown that strategic action on hard power issues remains the privilege and duty of nation-states, however much one opts for multilateral diplomacy and IOs as platforms of action.

Notes

1. 'France's Macron, UK agree to cooperate on defense and security after Brexit' .W Horobin and J. gross, *Wall Street Journal*, 18 January 2018.
2. US National Security Strategy, 18 December 2017.
3. Author's interview, 14 January 2018.
4. Interview with Prime Minister Orbán, 'Schengen siecht dahin', *Die Welt*, 14 January 2018.
5. 'Defense secretary Mattis says US policy against ISIS is no "annihilation"', *The Guardian*, 31 May 2017.

INDEX

NUMBERS AND SYMBOLS
1951 UN Convention on the Status of Refugees, 105
1994 Budapest Memorandum, 188
2010 Lancaster House agreement, 179
2010 Strategic Defence and Security Review (SDSR), 178
2014 NATO Wales Summit, 157
2015 Strategic Defence and Security Review (SDSR), 179

A
Abkhazia, 54
Adamsky, P., 49
Afghanistan, 18
Al Assad, Bashar, 40
Aleppo, 65
Al Gaddafi, Muammar, 134
Allied Command Transformation (ACT), 201
Allison, G., 19
Allison, Roy, 75
Al-Qaida, 25

Al-Shabaab, 133
Alternative für Deutschland (AfD), 110
Althea, 215
Anakonda-16, 254
Appeasement, 101
Arbatov, A., 76
Armenia, 8
Artemis, 215
Article 5, 8
Article 42.6, 198
Asmus, R., 50
Åtland, K., 53
A2/AD, 258
Azerbaijan, 8

B
Balance-of-power system, 23
Baltic, 40
Barkhane, 141, 208
Bataclan, 126
Bjørgo, B., 125
Blair, T., 6
Boko Haram, 133

© The Author(s) 2018
J. H. Matlary, *Hard Power in Hard Times*,
https://doi.org/10.1007/978-3-319-76514-3

286 INDEX

Border Control, 93–124
Breedlove, P., 82
Brende, B., 8
Brexit, J., 181
Bulgaria, 252
Bundestag, 273
Burden-sharing, 4
Burke-White, W. W., 55
Burkina Faso, 208
Bush, G., 8
Buzan, B., 12

C

Cameron, D., 14
Cardiff, 39
Carter, Sir Nick (General), 179
Chad, 208
Chechen wars, 53
Chilcot inquiry, 177
China, 7
Clausewitz, Carl von, 25
Coercion, 14
Colby, 259
Cold War, 23
Collier, Paul, 103
Cologne attacks, 101
Commissioner for National
    Minorities, 256
Common Foreign and Security Policy
    (CFSP), 222–223
Commonwealth of Independent States
    (CIS), 75
Compellence, 39
Congressional sanctions, 232
Co-ordinated Annual Review
    of Defence (CARD), 223
Copenhagen Criteria, 7, 219
Corbyn, J., 177
Council of Europe, 7
Counter-insurgency (COIN), 30
Counterterrorism, 207

Covenant, 176
Crimea, 6
Cross, Tom, 29
Cuban missile crisis, 19
Cyber technology, 249

D

Daalder, I., 82
Daesh, 3
Defence union, 229
De Maizière, T., 166
Détente, 247–269
Deterrence, 14
De Wiijk, R., 36
Directoire, 228
Dissuasion, 195
Donetsk, 54
Dublin system, 166
Dunford, Joseph, 66
d'Urbal, Victor, 30

E

Economic and Monetary Union
    (EMU), 218
Enhanced Forward Presence (EFP),
    164, 253
Erdoğan, Recep Tayyip (President), 116
ETA, 126
EU battlegroups, 216
Eurasian Economic Union (EAEU),
    48, 52
Euro-deterrent, 227
European Defence Action Plan
    (2016), 182
European Defence Fund (EDF),
    182, 223
European Neighbourhood Policy
    (ENP), 52
European Security and Defence Policy
    (ESDP), 218

EU's 2003 Security Strategy, 214
EUTM Mali, 207
EU-Turkey deal, 241
EU-Turkey Refugee agreement, 114
Executive power, 193

F
Fallon, M., 185
Finland, 252
Finlandization, 17
Fire-brigade, 30
Force de frappe, 195
Force for good, 6
Foreign policy prerogative
(FPP), 152
Framework Nation Concept, 157
Framing, 96
Freedman, L., 38
Friedman, T., 10

G
Gabon, 208
Gabriel, S., 158
Galeotti, M., 48
Game theoretic models, 23
Gates, R., 248
Gegout, C., 137
Geneva Conventions, 65
Geopolitics, 9
George, Alexander, 38
Georgia, 7
Gerasimov, Valery, 37
Global Strategy for the EU's Foreign and Security Policy, 219
'Good cop'/'bad cop' plan, 276
Gorbachev, M., 68
Gray, C., 25
Greece, 116
Grygiel, J., 260
Guerrilla, 15

H
Haftendorn, H., 41
Hakvåg, U., 53
Hampshire, 107
Hard power, 6
Hebdo, C., 125
Heisbourg, F., 71
Hezbollah, 36
High North, 104
Hobbes, T., 16
Houghton, Sir Nicholas
(General), 185
Human rights 'regime', 96
Hungary, 56
Hybrid war, 17

I
Identity politics, 13
Incirlik Air Base, 168
Innere Führung, 155
Intermediate-Range Nuclear Forces
(INF) Treaty, 68
International Organisation of
Migration (IOM), 117, 281
International organizations (IO), 250
International Security Assistance Force
(ISAF), 154
IRA, 126
Iraq, 142–143
Ischinger, W., 82
Israel, 36

J
Jacobsen, Peter Willy, 38
Joint Expeditionary Force (JEF),
179, 249
Juncker, Jean-Claude, 113
Jus ad bellum, 15
Jus in bello, 15
Justice and Home Affairs (JHA), 236

288 INDEX

K

Kaliningrad, 252, 274
Kelly, John, 65
Kennan, George, 24
  long telegram, 235
Kennedy, D., 16
Keohane, Daniel, 10
Kerry, John (Secretary of State), 58
Kissinger, H., 10
Koser, Khalid, 93
Kosovo, 34
Kriegslist, 155
Kroenig, M., 260
Kupchan, C., 9
Kurds, 40
Kurz, Sebastian, 108

L

Lavrov, S., 58
Le conseil de défense restreint, 193
Levada polls, 235
Levitte, D., 139
Lévy, B., 138
Libya, 18, 114–119, 242
Libyan Coast Guard, 117
Limited war, 28
Lisbon Treaty, 198
Lithuania, 275
Liu Xiaobo, 7
Löfven, Stefan (Prime Minister), 99
Loi de la programmation militaire, 194
Luhansk, 58
Luttwak, Edward, 33

M

MacFarlane, N., 57
Mack, A., 129
Macmaster, 65
Maghreb, 195
Maidan, 8
Malaysian Airline, 60

Malaysian Airlines plane, 277
Mali, 18, 195, 208
Mariupol, 60
Matlary, Sophie, 113, 241
Mattis, James, 65
Mauretania, 208
McDermott, Roger, 37
MENA, *see* Middle East and North
  Africa
Menon, A., 57
Merkel, C., 82
Merom, G., 129
Meyer, P., 177
Middle East and North Africa
  (MENA), 125, 195
Military Balance, 255
Military humanists, 16
Milosevic, Slobodan, 34
Minsk, 60
Minsk II, 162
Mistral, 204
Mogherini, Federica, 112, 227
Moldova, 8, 48
Multidimensionelle integree des
  Nations Unis a Mali
  (MINUSMA), 141, 207
Multilateralization, 256
Multipolarity, 9
Munich Security Conference, 74

N

National heroes, 154
NATO Force Integration Units
  (NFIUs), 252
NATO-Russia Council, 6
New 'Chindit' brigade, 186
Niger, 208
Nigeria, 18
Nobel peace prize, 7
Noble Jump, 254
Non-refoulement, 105
Nord Stream 2, 165

INDEX 289

North Atlantic Council (NAC), 262
North Korea, 250
Northern Group, 189, 249
Norway, 7
Norwegian, 275
Nusser, Karl-Heinz, 98
Nye, J., 10

O
Obama, B., 14
Observation force, 277
Operation *Chammal*, 208
Operation Enduring Freedom, 35
Operation *Serval*, 141
Orbán, Viktor (Prime Minister),
110, 238
Organization for Security and
Co-operation in Europe
(OSCE), 277
observers, 53
Ostpolitik, 159
Otto Brenner Institute, 100

P
Palmyra, 64
Paradigm shift, 28
Parlamentsheer, 155
Permanent Structured Cooperation
(PESCO), 198, 216
Pesh merga, 282
Poroshenko, P., 56

R
Rand Corporation, 38
Rationality, 24
Readiness Action Plan (RAP), 252
Reagan, R., 68
Realpolitik, 9
Republic of Congo (DRC), 215
Responsibility to Protect (R2P), 134

Revisionism, 16
*Revue stratégique de défense et de
sécurité nationale*, 196
Richards, Sir David (General), 139
Romania, 252
Rostoks, T., 258
Rules of engagement (ROEs), 153
Russia-NATO Council, 276
Russian-German trade, 160
Rutte, Mark (Prime Minister), 110

S
Sahel, 141–142, 195
St. Malo summit, 218
Saint-Nazaire, 202
Sanctions, 6
regime, 230
Sandhurst Military Academy, 272
Sarkozy, N., 50
Schelling, Thomas, 38
Schengen, 239
Schengen borders, 115
Schulz, M., 158
Sea Lanes of Communications
(SLOCs), 260
Security community, 11
See, H., 143
Senator McCain, 57
Serval, 207
Sevastopol, 53
Sherr, J., 48
Shirreff, R., 183
Simons, William, 38
Simpson, Emile, 25
'Small' war, 15
Smith, Rupert, 29
Snyder, J., 19
on Soviet strategic culture, 19
Soft power, 213–246
Solberg, 39
Solomon, J., 259
Somalia, 18

290 INDEX

South Ossetia, 54
Soysal, Yasemin, 107
Spetsnaz, 53
Sphere of interest, 50
Srebrenica, 55
State Tillerson, 266
Stavridis, J., 82
Steinmeier, F., 82, 159
Stoltenberg, J., 62
Strachan, H., 26
Strategic Arms Reduction Treaty
  (START) I, 68
Strategic culture, 27
Subversion, 17
Sun Tzu, 47
Sweden, 252
Syria, 64

T
Talbott, S., 82
Taliban, 127
Tamnes, R., 68
Tbilisi, 78
Thies, W., 247
Toft, A., 127
Train and equip, 80
Transponders, 71
Trip-wire, 261–266, 274
Trump, Donald, 4
Turkey, 40
Tusk, Donald, 238

U
Ukraine, 7
Une acte de guerre, 205

UN High Commissioner for Human
  Rights, 119
UN High Commissioner for Refugees
  (UNHCR), 97, 279
Unified Protector, 135
Unipolarity, 9
UN Pact of 1945, 15
UN Security Council's (UNSC), 6

V
Very High Readiness Joint Task Force
  (VJTF), 252
Visegrad states, 102
Vladivostok, 202

W
Wæver, O., 12
Wald, C., 82
Wandel durch Handel, 231
Warsaw summit, 275
Weber, Max, 95
Westbindung, 164
Western humanitarian intervention, 77
Westphalian, 12
Willkommenheitskultur, 166
The World is Flat, 10

Y
Yanukovych, V., 52
Yemen, 18

Z
Zapfe, M., 261

CPSIA information can be obtained
at www.ICGtesting.com
Printed in the USA
LVOW13*2053250518
578528LV00019B/462/P